FATHER ON THE LINE

FATHER ON THE LINE

Jim Hock

RARE BIRD
LOS ANGELES, CALIF.

THIS IS A GENUINE RARE BIRD BOOK

Rare Bird Books
453 South Spring Street, Suite 302
Los Angeles, CA 90013
rarebirdbooks.com

FIRST PAPERBACK EDITION

Set in Minion
Printed in the United States

10 9 8 7 6 5 4 3 2 1

Publisher's Cataloging-in-Publication data available upon request.

My Everything: Kellie, John, and William

My Inspiration: Dad #63, Mom and Jay, Mary, Sue, Lisa,
Anna, and Joe

CONTENTS

INTRODUCTION

I REMEMBER THE WORDS as if they were said
yesterday: "If you don't do this I will kick your
ass." As the youngest of seven kids, I had heard
this kind of threat my entire childhood. But this
time was different. Those words came from my brother
Joe as he leaned over to me at a memorial service in
Southern California for our father, John Hock, after he
passed away in 2000. It had been a few months since
he was diagnosed with lung cancer and the doctor said
that a person without his high pain threshold would
have noticed that this was no usual cough. But they
caught it much too late. Now we stood just a few short
months after that diagnosis and his passing. Following
the service, my siblings and I listened in rapt awe of
the stories of former NFL greats Les Richter, Duane
Putnam and others. Tears and laughs, and because we
are Irish, just a few beers. The stories provided comfort.

Friends of our father, sharing memories of their dear teammate and their days playing together for the Los Angeles Rams of the 1950s.

The "this" my brother referred to was to write and capture these stories, maybe even turn them into a book. I began writing it in 2002, and it took more ten years to finish. I started writing after the birth of our first son while working as the spokesman for US Senator Dianne Feinstein from California. I went in one direction and another with figuring out exactly what to write, and then started a business of my own and put the project on hold for a few years. Honestly, the book was never meant for an audience wider than my mother and our immediate family—and my two sons who never had the privilege of meeting their grandfather. The Rams were an integral part of our parents' lives; they grew up just blocks away from the Los Angeles Memorial Coliseum that the team called home. Both of my parents' families had settled within a short walk from the stadium seeking better lives after the Great Depression. Yes, the Rams loomed much larger than just a sports team in our family. They represented something bigger—a way to connect and stay connected—to the stories, to our family history, to the history of Los Angeles, a city my parents loved.

In 2016, after twenty years in St. Louis, the Rams moved back to their longtime home. It seemed hard to believe. Some called their return to Los Angeles a relocation. Yet it was more like a restoration. In August of 2016, it was surreal to walk into the Los Angeles Coliseum with my wife and two boys through the same Tunnel 8 that my mom had entered to watch my dad roughly sixty years before. Even though I tried to hide it from my boys, as the Rams took the field that day my eyes welled up with tears as I could feel my dad's presence in a place he loved so much and a team he loved so much.

I wanted to pass on stories of the Los Angeles Rams to my sons so they would learn not only about their grandfather, but about this incredibly dynamic and historic professional football franchise. Make no mistake, the Rams of the 1950s were innovative. They were glamorous. And most of all, they were exiting. And like the city itself, what I found most remarkable was that the Rams were comprised of big stars and everyday workhorses like my dad—a quiet, humble and stout offensive guard—that are needed make things run if any effort is to be successful.

The Rams were the first major professional sports team to move west of the Mississippi River. They were the first to integrate, roughly a full year before Jackie Robinson shattered Major League Baseball's color barrier. They were the first to paint a logo on their helmets. They were the first team to reach one million fans in a season. They were the first team with a television contract.

Their 1950's roster is a who's who of the NFL Hall Fame. Names such as quarterback Norm "The

Dutchman" Van Brocklin, wide receiver Elroy "Crazy Legs" Hirsch, Bob Waterfield, end Tom Fears, defensive back Dick "Night Train" Lane, and linebacker Les Richter. Other notables from the era was a wunderkind public relations man named Pete Rozelle who would go on to become the boy commissioner of the NFL at age thirty-three. Head coach Sid Gillman was an architect of the modern passing game. Owner Dan Reeves was a genius in business, but troubled by alcohol. Heck, even the iconic comedian Bob Hope was a part owner of the Rams and Walt Disney's son-in-law was on the roster at the time.

The Los Angeles Rams were indeed Hollywood's Team.

This is the story of that incredible team and my dad and his colorful teammates and coaches and of a team place in a very special time in place in our history. It's also a story that of simple, humble people like my dad and mom that were blessed and honored to be part of something much bigger and a game that has become such a fabric of our society. *Father on the Line* is about their story and how my dad sacrificed his body for a game he loved.

PART I

PART I

CHAPTER 1

The Rabbit Skinner Comes Home

CONSIDER THE WAY HOLLYWOOD would film the opening, this story of Los Angeles and professional football. Play at cinematography and place the cameras to show off our main character's best features. A giant, this guy, he wears an Army soldier's haircut, duffle bag strapped over shoulders that would fill a closet. For this—the movie version—he'd be wearing his Army uniform and corporal's stripes.

On location, outside a small bungalow in South LA, sunlight beats against the house's stucco. It's warm, this January day in 1953.

Imagine the camera shot from the sidewalk: our character's back fills the frame as he steps toward the house. He'd need to turn sideways to get through the front door. Who he is seems less important than where he's going, that house that seems too small. His age? About to turn twenty-four. Yet he's slow up the two steps to the porch, walking as if his knees are stiff. He lingers to look around, enjoying all he has missed for so long. The camera tightens its focus, catches a glimpse of a name tag pinned to his chest. Then Corporal John Hock's parents open the door...

Cut to our hero's grown-man face as he peers out the side-by-side windows of his childhood bedroom, small and west-facing and so bright with January sun that you know the room would bake in summer. Big-chested at 230 pounds, he makes the window seem small. The glass reflects cars rushing by on Western Avenue. John Hock—my dad—presses the palm of a hand against the pane as if to make certain the window is real. His eyes fix on a spot somewhere the camera can't see, and he searches the sky, a slight smile suggests that he's looking at all his best tomorrows.

Then he brings his hand to his jaw, that large hand with fingers thicker than most men's thumbs, thumbs wide as a Bible. He cups the chin as if he's taken by a thought.

Wait! the director shouts. *No! Not that!*

The jaw, you understand, my dad's jaw, already draws enough attention to itself. Though my dad was big, blond, and blue-eyed, what separates him in any crowd or photograph, what people always remember, what you can't help but see, is that jaw.

Broad and long, with a cleft dead center in the chin, it's a jaw you could imagine was made of granite, a jaw God intended for Mount Rushmore. Its cousins are the jaws Disney Studios gave to Mighty Casey as he swung the bat in the 1946 cartoon, or years later to Paul Bunyan as he cleaved forests with his axe. Dad's profile makes Kirk Douglas's famous jaw forgettable.

So, hand on the windowpane, please—and then the camera draws back. Begins to build distance between itself and my dad, shows the tiny house in its surroundings, only a few yards from the back door of a Roman Catholic church. From there, the camera rises high above the bungalow—a helicopter shot—dad and his world shrinking as the grid that is Los Angeles is revealed, streets and houses proliferating, endless sidewalks straight as sidelines, and palm trees tall as goalposts. At last the camera floats high enough to pan across several flat miles, and *there!* The Los Angeles Memorial Coliseum—just a long walk from the house where dad grew up.

The stadium sits empty now, in January, but a little film editing changes that. The picture grows hazy, and a fade-in fills the coliseum with tens of thousands of football fans who cheer and applaud. Under their roar is the grunting and thumping of men who fling their bodies hard against each other, a referee's whistle, a profanity shouted from a sideline. On the field, pass follows pass, touchdown follows touchdown. A newspaper headline spins into the picture to show a team familiar with glory (the banner reads: "THEY BEAT THE BROWNS! Rams win NFL Championship!"). And then, as if carved in marble, come the names of players who are already legendary: Van Brocklin, Tank, Crazylegs, Deacon Dan.

The future John Hock sees out the window of his childhood home has become clearer

If everything happens as it can in the movies, in a few months dad will suit up in blue and gold, don a helmet decorated with the Rams' famous curling horns. When the starters rush from the sidelines for their first play of the season, he'll come with them, fall into a three-point stance on the offensive line and await the snap. With my dad's brawn to shove aside a Colt here or a 49er there, the Rams will be on their way to another NFL championship.

Fittingly, this will all happen in his hometown. It is 1953, and the city he left for college seven years before has become something rare and strange, a place where the impossible can become real—a place so full of change that whole neighborhoods might seem unfamiliar to a man who has been so many years away.

This Los Angeles carries remnants of its Old West and Spanish colonial histories, but now strip malls and drive-in churches light the night with neon. Here, men design jet propulsion engines while others draw cartoons about sending a mouse into space. This Los Angeles is as fake as an African jungle on a stage set and as real as the concrete coliseum where a linebacker cracks the ribs of a quarterback; dangerous as big finned cars careening on a smooth highway, comforting as a suburb laid out in a perfectly predictable grid. Los Angeles is glamorous and middle class and poor. Full of promise, impossible to predict. It's a city so new that by the time the sun rises, it's already tomorrow.

The perfect sporting complement for that Los Angeles is the Rams: forward-thinking, impatient, innovative, gimmicky. Like their city, they are a feisty outlier challenging the nation's east-of-the-Mississippi establishment. From 1948 to 1951, the Rams played in the NFL's championship game, winning the last, and they hold just about every NFL record for passing and scoring. Yet those gaudy numbers aren't enough to satisfy Los Angeles, whose city leaders dream of something other than NFL football, who long to hear the crack of a major league bat and watch a summertime double play.

America's most exciting town. The nation's most exciting NFL team. And an affable giant of a man coming home and hoping to play for both.

A fast-talker could sell that script to Hollywood.

In the movie version, my dad turns from the window. My grandmaother—his mother—is calling; she's fixed him dinner. Steak with potatoes, the meat broiled to medium with enough gristle to put "hair on your chest," she'd say—his favorite. Football will come soon enough. For now, he can enjoy being a regular guy, a GI happy to be in his parents' house, sipping a cold beer, and hopeful about a new job.

◆

WHEN MY DAD FIRST left my grandparents—Harry and Elizabeth Hock's house for the University of Santa Clara in Northern California in 1946, he left behind a city still stunned by the Depression, exhausted by World War II. Seven years later and back from Army service during the Korean conflict in occupied Japan, he found that money and bulldozers and new ideas and new faces had scrubbed the city fresh.

People were betting on Los Angeles—and the bets were paying off. In truth, people had brought their hopes to Southern California since the turn of the century, but especially since the 1930s when Depression economies throughout the country convinced hundreds of thousands to move west. The Hocks were part of that migration, driving cross-country from ailing Pittsburgh in 1937 when my dad was nine years old. His father, Harry, worked for US Steel and was one of thousands laid off and looking for work for month after month. Losing all hope, Harry had moved out a month before the wife and kids, telling young John that he'd see them soon in California. At the time, it must have felt like the other side of the planet.

The Rams themselves landed in Los Angeles in 1946, having abandoned poor attendance and money problems in Cleveland to make themselves the first National Football League team west of the Mississippi River. Not even the combination of a rookie star quarterback (Bob Waterfield) married to a movie star (Jane Russell) and an NFL championship in 1945 had drawn enough paying fans in Cleveland to offset that season's reported $50,000 loss. At first, NFL owners vetoed the move. Los Angeles was some two thousand miles farther than Chicago, the closest NFL city, and an airplane could take eighteen hours to cross the country. League owners saw long and expensive road trips. But Rams president Dan Reeves, then only thirty-three years old, is reported to have shouted at them, "And you call this a national league?" When that logic didn't convince, he won their approval for his move by agreeing to pay other teams' travel costs for games played in LA—an early indication that Reeves and the team wouldn't play the game as others did.

Both the Hocks and the Rams added to a Southern California population boom that would for decades shape the region and even the nation. In 1930, seven years before my dad's family arrived, the United States Census had counted about 2.2 million people in LA County. The population estimate for 1953 when my dad's army service ended? More than double that at 4.6 million. *Four-point-six.*

During those years, Burbank added 70,000 residents and Long Beach, 110,000. In southeastern Los Angeles County, the area called Lakewood boomed from 980 people to an estimated 81,550—a spectacular growth rate of 8,221 percent.

LA, the city, also grew. The numbers for Van Nuys, where Rams quarterback Bob Waterfield and Jane Russell had met in high school, grew from a mere eleven thousand people in 1930 to about seventy-four thousand in 1953, the year Waterfield retired from the game. The Leimert Park neighborhood, just west of where my dad's family settled, doubled its population. As journalist Carey McWilliams wrote in 1946, "Every city has had its boom, but the history of Los Angeles is the history of its booms. Actually, the growth of Southern California since 1870 should be regarded as one continuous boom, punctuated at intervals with major explosions."

Many new residents had come from Texas, Oklahoma, Arkansas, and Missouri—states struck hardest by the Dust Bowl. Some people found work in the orange groves and agricultural fields east of the city, but perhaps six to seven hundred thousand came during World War II to work in factories to fuel America's war machine, such as those that manufactured aircrafts and parts in Long Beach and the San Fernando Valley. In a 1941 newspaper column, the famous reporter Ernie Pyle called them "Aviation Okies."

Other new residents were sailors and soldiers returned from World War II's Pacific Campaign. Many young men, aged nineteen or twenty or twenty-one—unmarried, looking for work—found that driving under a cloudless blue yonder was preferable to walking Boston's rain-splashed sidewalks, that tanning on a

Santa Monica beach was more fun than shoveling snow from a Toledo stoop. Veterans found work building little houses that pimpled what had once been farm fields in Lakewood and other suburbs, and veterans bought those houses, too. In *Holy Land: A Suburban Memoir*, Lakewood resident D. J. Waldie writes of how the federal government threw money at veterans so they could buy homes—no down payment and 4 percent interest. Waldie's Lakewood subdivision added 17,500 of these houses in three years. They were small, built rapid-fire, and equipped, according to Waldie, "With a Waste King electric garbage disposal, oak floors, service porch, stainless steel kitchen counter, and a stainless steel double sink." He quotes what the subdivision's sales manager once said: "We sell happiness in homes."

Los Angeles drew more than its share of dreamers, too—the people who saw money in the marquees, who hoped for fame through film. Victor Mature arrived from Louisville, Kentucky; Hedy Lamarr came from Europe; and Bob Hope, who would one day own a share of the Rams, arrived in 1938 via Broadway and a deal with Paramount Pictures. For each film-famous face, thousands of others appeared only as gofers on stage sets or as servers in restaurants and bars. All told, their numbers were dwarfed in the population boom by the WWII veterans and the immigrants from the western South, but the most successful of the dreamers became the image LA showed the nation and the world—that beautiful, handsome, funny, perfectly lighted, and charismatic face of Hollywood.

◆

ON AN ARMY BASE outside Tokyo, in the summer of 1952—six months before he would muster out of the army—my dad received a football player's version of a "Dear John" letter. His stateside team didn't want him anymore.

That team was the NFL's Chicago Cardinals, who had made him the ninety-ninth pick in the 1950 draft. He played in all twelve Cardinals games during his rookie season, when Chicago finished a less-than-mediocre 5–7. But then the government sent its own draft notice, so off Hock went.

First, the army sent him to Fort Ord in California for basic training and a season assigned to special services, the wing of the military meant to entertain the troops and raise morale. My dad's job, naturally, was to play football. From Fort Ord, he headed across the Pacific for more of the same: an assignment with Camp Drake's Bulldogs—the best team in the Far East Command. My dad, who had once faced the NFL's Eagles and Steelers, was now playing against Yokosuka Naval Base and the Tokyo Quartermaster Depot.

And that was fine. Heck, it was good. Each game provided a distraction for soldiers and sailors on R&R, a taste of stateside life, a safer violence. No complaints from John Hock. Sure, he'd expected that service ball wouldn't match up to the NFL, that his teammates might be a bunch of deadpans. But they weren't. They acted like pros. Did what was expected without asking too many questions. That's what he told a reporter from *Pacific Stars and Stripes* on a late October day in 1952, in a damp locker room just after drills had ended. The reporter had done the fly-on-the-wall routine while the Bulldogs practiced, then followed players into the locker room with pen and paper to gather tidbits. He chatted with an all-American from Tennessee while nearby Camp Drake's coach painted stripes on game balls so they'd be easier to see. Another player was tightening new cleats onto his shoes. My dad stood at his locker, giving his knees a rest. Even at the University of Santa Clara they'd given him trouble—he'd worn a large knee brace for the team photograph his senior year. He didn't talk about the pains, but he knew he needed to take care. His career as an offensive lineman would last only as long as those knees. Could be years. Could be tomorrow. He babied them when he could.

Knowing my dad had played in the NFL, the reporter wandered over. He wanted to know what the pro thought of his new teammates.

Most of these boys have played some good college ball, my dad said. They do things right. They really surprised me.

And that was that. Stoic and humble, my dad had never been one to jabber with a lot of words.

If the reporter had pressed, though? If he'd asked more questions? My dad might have acknowledged that heck, well, sure it was better to be with Camp Drake than a team like Quartermaster Depot, which Drake had beaten, 74–0, the week before. Seemed every one of Drake's Bulldogs had scored a touchdown—even dad, getting a turn on defense and falling on a dropped lateral in the end zone.

Seventy-four to zip? You didn't find such lopsided scores in the NFL.

Comparisons are a strange thing in wartime, though. You start making them, you can't stop, and each one added to the next seems to make less and less sense. If you start comparing the NFL to the Far East Command Football League and Camp Drake to Quartermaster Depot, you can't help but compare serving in Japan to serving in Korea, showering in a locker room to shivering in a foxhole. You take the field in a small stadium to cheers from guys who have battled back and forth across the thirty-eighth parallel, and you can't help but wish the Chinese and North Koreans could be swept 74–zip. And that's when you know none of it makes sense. Best, then, to put aside comparisons, follow orders, do what the United States government wants you to do, and be grateful to be spared bullets and bayonets and grenades.

Gratitude matters. Guys in foxholes sometimes get real "Dear John" letters. Cold, brief *sayonaras*. Dad's kiss-off from his team had been perfunctory, too. But it had come with a pretty big postscript.

Chicago didn't want him anymore, that was true. But the Cardinals had swapped him to Los Angeles for a rookie linebacker from Tennessee and a tackle out of Texas Tech. His new bosses had been willing to give up two players for him, and those boys could suit up right then, didn't have to miss one more season while playing the likes of Yokosuka Naval Base. Maybe that's why Chicago had traded him—for the chance to get help right away.

The Rams? They had wanted him even knowing they'd have to wait—like a sweetheart who takes your ring and says she won't date anyone while you're away.

◆

IT WAS SMALL, THAT bungalow on Fifty-Second Street at the corner of Western, so tiny he did not have a bedroom and slept on the back porch. Not much changed from when he was a boy, when he'd so often wake from a deep sleep to a tap on the siding or the window glass. Outside, a priest from neighboring St. Brigid's would motion with a finger, and my dad would know that some other altar boy hadn't shown for Mass. Within a few minutes, he'd be out the back door, past the my grandparents' rabbit hutch, and into the sacristy, dressed in a surplice, ready to play his role. He knew the game plan: when to kneel, when to pour water over the priest's hands, when to ring the bell during the Eucharist. *Amen.*

Then, back home to do his part there, to feed and give water to the rabbits. Selling furs was how a boy could earn pocket change, maybe contribute to the family. Pittsburgh had been devastated by the Depression, so my grandparents had left, but Los Angeles didn't hand them thick rib eyes and an easy chair. In fact, answering the census worker who arrived at the door in 1940, my grandparents reported that only one person in the household held a job: daughter Ruth, ten years dad's senior, who had worked the previous year as an office clerk for a credit collection bureau. My grandfather, Harry, had been out of work for eighty-six weeks, nearly two years. His last job, the census worker noted, had been an assistant at a filling station.

Dad was twelve. He didn't have a job. He had rabbits.

Decades later, when he talked about the rabbits, the story would take a comedic turn—how young John sold rabbit skins! He'd tell the story and chuckle, and his kids, themselves grown, would consider the spectacle of some miniaturized version of their father, going door-to-door with a bag or a sack full of fur, or maybe to a shop somewhere, asking a nickel or a dime a pelt. *Dad did that? Can you imagine?* My siblings and I would often ask ourselves. It seemed kind of crazy in the middle of Los Angeles.

Take a moment and step up to the rabbit hutch with my dad, the boy. It's morning, still cool. If the rabbits acknowledge him, it's difficult to tell; mostly they stay where they are, legs tucked beneath their bodies, whiskers twitching. He begins as his father taught him, reaching into the cage with one hand and grabbing one by the soft scruff, calming it with caresses as he takes it against his chest and with his free hand fastens the hutch door. Dumb, harmless—the rabbit knows nothing about the knife. He sets the rabbit down—on a table or on the ground—but doesn't let it go. Pets it, talks to it until it is calm. With his free hand, he grips the pipe, what he always uses. The blow needs to be quick and accurate, just as he was taught. Hit that spot behind the ears where the head meets the neck. Hit it hard, to stun. Now, move fast—knife to throat, slice. Blood spurts, and he doesn't want it on the fur, so he lifts the body by its rear legs, hangs it with wire or a peg, lets the blood drain. The rabbit is already dead, and soon the legs stop kicking, the body gives up its twitch. Now, with the knife, which must be sharp, he cuts circles around the rear legs and with his fingers yanks the fur down, first past the legs, then the torso. To knick the fur here and there with the knife makes everything easier. There's a soft tearing sound as the meat lets go of its skin. Some call this stripping the jacket, and when the job is finished, what's left is a handful of rabbit fur and a purplish carcass.

It's a small violence, maybe more than most boys could stomach. But my dad isn't most boys. He'll never object to a chore, never complain about a job. It's in him to help his family, his church—later his teams and his country. It would always be in him to help, and he would do whatever needed doing. Show him the Xs and Os of serving a Mass or skinning a rabbit or blocking a linebacker on a sweep left, and he'd follow the plan. It didn't matter whether he was sleepy, or the rabbit twitched, or his knees ached. In his quiet, you'd never know if he was troubled; he'd never say. He'd do what was expected.

These boys, he had told the newspaper reporter in Japan, *they act like pros, they do what's expected. They do things right.*

In January 1953, the man who had been that boy was home. He had become strong, quick. Having wrestled some in college, even good enough to go the Olympic trials, he had moves and balance. But the world was full of strong, quick men. Some with healthy knees. Not all of them made it in professional football. If he was to succeed with the Rams, my dad needed something all the other strong, quick men didn't have. If he was to play for the NFL's most exciting team in what was probably America's most exciting city, he would need to bring to bear that talent he'd shown as a boy who skinned rabbits. It was perhaps his greatest gift: a willingness to take up any load, to tolerate any pain.

CHAPTER 2

Training Camp

THE SUMMER SUN, THROWING its first light from behind the San Bernardino Mountains, promised a sweltering day in Redlands. Seventy miles inland and planted amid desert brush and fruit orchards, Redlands often simmers ten to twenty degrees hotter than Los Angeles with its blessed ocean breezes. Mornings, though, can be cool, sixty-something, like this one in July 1953. Farmers checked irrigation systems, fed chickens. At the University of Redlands campus, inside Melrose Hall dormitory, my dad and other football players slept. Outside their closed doors, coaches padded past; some might have grinned or suppressed a chuckle, knowing the ruckus to come.

At the controls of the dorm's public address system, a coach flipped a switch, spun up the volume, pressed a button.

"READY-SET-*HUT*-TWO-THREE-FOUR!"

Like a football version of reveille, the recorded voice boomed into every corner of Melrose Hall. Loud and fast, less a quarterback's voice, more an auctioneer's.

"READY-SET-*HUT*-TWO-THREE-FOUR! *HUT*-TWO-THREE-FOUR!"

It's six thirty in the morning, rookies. Welcome to training camp.

Up and down the hallways, players bolted awake, grumbling. My dad stirred in his bed. You expected to rise early at training camp, but not to the crowing of a rooster this rude.

"*HUT*-TWO-THREE-FOUR! READY-SET-*HUT*-TWO-THREE-FOUR!"

In all Hock's years of football—high school, college, pro, and military—he'd never heard a snap cadence this fast. Or this loud. And never before coffee.

"*HUT*-TWO-THREE-FOUR!"

An air raid siren would be more melodious.

It had been almost six months since dad's return to Los Angeles from Japan. Since then, he'd signed a contract with the Rams, rested his knees, and worked himself into shape for training camp. Though he had a year of NFL experience, the Rams' coaches wanted him to report early with the rookies. He was, after all, in his first year with the team, and he'd been out of the NFL for two years. So, on Monday he'd driven from Los Angeles, heading for that Redlands furnace where the Rams had held their annual training camp since '49. Their home for the next several weeks would be Melrose Hall with its thin mattresses and even thinner pillows. Like other dormitories at the University of Redlands, Melrose was built to take the edge off the heat: with high ceilings but only two stories, long and wide with shallow-pitched tile roofs, and lots of windows to open for a breeze. The long porch was sheltered, too, not for worry of rain, but to offer shade. Paired ionic columns framed the entry from the college's quad. Out back, a short stroll away, were the practice fields.

Dad had arrived with rookies who'd come from as far and wide as Spokane, Washington, and Lewisburg, Pennsylvania, hoping they might turn their love of a violent game into a paycheck. Among them was Verdese Carter, an offensive tackle who had been a Negro all-American at Wilberforce University, and who had lined up beside my dad with the Camp Drake Bulldogs. Carter was taller than dad by an inch and a half, outweighed him by twenty or so pounds. Together, they'd helped Camp Drake to the first-ever Far East Interservice championship game, what the military had called the Rice Bowl, as if it were an Asian cousin to the Rose Bowl or Orange Bowl. The military even scheduled the championship on New Year's Day, when all the big bowl games were played. The 1953 Rice Bowl pitted dad and Carter's Bulldogs against the Yokosuka

Naval Base Sea Hawks, the teams meeting in a Tokyo stadium the Japanese had built but the Americans had commandeered and renamed for New York Yankee great Lou Gehrig.

Camp Drake scored first, near the end of the first half, then again at the start of the second, and eventually won, 25–6. A mere twenty days later, Corporal John Hock had traveled the breadth of the Pacific Ocean, arrived at Fort Ord in California, and received his discharge papers. Now, he and Carter were competing for a spot on the offensive line where both had primarily played tackle.

Despite the name, an offensive tackle never tackled anyone. He played on the offensive line—that group of oversized men whose job was to be both battering ram and wall. On running plays, offensive linemen threw themselves at opponents in carefully choreographed patterns intended to clear paths that their fleet-footed teammates could rush through, carrying the ball. On passing plays, the line formed a protective circle around the quarterback, intending to give him an uninterrupted second or two to find an open man downfield to catch his pass.

In the middle of the offensive line were two guards and a center—men who were generally stouter, harder to move, but also gifted with better balance and dexterity. Imagine a dancing elephant, and you've got a guard. The two tackles, on either edge, needed to be rangier—generally bigger and taller—and needn't be so nimble-footed. After all, it's easier to walk on the edges of a crowd than it is to walk through the middle. Since college, John Hock had regularly played tackle on the left side, protecting the quarterback's blind side. So had Verdese Carter.

When Hock and Carter and other first-year players arrived at Redlands, they dressed out in Rams practice jerseys and helmets, then participated in a few easy drills and posed for newspaper photographers. Redlands locals gathered for the hubbub; ten- and eleven-year-old boys played at tackling the rookies, but mostly hung on their legs. That first day was a get-to-know-you affair. Tuesday would be the first true day of camp: workouts in hundred-degree heat.

But first:

"*HUT*-TWO-THREE-FOUR! READY-SET-*HUT*-TWO-THREE-FOUR!*"

Though the recorded voice belonged to an assistant coach, the idea to wake the rookies this way came from the top man, Coach Hampton Pool. Beyond the welcoming prank, he wanted to make a point. Later that day, he would explain how every scoring record in the NFL belonged to the Los Angeles Rams, and he wanted the team to break its own marks. The way to do that, he theorized, was to speed up the offense. If you thought of a football team as a factory that manufactured points, and there were only sixty minutes in a game, the way to score more points was to speed up the production line. Every touchdown or field goal needed to come quickly and efficiently, so you'd sooner have an opportunity at another. Therefore, each play had to be quick—and each play started with the snap count.

"The faster you run off your plays, the more plays you can squeeze into a ball game," Pool told reporters, two of whom also stayed in Melrose Hall and were awakened with the rookies. "By increasing the tempo, you run less chance of being penalized for delaying the game. Also, the slower the cadence the more margin for error. If a player misses the beat by a fraction of a second, he can jam up the whole play."

Hamp Pool spoke as if what he'd come up with was an innovation that would change football.

Or was it a gimmick?

Maybe the rookies wondered themselves. For Hock, especially, and for other Angelenos, it was likely a familiar conundrum, an ongoing existential question, because in postwar Los Angeles every day seemed to bring a new something: gimmicks that could be innovations in disguise and innovations promoted with gimmicks. Which new things should you take seriously? Which could you ignore? Take, for example, night golf. A year before, a rich toy manufacturer hosted a golf-under-the-lights tournament at the Inglewood Country Club, hoping to prove that Americans in the Philippines or elsewhere could tee-up in equatorial jungles during the cooler after-hours. He paid Joe Louis, the former heavyweight champion, to play under a portable seven hundred thousand–beam candlepower lamp. "A light-bearer wears the spotlight on his head in a man-from-Mars effect," reported the *Los Angeles Times*, "and covers the course on a scooter-type affair." Take it seriously? Or laugh about it?

What about the humongous four-level stacked freeway *whatsit* opening that summer near downtown? The idea was to connect Highways 101 and 110, and politicians said it would be the first interchange of its kind—meant to use less land than a cloverleaf. An interchange for the future! Sure, but even drivers with a good inner compass struggled to understand how this ramp led to that direction. They merged lanes into the stack with a prayer on the lips: *Please, God, help me find a way out.* Would the interchange prove to be an innovation or a Rube Goldberg version of highway design? Or this: a few months before training camp, Warner Brothers Studios released the Vincent Price film, *House of Wax*, the first full-length 3-D stereoscopic film in color. Theatergoers had to wear flimsy red-and-blue cellophane-lensed paper eyeglasses to see that waxy-faced fellow in cape and hat run right toward them. Gimmick or innovation? Few, if any, were better than Hollywood at blurring the lines.

Was it money? Fancy? Optimism? Perhaps it was the newness of Los Angeles itself, all that originality generating new problems the way the city's pioneering highways had created smog a decade earlier. New problems called for new solutions. So, week in and week out, Los Angeles became a place where eager, hungry minds looked for problems to solve—and innovation and gimmicks thrived. Not only thrived, but were in demand. Because if you didn't have the next big innovation or a gimmick to sell, someone else did.

"However," wrote Frank Finch, the Rams' beat writer for the *Times*, "if they turn on that blasted recorder tomorrow at sunrise, I'm moving downtown."

◆

THIS TRAINING CAMP WAS Hamp Pool's first as head coach; maybe the wake-up call was him trying to make his mark. He couldn't have felt comfortable in his new position.

A year before, he'd been feuding with his one-time friend and his predecessor, "Jumbo" Joe Stydahar. Pool had won that go-around, and the head coaching job with it, but he was the Rams' fifth "boss coach" in eight seasons. All but one predecessor had been let go with a winning record; several had led the team to championship games, two had won it all.

Adam Walsh had coached the Rams in Cleveland and in their first Los Angeles season. Back east, he'd led the team to its first championship, beating Washington, 15–14, for the title in a game played in snow with a temperature around zero. Fans burned hay in barrels to stay warm. Players slipped around the field in rubber-soled shoes. But the next season, out in the sunny west, Walsh's Rams went 6–4. Dan Reeves, the team's principal owner and president, fired him.

The Rams promoted an assistant coach, Bob Snyder, who became at age thirty-four the youngest coach in the NFL at the time. He went 6–6, but a four-game losing streak ended his first season. Following an exhibition-game loss the next season, he resigned, citing ulcers.

Clark Shaughnessy, another assistant and already admired as a football innovator, was next to plant his backside onto the hot seat. More than a decade earlier, Shaughnessy had needed only one season to coach Stanford University from a 1–7–1 joke into a 10–0 Rose Bowl champion. The change was so rapid that Shaughnessy's Stanford team became known as the "Wow Boys." Shaughnessy, nicknamed "Shag," worked that miracle by resurrecting an old, seldom-used offensive formation based on bulk and strength—the "T," which put three running backs behind the quarterback to make a shape like the capitalized letter. But instead of power running, Shaughnessy emphasized speed. The scheme confounded defenses relying on misdirection to mask which player would get the ball and which direction the play would go.

As head coach for the Rams, Shag kept innovating. He moved one of those "T" halfbacks up to the line of scrimmage so that particular halfback would be eligible to catch a pass. With that move, Shag created what was to become the wide receiver and the modern passing game. The change was so revolutionary and successful, especially with future Hall of Famers' Bob Waterfield and Norm Van Brocklin sharing quarterback duties, that other teams tried (and failed) to outlaw it at a meeting of the NFL rules committee. "There's nothing wrong with the play," Shaughnessy scoffed, "except some teams can't stop it!"

Yet after Shaughnessy's second season, with the Rams finishing 8–2–2, Rams president Dan Reeves fired Shag.

Reeves cited "internal friction," according to a *Times* report. The source of tension might have been an overly complex playbook that had begun to annoy the players. Or it might have been a postgame tongue-lashing Shag gave to some assistant coaches who been drop-down drunk in front of players after a game. Or it might have been all that and more. In *NFL Head Coaches: A Biographical Dictionary, 1920–2011*, author John Maxymuk describes Shaughnessy as "a milk shake drinker who neither drank nor smoked," and "aloof with a superior attitude and a penchant for cutting, sarcastic comments." Shaughnessy sued the Rams for more than $33,000, what he said was owed on his contract.

Reeves promoted Shag's assistant, the six foot four, 260-pound "Jumbo" Joe Stydahar. Said Shaughnessy, proving his cutting, sarcastic ways: "When Stydahar gets through coaching the Rams, I can take any high school team in the country and beat them."

Stydahar was no milk shake drinker. The son of a West Virginia coal miner, he was said to be capable of drinking whiskey while smoking a cigar and chewing tobacco, all at the same time. The press enjoyed his palaver. Stydahar took Shaughnessy's ideas about passing and, with the help of assistant coach Hampton Pool, pushed them further. In 1950, under Stydahar, the Rams scored sixty-four touchdowns. Van Brocklin threw for 554 yards in one game, breaking the record at the time by 86 yards (a record still standing more than six decades later). In two seasons under Stydahar, the Rams went 17–8 and won the 1951 NFL championship. (Still the only title in LA to this day.)

But even that couldn't save his job.

When Stydahar left the Rams at the start of his third season, he accused Pool of betrayal. The two had been teammates with the Chicago Bears, longtime friends, and Stydahar had given Pool oversight of the Rams' offense and defense. Pool, who had played offensive line but was a running back at heart, loved designing schemes and strategies based on speed. He had a master's degree in education from Stanford, and he relished study, staying up nights, and waking early to devise new game plans. The first photo of him as a Ram to appear in the *Times* showed him sitting at a desk with his necktie loose and with a sharp pencil in hand, reading an open three-ring binder. "Joe was a big, happy guy, the nice guy," Rams linebacker Don Paul later told Mickey Herskowitz, the author of *The Golden Age of Pro Football*. "Pool was the guy who worked his butt off."

Eventually, Stydahar came to believe he'd given away too much responsibility. "Pool wanted to run the club—

the whole works—his own way," he told the *Associated Press*. "I went to Dan Reeves on several occasions and asked him to do something about it. He refused. I asked for a showdown—and it went against me. That's well and good. It's probably good for the ball club. I'm glad I got out."

Professor Pool, as local sportswriters called him, finished that 1952 season, his first, with a 9–3 record. The Rams' last game was a playoff loss to the Detroit Lions. For the league's defending champs, it was a disappointing finish.

Now, it was training camp, and the professor needed to show something so that he could keep his job.

"READY-SET-*HUT*-TWO-THREE-*FOUR!*"

◆

BACK IN LOS ANGELES, football wasn't Rosalind Wiener's first concern. Probably, it wasn't even her twenty-second. Or eighty-ninth. Pick any number. Football wasn't on her agenda. Instead, Roz Wiener—staring hard into Los Angeles's future—saw baseball.

The Wednesday before the Rams training camp began, she had won an historic election to the Los Angeles City Council. At age twenty-two, she had become the youngest person ever elected to the job; like Van Brocklin's passing yards in a game, it is a mark that still stands. Nor had any woman served on the council since World War I, and no one Jewish since the turn of the century.

Months earlier, no one—not even Wiener—would have envisioned this happening. Though active in campus politics at the University of Southern California and with the local Democratic party, she had been thinking law school in 1953, not elected office. But she'd joined a committee to pick candidates who might run as Democrats for city council vacancies. "We didn't like anybody," she recalled years later. Then someone on the committee said to her, "You talk so much, why don't you run?"

So she did, fresh out of USC, where she had graduated with a degree in public administration. She had no platform when she started, no funds, no natural constituency. She filed her candidacy papers five minutes before the deadline. But Roz Wiener ran for LA's fifth council district as if she'd been preparing her whole life for the role—and perhaps she had been.

A photograph of a two-year-old Roz shows her standing by a billboard of Franklin D. Roosevelt. Her mother put the picture in her baby book. Mom and Dad were New Deal Democrats, and Sarah Wiener was a fierce champion for FDR, using the drugstore and soda shop she and Oscar owned on Western Avenue to campaign on Roosevelt's behalf. Roz grew up writing "Dear Mr. President" letters in the same tone she'd use to write an uncle. One of FDR's secretaries would write back: "Dear Roz, The President is very busy." When Roosevelt died, she—in her own words—went to pieces. She had loved FDR the way other girls loved Frank Sinatra.

To help fund Roz's city council campaign, her mother hosted card games. A nephew sold polliwogs and donated the money. Throughout her district, Wiener walked: door-to-door through the heart of central Los Angeles out to Sepulveda Boulevard, seven to eight hours a day, scheduling her visits around *I Love Lucy* episodes because the television show was so popular she knew people would be home watching. She walked so much she wore out thirteen pairs of shoes, which *LIFE* magazine captured in a photo published that year. The young woman who arrived at voters' doors showed herself to be energetic and full of ideas, a short brunette with green-brown eyes and an infectious smile. With voters, she left a bar of soap wrapped with a business card that read, "Let's Clean Up City Hall." On those cards, she put check marks next to her goals, including: "Bring Major League Baseball to Los Angeles."

As a native Angeleno, Wiener knew that in the eyes of the country—and even to many locals—Los Angeles was a second-class city. New York was the cream, the big brother with whom Los Angeles (and others) had a one-sided rivalry New Yorkers hardly noticed. After all, New York was busy being New York: catching theater on Broadway, enjoying a ticker-tape parade, spending Wall Street money to catch the Yankees in the World Series… Why would New York even notice Los Angeles?

Los Angeles cared what New York thought, but if Los Angeles wanted New York to come out and play, it needed a game worth The Big Apple's attention. If

Los Angeles wanted to be a top-tier US city, Wiener believed, it needed Fortune 500 companies and a major opera house. Most of all, it needed major league baseball.

Los Angeles was home to the national pastime, but the Hollywood Stars and Los Angeles Angels played in the minor leagues. That put LA on a field with Oakland and Seattle, not Chicago and New York. Sure, the Rams played teams from back east, but in 1953 the National Football League was a sports afterthought. Maybe the Rams won championships and regularly drew some eighty thousand fans to games, but the nation didn't care. When the weekly *Sports Illustrated* was founded in 1954, it gave only about a page each fall issue to pro football. College football warranted several pages. So did horse racing, golf, boxing, and even fishing. Only professional ice hockey might have mattered less than the NFL.

If the Rams were at all useful to Los Angeles and Wiener in the effort to become top-tier, it was mostly as an example showing that pro sports could succeed in the Pacific Time Zone. No major league team played in a city farther west than St. Louis. Any baseball club would face a financial risk by packing up the moving trucks and driving out Route 66, just as Dan Reeves had taken a big chance when he moved the Rams from Cleveland. But if an NFL team could succeed in Los Angeles, surely the Dodgers or Cubs would draw!

For her first act as a city councilwoman, Roz Wiener introduced a resolution encouraging the LA

Memorial Coliseum's governing commission to let the local American Legion stage a baseball game in the coliseum. Though the coliseum had been used for track and field along with football, Wiener wanted to show major league owners and local skeptics that the great oval, Los Angeles's largest public gathering space, would serve well as a baseball venue.

The resolution was a gimmick, sure, but it was a gimmick with a purpose. Maybe it would take years to bring baseball west. (*Let's be realistic*, she might correct. *Probably it will take years.*) But she had to start her efforts somewhere.

That's how Roz Wiener began her quest to change Los Angeles sports history.

◆

NORM VAN BROCKLIN NICKNAMED my dad "Lantern Jaw," as in: "Hey, Lantern Jaw! Don't you know who you're supposed to block?" Other players called him "The Hooker," playing off his last name. Tank Younger called him "Cotton" because he would sometimes foam at the edges of his mouth during games.

Perhaps more importantly, Professor Pool started called him an offensive guard, shifting my dad away from his familiar spot at left tackle. Maybe the Rams had too many tackles and too few guards. Big as my dad was at the time, when compared to other Rams tackles he proved a few inches shorter and pounds lighter. Today, he would been the size of an NFL fullback. Maybe the balance and footwork he'd learned as a college wrestler made him better suited for guard, especially in the system Pool wanted to use, emphasizing speed on the offensive line over size. Whatever the reason, shortly after training camp began, Pool told my dad to get used to playing one step to his right at guard, in the heart of the offensive line.

Naturally, John Hock obliged.

Come serve the Mass, John. John, feed the rabbits. Ship out to Japan, Corporal Hock. Learn a new position, Hooker.

When you belong, my dad always told us, you contribute. Family or church, country or team. Do the right thing he'd always say, even when no one was looking. It was something he lived by—doing his duty. If you think about it, it's a blessing to be instructed in that role, that liturgy, the military's regulations, the footwork and timing. It's a comfort. After depression and world war, and now with politicians talking about Soviets and city-destroying bombs, with so much changing so haphazardly—it's a blessing and a comfort to have directions to follow, a part to play, to know that some outcomes are predictable if you do your job.

Dad turned the page in the playbook.

◆

THE NEXT TWO WEEKS of training camp, dad's lessons were a combination of where to go and how to get himself there, who to hit and how to hit him. "When" to hit also mattered. In Pool's system, much of my dad's job would require clockwork timing, then violence: charging to his assignment and crashing into whatever snarling, roaring Eagle or Steeler or Giant he found there—before a Rams halfback arrived.

When lessons were over, there was running to be done. Coaches worshipped at the church of running. Leg strength was built by running. Endurance was built by running. Run laps. Run a mile. Run another. Run under the glare of that desert sun. Run through that desert heat. At training camp, no one escaped running. No one escaped the sun. There were no tents, no shelters. Sun glared off windows hundreds of feet away. It made the grass hot, the dirt dusty. It licked up sweat and burned skin. Sun burned in the players' eyes and in their mouths and ears; probably it burned in their dreams…while they ran.

Each night, a dinner. Maybe a letter written home. A game of cards on the dorm's porch. Days passed. Then, two weeks into camp, Van Brocklin and the veterans arrived.

With them came a different atmosphere. More joking, more insults, more pranks—all part of a shared history, a common language earned through years of bruises, ass-kickings and asses kicked, a shared expectation of the right way to win games. Van Brocklin, the quarterback known for what one sportswriter called his "carbonated remarks," might chew out the newbies. Kinder players—like Duane Putnam, a guard playing on the right side of the line opposite my dad—offered tips.

Putnam, aka "Putter," had been the rookie sensation among linemen in camp the year before. Though at six feet he was smaller than most NFL guards, Putnam had drawn praise from his coaches. "Duane is a deadly blocker," Stydahar had said. "He not only has speed but he has quickness in getting to his man… [H]e can maintain a drive after the initial contact. Once he gets an opponent on the run, he chases him right out of the ballpark."

Putnam, already married and with a daughter, played guitar, dipped tobacco, and liked to laugh. He had dark hair buzzed flat on top and a face so boyish that when he tried to look mean people chuckled. He liked it when people laughed. Putnam, Stydahar had once said, knew how to have fun playing the game. But "he wants to be the best man at his position in the league. He doesn't come to you and tell you that, but that's the impression you get from watching him play." As guards on opposite sides of the line, Putnam and my dad weren't competitors so much as partners. They were like the two bishops on a chess board, lined up on either side of the king, greater if they worked in tandem than separately. Aside from playing guard, the men had other things in common. Both had played high school and college ball in California, and both had gone through tours in the Army. Both were in their second season as pros. Neither liked to talk much about himself. Both enjoyed a cold beer and someone else's jokes. Naturally, Putter and the Hooker hit it off. They would end up being lifelong friends.

One other very important thing changed when the veterans arrived. Putter and Van Brocklin and the rest? They knew about a little burgers-and-beer place outside town that could help a guy forget Redland's heat.

◆

HARRY PATTISON WAS A boy, probably twelve years or so, when fiery Jane Russell threw open the door of his parents' corner restaurant-bar and started yelling at her husband. Bob Waterfield, by then one of the best quarterbacks in the NFL, rose from his seat beside Van Brocklin at the end of the bar and headed outside.

"Bob Waterfield and Van Brocklin would always sit down by the far door there," Pattison says, recalling those summers the Rams sought refuge at Ed and Mary's, his parents' place.

He remembers how his mom once invited them all to the Pattisons' house up in the nearby mountains so they could taste her fried chicken. And the Rams came, too. A few went hunting for cottontails with Harry's dad.

Decades later, Harry still has a football that Rams players signed and gave him.

But when at the tavern his dad pulled him behind the counter and said, "Don't bother the players." Harry didn't.

He knew why the Rams ("the boys," he calls them) came out to Mentone, a tiny farm town a few miles east of the heart of Redlands. Down in Redlands, if the Rams stopped in at a bar, people would come by to gawk and not even buy beer, just try to chat up the Rams. What the players wanted to do was relax, forget the heat, and forget football.

At Ed and Mary's, everyone knew the house rule: no one bothers the boys.

"When the boys would come in," Harry says, some sixty years later, "my mom would have two or three of the waitresses working. 'Keep those pitchers coming,' my mom would say. 'Don't turn the taps off. Just keep 'em coming.'"

The Rams crowded around the bar, a small space maybe six feet wide and twenty feet long, room for a half dozen circle-tables.

Lucky Lager. Even now, if you ask Duane Putnam about Ed and Mary's, Lucky Lager is what he remembers.

"It was just so good," he says one morning at his house in Ontario, California. He cups his hands as if placing them around a mug. "It was so cold, the pitcher would end up with frost around it—and it was so *good*."

The Rams would come by Ed and Mary's after practice in the late afternoons, happy hour time. They needed to drink fast if they wanted to drink a lot, because they were always due back at the university for the team dinner. Harry remembers them ordering 7-Up soda, too, the green bottles standing amidst the beer glasses. "They liked to pour that into the pitcher after they took the first draw," Harry said. The Rams, apparently, believed 7-Up's carbonation made it so "they could belch louder and drink more beer."

"*READY-SET-BURP-NOW-DRINK-FOUR!*"

Bottles of 7-Up! Every new problem awaits its innovative solution.

◆

NOT ONLY WAS THIS summer Pool's first training camp as head coach, it was also the first time in eight seasons that the Rams had assembled for camp without Bob Waterfield, the UCLA legend and the team's top quarterback through two national championships. If there had ever been a Mr. Ram it was Waterfield: a physical marvel who not only played football but had been on the gymnastics team in college (in her autobiography, Jane Russell recalls him doing one-armed handstands on roof corners). During Waterfield's tenure he twice led the league in passing yards. He'd also kicked field goals and played defense. As a local boy who had led UCLA's Bruins to a Rose Bowl, he proved a big draw at the LA Coliseum. Wags often quipped that Dan Reeves moved the team from Cleveland to take advantage of Waterfield's celebrity and that of his movie-star wife.

Not that Waterfield enjoyed the spotlight. He didn't. Taciturn, stiff-jawed, more Humphrey Bogart than Cary Grant, Waterfield wanted to play football and drink beer with friends and not much else. Talk? He'd as soon tear his own tongue out. In the *Los Angeles Times*, one friend described a round of golf with Waterfield:

"He used to say to me just five words all day… On the first tee he'd say, 'Hi, Greek.' And on the eighteenth green he'd say, 'So long, Greek.'"

Nor did he say much during games. Waterfield, wrote legendary LA sportswriter Melvin Durslag in a 1953 *Colliers* magazine article, "bottled his emotions perfectly for eight years on the field and never exchanged a cross word with anyone."

That might explain why he only lasted eight seasons. In *Jane Russell: My Paths and Detours*, Waterfield's wife writes that a duodenal ulcer ended his career: "He took the responsibility for the team's success too personally," Jane Russell wrote, "and while it made him the great player he was, it could also kill him if he didn't get out."

So he got out. And the quarterback who remained was the anti-Waterfield.

Norm "Dutch" Van Brocklin couldn't run and didn't kick well. He couldn't play defense. It's unlikely he ever attempted a handstand.

"Afoot, he was very inept," recalls Durslag. "He had no speed."

For some old-school coaches, that meant Van Brocklin was a poser, one-dimensional, and not a true quarterback. Or as the legendary coach George Halas said: "Van Brocklin can throw. Period. In the full sense of the word, he is not a professional player."

Retorted Van Brocklin: "And Joe Louis wasn't a great fighter…all he could do was punch."

Van Brocklin could throw. Despite small hands with fat fingers, he tossed elegant, lofty, on-target passes—what Hall of Famer Elroy "Crazylegs" Hirsch compared to catching "floating bubbles." Another player at the time said Van Brocklin could make passes that "belong in a museum." His form was like that of a javelin thrower, his whole body making the pass rather than just his arm.

And, unlike Waterfield, he talked. You couldn't shut him up.

"His reaction to anything could have been almost anything," said Durslag, who covered the Rams as a columnist for the *Los Angeles Examiner*, which later became the *Herald-Examiner*. "He was a very erratic type of guy. He was an outstanding player. He was a little nuts, you know?"

But people liked him as often as they didn't. A giggler, he'd laugh at anyone's joke, no matter how schmaltzy. A teammate, Durslag once reported, called Van Brocklin "the man most likely to be babied by an airline hostess."

Charming, loquacious, vicious, mean, and unpredictable as Los Angeles itself. Any moment could give rise to a new Norm Van Brocklin. Hall of Famer Baltimore Colt Art Donovan told me that he and Van Brocklin would cuss so much across the line of scrimmage that players on both sides thought they were nuts.

Decades later, Durslag still remembered a time he was in the coliseum locker room after a game interviewing Van Brocklin. A radio reporter—"a nice guy," Durslag said—came over to ask for three minutes from Van Brocklin. Dutch grabbed the radio guy's shirt, pulled him near and growled, "One of these days I'm going to hit you so hard your ass will bounce like a golf ball down a paved road." Another time, Durslag recalled, Van Brocklin was riding in a taxi with a reporter who'd been given a championship ring by the Rams. "Where'd you get that?" Van Brocklin said, then asked to hold it for a closer look. The reporter slipped off the ring and handed it to Van Brocklin, who flung it out the cab window.

"You're talking about a guy that's a little cuckoo," said Durslag.

Harry Thompson, who played offensive line for the Rams, remembered Van Brocklin's reaction during a game when the quarterback heard the play Pool wanted him to run. "Where did he get that?" Van Brocklin asked his teammates in the huddle, "from his asshole?"

Reportedly, Coach Pool said, in turn, of Van Brocklin: "He is not a picture passer like Bob Waterfield…but he is the most skillful of all. He will break every record—if some lineman doesn't break his neck first."

Waterfield and Van Brocklin had competed against each other—while playing for the same team—for four seasons. Most NFL teams used one quarterback and kept another in reserve, but Waterfield and Van Brocklin were both too good to keep one on the bench for too long. They played fifty/fifty during games. Dutch played half and Waterfield had played the other half. The pair were more like coquarterbacks, a two-headed coin that paid off with three NFL championship games, including one victory. But neither man liked the herky-jerky nobody's-the-big-dog approach. Naturally, Van Brocklin was the one to complain. When he argued with "Jumbo" over playing time, Stydahar benched him for the 1951 championship game. But with eight minutes left and the Rams and Browns tied at seventeen, Stydahar knew Waterfield wasn't going to win the game for him. He needed Van Brocklin's arm. So Van Brocklin took the field, and three plays later, he tossed one of those floating bubbles to Tom Fears who caught it and scored. Pretty soon, Jumbo Joe was gone. Dutch stayed.

When Waterfield's ulcer finally settled the competition, Van Brocklin knew, as Durslag wrote in *Colliers*, that without him, their one remaining quarterback, "the Rams would be dead." Van Brocklin's contract was supposed to pay him $14,500 for the 1953 season. He wanted more. Durslag reported how the negotiations went.

First, a sportswriter quoted Van Brocklin as stating he would demand $25,000, an unprecedented figure for professional football. Then Norm got hold of an advertising folder which the Rams mail each year to their season-ticket prospects. He returned it to the club, writing under the section marked "Suggestions":

"Pay Van Brocklin one-and-a-half-milion dollars a year."

They settled, finally, for about $20,000, and since Norm felt he went too cheap, he insisted on a mere one-year contract, with the idea of asking for more in 1954.

This was the man dad—"Lantern Jaw"—hoped he'd be paid to protect.

◆

THE NFL IN THE 1950s was no way for anyone to get rich—not the owners and especially not the players. Most didn't earn anywhere near the five figures Van Brocklin made in 1953. Linemen like my dad made five or six thousand dollars. Most needed off-season jobs to get by. Duane Putnam threw kegs in trucks for a Budweiser distributor. Woodley Lewis worked with juvenile delinquents through the LA police department. Andy Robustelli owned a sporting goods store in his native Connecticut. Because they were young men and athletic, some Rams showed up as extras in Hollywood films; Elroy "Crazylegs" Hirsch even starred in a couple (including a biopic of his own life and a prison flick that introduced the world to the famous ballad, "Unchained Melody"). New York Giant Hall of Famer Frank Gifford grew up in Los Angeles and spoke to me of his off-season routine, "You know, I wasn't even going to play pro football. I mean I could have made more money working as an extra and doing stunt work in the movies, which I did while I was at USC." Former Redskin and Giant Sam Huff was employed by the J. P. Stevens Textile Company selling men's fabrics reporting "I was there to learn how to deal and succeed in business. I learned how to maximize profit and such."

Fred Gehrke, a halfback with the Rams until 1949, had worked as an industrial illustrator for an aviation company. Putting paint on metal all day gave him the idea to paint sleek yellow Rams' horns on the players' helmets. Owner Reeves liked what he saw and paid Gehrke a dollar per helmet for his paint job—the first time any pro football team put an insignia on its hard hat. Creating an iconic logo, it was years before the rest of the NFL caught up.

At training camp in Redlands that summer, no player earned any money. That's how the contracts were structured. No pay until you play. Practice didn't count. Neither did those half a dozen or more games called "exhibitions," warm-ups that pit the Rams against other teams before the start of the real thing, the "regular" season.

So what happened if a coach says a guy's not good enough and sends him home from training camp? Sorry, Charlie. No money for you. What if a fella gets hurt in practice or an exhibition? It happened that summer to a rookie guard from the University of Houston. Rams players visited Frank James at Redlands Community Hospital, but if Frank got a penny for his troubles it was an aberration. Only those who made the roster for the regular season's opening kickoff could expect to get paid their contract salary.

Heading into the first exhibition game, my dad was healthy and scheduled to start at left guard, a good sign even if not yet earning a paycheck. The Rams would face Fort Ord's football squad in a game to be played in Long Beach, a short drive southeast of Los Angeles. Fort Ord's defense didn't intimidate the Rams, but its offense featured Ollie Matson, a renowned running back who had led the nation in rushing yards as a college senior, then gone on to win a bronze medal in the four hundred meter and a silver in the four-by-four-hundred-meter relay at the 1952 Olympics in Helsinki.

That night at Long Beach, the Rams offense performed as if cockeyed, but Fort Ord and Matson didn't offer much of a threat, either, never getting closer to the end zone than the Rams' twenty-one-yard line. The Rams beat the soldiers, 24–0, before a small crowd of twelve thousand. The warm-up showed that the Rams were still a few spark plugs short of an engine. Even six days later, in a 72–19 rout of Navy and Marine all-stars, the pros didn't dazzle.

Probably the coaches would have liked a few more easy exhibitions to help new guys find their way and veterans shake the off-season stupor. But it didn't matter what anyone wanted. The next exhibition would be the Rams' first true test, less a simulation and more of a donnybrook.

The game had become an annual grudge match. Always, it was played for charity, but nothing charitable happened on the field. Always, it was the Rams' debut at LA Memorial Coliseum, one of football's historic palaces. Fans filled the stadium, wanting to be impressed by that year's team. Rookies hoped to impress coaches and coaches hoped to impress Reeves. For the first time, the Rams would match up against another NFL team. Always it was the same opponent: Washington's Redskins. Seven times the Rams and Redskins had met this way, and the Rams had won four.

Even without pay, players on each team hit each other as if this exhibition were the real thing. To heck with waiting for the regular season. This game *was* the real thing. In the previous year's match-up, Washington's star running back suffered a broken arm.

For dad, the *Times* Charities Football Game would be, in the words of TV personality Ed Sullivan, "a really big show." For the first time in two years, he'd be tested by a professional defensive line, pitting himself again players heavier, taller, faster, and meaner than those the Far Eastern teams had offered. Those boys across the line would be fighting for their jobs, too, wanting to knock dad on his ass and crush Van Brocklin or any running back daring to carry the ball. That night, dad would need to prove to Hamp Pool that he'd learned his plays, that he could hand out licks and take 'em, too.

And there was this, a tender prick to however much sentimentality resided in my dad's very Irish Catholic heart: for the first time he would dress out in the uniform of a professional football player, then run onto a grassy field under the lights in his hometown. He'd hear cheers from a crowd of eighty thousand fans welcoming its team, and maybe there'd be a few faces among them he'd recognize: his father, Harry, or a priest from St. Brigid's, maybe old high school chums. He'd look up into the blackness beyond the lights and know the particular thrill of game time. Feel how different it was from games in any other city, like Pittsburgh or Chicago, where he'd played his rookie year. This was Los Angeles in 1953. Maybe Los Angeles wasn't so special to merit major league baseball, but the Rams were still the best pro game in town—Hollywood's team and worthy of a five-star premiere, with celebrities on hand to make fans laugh, and a five-ring circus featuring aerialists and trampolinists and performing elephants and Hap Henry with his trick dogs.

My dad, aka the Hooker, would fit his helmet with its golden horns over his head, snap in place the chin strap that stretched across his impressive jaw, then take the field and crouch in a three-point stance at the line— legs bent at the knees, fingers of his right hand in the grass and soft dirt. For a moment he'd become all heart and muscle, awaiting the "hut!" that would launch him like a rocket, his whole self exploding up and onward...

A night, as the shills like to say, to remember.

CHAPTER 3

"Git-gat-giddle with a geet-ga-zay!"

O N GAME DAY AT the Los Angeles Memorial Coliseum a groundskeeper finishes chalking the field's yard lines. Up high in the press box, a radio announcer stubs out a cigarette in an ash tray, lights another. He pencil-marks rosters, practices the pronunciation of names, especially those of Washington's Rykovich and Tershinksi and Ulinski. A wandering *Times* columnist notes the players from each team who have railroad nicknames: "Night Train Lane" and "Choo-Choo Justice," "Day Train Dwyer" and Chuck Drazenovich, aka the "Pennsylvania Flyer." Don't forget "Mule Train Heath," though his is not, technically, a railroad name.

No, Danny Kaye hasn't arrived yet, but don't worry, he's not performing until halftime.

Over on the southwest side of the stadium, circus folks are readying themselves for the pregame show, their trucks and wagons parked so they can roll equipment and animal cages down the ramp that cuts underneath the stadium and onto the field. Musetta, the heel-and-toe trapeze artist, touches up her mascara and chooses a lipstick to match her outfit, one a cigarette girl in Vegas might wear.

Fans come early, paying $3.90 for a reserved seat, a quarter for a game program. This morning's newspaper reported that the Russians have, for the first time, detonated a hydrogen bomb. Now we can blow them to smithereens, and they can send us to kingdom come. The uncertainty and worry is enough to make anyone want to get to the stadium and its distractions ahead of schedule. In the game program, a full-page advertisement from California Rent-A-Car promises that tonight somebody will win a two-door Ford sedan. "Your number is on the front of the program," it informs. A fan checks to see if his number looks lucky. It would be nice, like the ad says, to drive some cares away….

In the Rams locker room, a fellow in a T-shirt and slacks arranges bandages and wraps in case of injuries and checks to make sure there's plenty of ice for swollen ankles or shoulders. Hampton "Professor" Pool, the head coach, coughs and clears his throat. An ice pack might feel good to him right now, feverish and achy as he is with either a cold or the flu. Whichever, the sickbed will have to wait. He's got reminders to write on a chalkboard, players to coach.

First big game of the season, first big crowd. So who's nervous? Maybe the rookies. The Rams have nine. Some came straight out of college, but a few are NFL veterans new to this team, including Ben Agajanian, the kicker, there beside his locker, knotting the laces of his cleats—and likely the radio announcer is working his lips around that moniker, too. *AG-a-jay-nian? A-ga-JAYN-ian?* Maybe he'll just say "The Toeless Wonder," Ben's nickname since the accident. It involved a freight elevator, and it cost Ben four toes on his kicking foot. Now on one foot he wears size eleven. On the other, 7.5.

Agajanian is one of the rookies lucky enough—or good enough—to start tonight. The other two are Tom McCormick at halfback and my dad, while not a rookie but first time as a Ram, at offensive guard.

No player wants to lose a knuckle catching a ring on someone else's equipment, so Dad, at his locker, slips a gold band off the finger where a married man would sport his wedding ring. It's big, sized for his thick finger, and an oval stone dominates the face—without facets, bright red as a cardinal and bigger than a dime. Embossed on the edge reads the Latin *Universitatis* harkening back to my dad's days with the Jesuits at Santa Clara University. He wears the ring as a matter of course, and it has become part of who he is. He wore it while in the military, and he wore it during his season with the

Chicago Cardinals. Santa Clara University, which had its beginnings in a simple Spanish mission dedicated to Saint Clare of Assisi, gave him an education and a degree in history so one day he might become a high school teacher. It deepened his appreciation of the Mass and its mysteries, and it provided an opportunity to excel in football. Santa Clara shaped him—body, mind, and soul—and had more to do with the man he became than either the military or the National Football League did. As a priest wears a collar and a police officer carries a badge, Dad wears Santa Clara's ring, and, as far as he's concerned, he always will.

Today that ring is a reminder, too, of the last time he played in the LA Coliseum. It was nearly six years ago, on a Saturday—October 15, 1949. The Santa Clara Broncos were almost midway through my dad's senior season, with three victories against one loss, a team from a small school with players still unsure of how good they might be. At the coliseum, they were the visitors and the underdogs, facing UCLA's Bruins, who were 4–0 and predicted to be Rose Bowl–bound.

Tiny Santa Clara against mighty UCLA.

That was a good game. Turned into a heck of a season, too.

And because my dad is a student of history, a man for whom history matters, he knows that in another part of the coliseum, in the visitor's locker room, there's a defensive back for Washington who might also be thinking about that game against the Bruins. Dad knows that when the Rams take the field, the defense they face will include an Oklahoma-born halfback more familiar to him than most of his current teammates. Hall Gibson Haynes, dark-haired with an everyday handsomeness, was one of two team captains for the Santa Clara Broncos in that magical 1949 season.

My dad, naturally, was the other.

◆

THWARTED, CURBED, FRUSTRATED—THAT WAS UCLA in 1949 against my dad, Haynes and the Broncos. Said Red Sanders, UCLA's first-year head coach: "We were simply outplayed by a tough team that earned its victory."

The teams had last met in my dad's freshman year, a 33–7 victory for UCLA. Perhaps the Bruins expected another easy go against a school so small it had cancelled its football program during World War II. If so, the Bruins were wrong.

When did they first consider that these Broncos were no easy mark? Maybe it was a few minutes into the game after UCLA recovered a Santa Clara fumble, giving the Bruins the ball thirteen yards away from a possible touchdown. Most teams would hope to keep the Bruins in check, give up a few yards, force them to settle for a three-point field goal rather than a six-point touchdown. But Santa Clara did better, driving UCLA *backward*—all the way to the forty-two-yard line. Neither field goal nor touchdown was an option from so far away. The Bruins punted.

Or maybe it was after the second time the Bruins recovered a Santa Clara fumble—this time even closer to the end zone, only nine yards. Three plays later, UCLA had nudged forward to the two-yard line. On the fourth down, the last chance to score, Coach Sanders opted against the field goal and the Bruins again tried to run. Santa Clara allowed them only a foot.

Nearing the end of the third quarter neither team had scored, and UCLA's defenders were gassed. The Santa Clara lines—offensive and defensive, each led by my dad—had pushed and shoved and shoved and pushed until Bruins legs got wobbly. That's when Santa Clara scored the game's first points, the Broncos outmuscling UCLA on a quarterback sneak for the touchdown. Five minutes later, the Broncos scored again.

Final score? Santa Clara, 14; UCLA, zip.

"The statistics," wrote someone on the Santa Clara yearbook staff, "truly indicated the superiority of the fast-developing Broncos."

The nation noticed, too, and when Santa Clara finished the regular season at 7–2–1, the Broncos were ranked the fifteenth best college team in the country by the *Associated Press*. The committee for the renowned Orange Bowl sent an invitation, and Santa Clara accepted.

That Christmas night in San Jose, players and coaches, school officials, and some two hundred friends and family boarded a Southern Pacific Special with nearly twenty cars, bound for Miami. The trip lasted four days and covered 3,300 miles. The Bronco express arrived only a few days before the game, but according to Santa Clara–lore this was intentional. Coach Len Casanova had received a tip from one of his assistants that the fellow's father ran greyhounds at races in Florida and had discovered that the dogs fared better in the gauzy, steamy heat when he limited their workouts before a race. Maybe it was loopy to base a football team's future on what one man had to say about dogs, but Casanova took the advice seriously. In Florida, he kept workouts easy. Instead of sweating it out with tackling dummies, Casanova's young men hung around poolside in floral shirts and slacks, and they played shuffleboard like bona fide Florida pensioners.

Having arrived in early December, their opponent—the University of Kentucky Wildcats—had taken a different tack. That team's young coach worked his players hard. Bob Gain played on that team, and he'd eventually win the Outland Trophy for the nation's best college lineman. Years later, he recalled that Kentucky's coach, Paul "Bear" Bryant—who would one day become a college coaching legend and of the famous "Junction Boys" training camps of Texas A&M—brought the team to Cocoa Beach, woke the players each day at 5:00 a.m., and made them scrimmage twice a day. He squeezed practice sessions in between those. He forced his players to run wind sprints "like crazy, ten to twenty of those after practice," Gain said. The day after Christmas Bryant told his players, "You ate like a bunch of pigs. You better run it off."

Apparently Bear Bryant had no connections at the dog track.

But he and Kentucky did have the nation's confidence. The Wildcats were ranked eleventh in the country by the *Associated Press*, and Las Vegas oddsmakers had deemed them an early thirteen-point favorite, even though that point spread shrank to 5.5 points by game day. A young Jimmy Snyder, already a successful gambler but not yet the famous television personality "Jimmy the Greek," bet $265,000 on Kentucky.

The smart-money guys had good reasons to favor the Wildcats. As an article in Santa Clara's alumni magazine noted sixty years later, Kentucky's advantages were obvious—starting with the team's helmets. The Wildcats protected their heads with streamlined, light, and durable white plastic—the latest technology. The Broncos, as if from the mists of history, strapped on leather headgear that my dad used to say could "fit in your back pocket." To see the teams together on the field was like watching a horse-drawn wagon line up to race an Oldsmobile Rocket 88.

The most significant difference, though, might have been this: Bryant had two teams to Santa Clara's one.

In 1949, some coaches, including Bryant, had begun what would eventually become common practice: platooning their players. Traditionally, players had stayed on the field all the time, playing both offense and defense. Even for the Los Angeles Rams that year, Bob

Waterfield was playing quarterback and defensive back (and punting and kicking field goals). The old system favored the best all-around athletes.

But coaches who platooned had decided that offense and defense required different skills and different mindsets. A good offensive lineman, for example, followed directions, cared about timing, protected his quarterback. But a good defensive lineman caused chaos, surprised and improvised, and played as if he were a wildly swinging wrecking ball. Players who platooned could focus on the particular skills and attitudes suited for their positions. As an added bonus, during games one group could rest while the other took the field.

Kentucky platooned; Santa Clara did not. Dad played both offensive and defensive line. Hall Haynes, his cocaptain, was a halfback on offense who tried to break up passes on defense. Hardly a play went by with the captains on the bench. Oddsmakers must have figured Santa Clara's boys' would wear themselves out.

The Wildcats and Broncos met in the Orange Bowl on January 2, 1950, before some sixty-four thousand fans. The day promised a high of seventy-five degrees with humidity around 62 percent: less than sweltering, but still damper than the California air my dad and the other Broncos usually breathed.

As expected, Kentucky dominated the first half, building a statistical advantage in yards gained. But just as in the UCLA game, Santa Clara's defensive wall held.

At halftime, Santa Clara trailed, 7–0, but the Broncos had ended the half by stopping the Wildcats just yards from the end zone. A Broncos' halfback, Bernie Vogel, spoke of that defensive stand sixty years later. "It was a big moment," he said, as quoted in Santa Clara's alumni magazine. "You could just feel it was starting to go our way."

Back on the field for the second half, the Wildcats fumbled on their own thirteen-yard line. A few plays later, Santa Clara tied the game with a touchdown. Later in that same quarter, Santa Clara, again, had the ball and worked its way to the Kentucky two-yard line. Vogel was correct. Something in the game *had* shifted. The Wildcats, though platooning, played as if exhausted—and they were. Santa Clara's boys, though they were playing both ways, didn't seem at all fatigued. An *AP* reporter later described them as "iron." Solid and unyielding.

When the next play began, my dad lunged forward, taking a Wildcat low as the Broncos left end hit another man high. Both Wildcats toppled, and Haynes, taking the ball on a handoff, scooted around the block into the end zone. The nearest referee raised his hands to signal the touchdown and Santa Clara's lead. My dad scrambled up from under a pile of Wildcats, hopping in celebration and clapping twice to punctuate the play.

Kentucky eventually scored on a pass play, though the Wildcats kicker missed his extra-point attempt. Then, with Santa Clara leading, 14–13, and less than thirty seconds left in the game, halfback Vogel took a handoff from quarterback Johnny Pasco and ran sixteen yards through a gang of flat-footed Wildcats for a final Bronco touchdown. Santa Clara, 21; Kentucky, 13.

The upstarts from California had won the Orange Bowl. It was a noteworthy victory—but only that. For people outside of Santa Clara it wasn't even the day's biggest college football story (not with Oklahoma and Notre Dame arguing about which of them should be awarded the national championship). In years to come, football historians would call the Santa Clara-Kentucky Orange Bowl an upset, but nothing in the Broncos' victory was history making—fancy or forward-looking. It wasn't a landmark contest that changed how football could be played. In a way, the Broncos had approached the game as Jesuits would have them do: traditionally, relentlessly, and with rigor—one group of young men throwing their bodies at another in proven ways, winning because they were tougher than their opponents, more rugged, able to endure. It was a playing style that suited my dad's temperament and rewarded it, and it was satisfaction enough.

The train ride back home "was like a party from Miami to the Bay Area," recalled Len Napolitano, a reserve quarterback, in *Santa Clara* magazine. The Broncos were welcomed by more than ten thousand fans and with a victory parade. Cocaptains Haynes and my dad put on dark corduroy sport coats, and rode sitting atop the backseat of a convertible, California

Governor (and future US Supreme Court Chief Justice) Earl Warren squeezed between them. Haynes wore his shirt collar and coat open. Dad, always aware of the right way to do things, kept his coat buttoned and wore a tie with a tight knot.

Three weeks later, NFL coaches and executives gathered to draft the best college players. Of Santa Clara's Broncos, five were taken, and three would go on to make NFL teams: Hall Haynes, the 19th pick for Washington; Dad, 99th for Chicago's Cardinals; and Jerry Hennessy, 165th, also for the Cardinals. Hennessy and my dad must have been astonished to see themselves chosen by the same pro team. They'd been on the same team at Mount Carmel, a Roman Catholic high school in Los Angeles, then played together in college, and now had the chance to be teammates as pros.

In March, the new coach with the Chicago Cardinals traveled to Santa Clara to get Hennessy and my dad to sign contracts. Earl "Curly" Lambeau was as well-known a football ambassador as anyone could be. A frozen tundra named after him, he had played college ball under Coach Knute Rockne at Notre Dame, then in 1919 founded the Green Bay Packers for whom he played and coached over the next thirty years. The Cardinals hired Lambeau and gave him a piece of ownership at the twilight of his storied career. And now, he was sitting on the edge of a bed in my dad's dorm room checking out the man for himself, then reciting for the young man the terms of a proposed professional football contract. But my dad, in a chair nearby, couldn't concentrate. He was thinking about the priests at Santa Clara and their rules, particularly the strick prohibition against smoking.

Because here was Curly Lambeau propped on the edge of my dad's neatly made bed, waving around a lit cigarette stuck into the kind of extended holder FDR had used, as he explained how life would be with the Cardinals in America's second city.

What did Curly Lambeau care that each day a priest came to inspect the student rooms? But my dad knew that the priest would check the bed, if made and crisp. What if he smelled the cigarette smoke? What if he saw that dusting of gray?

Open a window? That would be impolite, and a priest outside might notice the smoke.

Was there a dish to offer as an ashtray? Of course not; smoking wasn't allowed. Why would my dad keep an ashtray?

So he stayed where he was, his eyes moving from Lambeau to the tip of the cigarette to the growing gray-white ash, the now-spilling ash. Lambeau was oblivious. And whatever he was saying, Dad didn't really hear, distracted by a future that might have had him reciting a hundred "Our Fathers." Maybe two hundred. Maybe the priests would just expel him. Ashes to ashes, as they say.

In my dad's life, a priest's direction would always trump that of an NFL coach. When Lambeau left Santa

Clara, he had Hennessy's signature, but not Dad's. Dad would eventually study his contract and sign with the Cardinals, but his first priority had to be exorcising his room of Lambeau's transgression.

◆

ON GAME DAY IN 1953, the Los Angeles Memorial Coliseum is a small world within a small world. The NFL is a dozen teams, not the thirty-two it will one day become. Each of those twelve teams carries about thirty-six players on its roster, and when you add coaches that gives the league a population of about five hundred. The NFL in 1953 is not a city; it's not even a small town. It's a neighborhood.

Duane Putnam, for example—the guard who will start tonight for the Rams on the left side of the offensive line—played college football with Washington's five-foot-seven-inch quarterback, the "Little General," Eddie LeBaron. And Leon McLaughlin, the Rams center, played for UCLA the day the Bruins lost to my dad's Broncos. As my dad fits pads over his shoulders in the Rams locker room, his ash-spilling coach with the Cardinals, Curly Lambeau, is a quick walk away, now in his second season as Washington's head man. Jerry Hennessy—my dad's good friend and teammate from Chicago, Santa Clara, and Mount Carmel High—is also in the visitor's locker room, having followed Lambeau from Chicago. Maybe my dad and Jerry will get together after the game. The hour will be late, but it would be pleasant to sit in the dark of the backyard next to St. Brigid's Church and listen to the city's night sounds and let my grandmother's cooking and a few beers ease the aches and bruises.

So, yes, the NFL is a neighborhood—but it's a neighborhood of a particular kind. Only men live there, and they know each other not just by shared histories, but through weekly collisions, a repeated violent intimacy. Forget who mows the lawn each week and who doesn't, whose car left an oil stain in the driveway, and who voted for Eisenhower. What these men know about each other is deeper. They know each other's weight and speed, their breath and sweat. They know soft flesh and sharp bone. They know where each other has been broken. They know, especially if they are offensive linemen, that it is true what a poet will one day write: *they live in a closed world, a small space few can share.* It exists, that space, in moments. A few seconds of strain, of giving everything you've got, and then it's over. To live in that space requires you to live in it again and again, play after play, through practices and games, everything you've got, and then again, everything, and again. No matter how it hurts, you tolerate the pain, and you endure the repetition for only one reason: you feel alive in that small space, which becomes something like home.

Now, the five-ring circus is finishing its act. The tumblers have tumbled, the clowns clowned. Time for the players to don their helmets and jog out through a dark tunnel to emerge where the lawn is green and mown, the fans eager, and the stadium lights ablaze.

◆

THE RAMS KICK OFF, and Washington needs only four plays to get two first downs. On three of them the runner is Charley "Choo-Choo" Justice. In this same game a year before, Justice rampaged through Los Angeles's defense, averaging eighteen yards with each carry. That ended—along with much of his season—on a play in the third quarter when two Rams tackled him and his left wrist fractured. Now he's running right and left, shifting and shaking Rams defenders as if he wants payback. Add a pass from the Little General, and the visiting team has its first touchdown on its first possession, and a 7–0 lead, just that fast.

The Rams run right back—literally. In a series that doesn't include a single pass play, Los Angeles running backs follow blocks made by my dad, Putnam, and company. After a twenty-three-yard rumble by Paul "Tank" Younger puts the Rams in range, Professor Pool sends the Toeless Wonder out to kick a sixteen-yard field goal, and Los Angeles trails Washington, 7–3.

Back and forth they go, Younger and Justice leading each team's efforts. Now and then LeBaron and Van Brocklin try a pass, but their coaches call the plays, and tonight Lambeau and Pool seem most interested in the ground game.

But look at the Rams' jerseys! Those guys can't keep their shirts on. Turns out somebody with the organization had the not-so ingenious idea to save money with jerseys that would tear away rather than rip. Seems like every down the Rams are reattaching their uniforms. Betcha those won't catch on.

Wait. Look. There goes Skeet Quinlan for the Rams! Twenty-four yards and a touchdown! Los Angeles takes the lead, 10–7, heading into halftime.

Now the football players have cleared the field, and here's Art Linkletter, our master of ceremonies, to say a few words about the *Los Angeles Times* Charities and the *Times* Boys Club. More than 2,500 boys have enjoyed the lessons and activities they've found there, and this game, played annually since the Rams arrived in Los Angeles in 1946, has raised more than six hundred thousand dollars, which built the boys club, and now equips and maintains it.

A good man, that Mr. Linkletter. A gentle soul. He's like the next-door neighbor you wish you had. In fact, because of his radio and television programs, such as *Kids Say the Darndest Things*, people here at the coliseum do have a sense that they know him. He might be famous, but he's not untouchable like a Rockefeller or a Queen Elizabeth.

You could say the same for Ann Miller, who danced with Fred Astaire in *Easter Parade* and who is out there on the field performing now. She was raised by a single mother who moved with her daughter from Texas to right here in Los Angeles. One time, Ann might have *actually* been the little girl who lived next door. Her mother might have borrowed sugar from you.

And Danny Kaye? He's a stitch, with that nonsense "git-gat-giddle with a geet-ga-zay," sounding like something you'd get if you recorded a toddler trying to speak Yiddish and then sped up the voice ten or twelve times. But his parents were immigrants, his father a tailor. In that movie *Walter Mitty*, he played a Joe Schmoe who dreamed of ways his life could be different, and isn't that just like you and me?

Sure, they're celebrities, and maybe their lives are a little easier for all that, or maybe not. The Rams are celebrities, too, but Duane Putnam served in an army artillery unit just like any guy might have. And my dad, he lives with my grandparents a few blocks from here and goes to Mass every Sunday.

Celebrity is a funny thing these days. It doesn't seem to mean you're untouchable. In fact, maybe it means you're more touchable. You're everybody's neighbor. Football player or movie star, you really are just like us.

◆

"A jester's chief employment is to kill himself for your enjoyment."

—*Danny Kaye*, The Court Jester, *1955*

THANKS TO BOB WATERFIELD and Jane Russell, the Rams arrived in Southern California already married to Hollywood.

Reporters joked that President Dan Reeves had moved the team from Cleveland just to keep the Waterfields happy. Even if that wasn't true, Reeves must have recognized the advantage in publicity and ticket sales that could come with bringing a quarterback married to a silver-screen bombshell into Hollywood's backyard. Maybe their marriage also gave him an inkling how enterprises that seemed so severely different—showbiz and football—could make a connection as natural as the ocean with the beach.

After all, pro football and Hollywood's concerns met at the same place: the ticket booth. The common goal was to get Mr. and Mrs. Main Street through the turnstile and into the seats. Entertainment for the populace. Let high society have its tennis clubs and opera; football and showbiz were for everybody else.

And those folks at the movie theater on Saturday night, who might also be at the game on Sunday, got much the same thing from both experiences. Good guys to cheer and bad guys to boo, drama and stories, climactic moments, and a glimpse of people who could do what others only dreamed of. Tank Younger's footwork and Norm Van Brocklin's floating bubble passes were in their ways just as astonishing as Danny Kaye's inimitable "git-gat" and Ann Miller's super-speed tap dancing. Westerns demanded that actors ride horses, throw punches, get shot. Comedy depended on a poke in the eye, a bump on the noggin, a pratfall. As Kaye once sang in a film, his job was to kill himself for the audience's enjoyment. Football players did that, too. In the end, movie or television star, quarterback or offensive guard, they were all entertainers, all workers in an industry. They were labor, not capital.

This was an important distinction in LA society. Hollywood's talent, no matter how famous or rich, was more likely to chum around with a bunch of football players than with Los Angeles's wealthy elites. Historian Kevin Starr has described Los Angeles in the 1950s as a city shaped by an oligarchy, built and ruled by people who had money from sources other than Hollywood. Some had earned their fortunes through land development or railroads or oil. Others had inherited it from family, or brought it with them when they left the East Coast to retire to California. The oligarchs were often Wasp-ish, sometimes anti-Semitic, concerned with reputation and background. They were wary of a movie industry that still carried a whiff of immorality dating back to nineteenth-century burlesque and vaudeville, a taint kept alive by scandal sheets that reported Hollywood's crime, vice, and broken taboos. Even movie and television stars who remained scandal free might not find themselves mingling with the Pauleys or the Firestones or the other movers and shakers. Having money was not the same as having a history of money, and many entertainers, like players for the Rams, had come from humble origins. Jane Russell's dad was an office manager. Art Linkletter left home after high school to hop freight trains, finding itinerant work as a meatpacker and busboy; before hitting it big, he broadcast from state fairs. Few Hollywood or television stars had been raised on art openings and opera and debutante balls.

But football? Many a marquee name could feel at home watching from the fifty-yard line.

In fact, even before the Rams arrived in Los Angeles, another pro football team had won the backing of some of Hollywood's biggest names. The Los Angeles Dons, part of an upstart league called the All-America Football Conference, played its first game in the Los Angeles Memorial Coliseum two weeks before the Rams kicked off their season. The Dons' owners included Bob Hope, Bing Crosby, Don Ameche, and Louis B. Mayer, the studio chief. But the Dons and the AAFC only lasted four years, and when the league shut down it left the Rams alone as Hollywood's Team.

Each party conveyed to the other a particular kind of celebrity. When Hollywood showed up for Rams games, it was as much an endorsement as when Elizabeth Taylor appeared in an ad for shampoo or John Wayne in one for cigarettes. A movie star in the stands or in the press box also brought a level of festivity and excitement to games.

For the movies, an industry based on faked sets and faked deaths and faked love, football players offered a sense of bruising physical reality to counter Hollywood's obvious artifice. A cameo from a handsome guy who really did get tackled, who really did suffer bruises and sprains, gave the movies grit and toughness. There was the novelty, too, of a football player acting—or trying to.

When the Rams held season-ending banquets, the entertainment could include Harry James and Betty Grable. Jerry Lewis and Bob Hope, who would also become a part-owner of the Rams, might make a few jokes at a player's expense. In the game program that night when Dad made his Rams debut against Washington, special note was made that three Rams— Leon McLaughlin, Jim Winkler, and Tank Younger— earned off-season money working as extras in films. By 1953, Woody Strode, who played briefly for the Rams after their arrival in Los Angeles, was deep into a long film career that would see him in several westerns and as a gladiator who fights Kirk Douglas in *Spartacus*.

Twice, the entire Rams squad portrayed football teams in film, including in a 1949 effort called *Easy Living*, starring Victor Mature as a quarterback facing the end of his career and dealing with a wife who doesn't love has-beens. "Loving you is like getting kicked in the heart," Victor Mature seems to say on a poster advertising the movie, "—only in football, I get paid for it!"

And, of course, there was Jane Russell, sitting in section eight of the coliseum with the other Rams wives, then with them again at the locker room as they waited for their husbands to emerge.

"She was always with us after games," recalled Patty Putnam, Duane's wife, years later, "and she was just as common as anybody else. She never got all dressed up, she never put on airs."

Hollywood: at a Rams game, it was just the good-looking guy and gal next door.

◆

AT HALFTIME ON THIS night of the *Times* Charities Game against Washington, the Rams locker room is not a happy place. Sitting players look at their knees. Hamp Pool clears his throat. His team played as bad in the first half as he'd felt that morning.

No. The team played worse.

Sloppy. Jittery. Embarrassing. The Rams had been one of the league's best teams the season before, losing only three games and each of those to same team: the Detroit Lions. Washington had been one of the league's worst teams. Tonight's game should be a drubbing.

Yet Rams defensive tackles can't seem to catch anybody running in a burgundy uniform. Washington had used some nine different running backs, and it didn't matter who carried the ball, the Rams couldn't grab them. In fact, the visitors have already amassed 171 yards by running the ball, almost twice as much as the Rams. One hundred seventy-one! That's a good night for most teams, and there's still a half to play.

It's amazing, really, that the Rams even have the lead. For that, they can thank Washington's coach, Curly Lambeau. Leading 7–3 and poised five yards from the end zone, Washington and Lambeau were looking at fourth down and a decision. The conventional thinking is to take the easy points— kick the field goal—when your team holds the lead. Why risk trying for the touchdown and failing? But to Pool's surprise, Lambeau kept his place kicker on the bench. He was going to go for the touchdown. "Boy, there's a break," Pool said, turning to an assistant coach with him on the sideline. Then the two watched as Washington's LeBaron dropped back to pass for the touchdown, only nobody caught the ball. The visitors had squandered their opportunity.

Now, if only the Rams can rack up a few more points in the second half. Where's that speedy, high-scoring offense Pool envisioned in training camp? With the exception of Tank Younger, the Rams look as if they're playing in cement shoes. Worse, the offensive linemen have missed assignments and even blocked the wrong players. How many passes has Van Brocklin completed? Six? Only *six*? But how's he supposed to throw if he's got Washington's linemen chasing him all over the field. C'mon, guys, make your blocks. You play this badly in the second half, and Dutch might finish with only twelve pass completions.

When was the last time he completed only twelve passes? Fifth grade?

Maybe Waterfield would have made a difference, but Waterfield isn't here, and he's not coming back. The

Rams have to learn to live without him. To win without him. To win a championship without him.

Halftime's almost over. Time to stop staring at those knees, boys. Rookies, you want a spot on this team? Earn it. Veterans, show them how. If you've got people in the stadium who know you, like my dad here, give them a reason to be proud. Now's the time. Get out there and hit somebody. Hit 'em hard.

And for God's sake, offense, make sure it's the *right* somebody.

CHAPTER 4

Grids and Gridirons

ALL THROUGH THE THIRD quarter and into the opening seconds of the fourth, Rams do indeed hit Redskins and Redskins hit Rams, but nothing much changes—especially not the score. But then, with his team trailing, 10–7, Washington's "Little General," Eddie LeBaron drops back to pass. It's a desperate ploy; he's only completed two passes all night, and there's no reason to believe he'll succeed this time.

LeBaron is tiny. Though the program lists him as five foot nine, he's really two inches shorter, something Washington's owner doesn't want the world—and especially opponents—to know. Thus, every program and roster sheet print the five foot nine lie. But reality is reality, and when a Ram rookie who is seven inches taller and some sixty pounds heavier crashes into LeBaron, the Little General sees stars. On the sidelines, the diagnosis is concussion, and Eddie LeBaron is out of the game.

Washington's coach, Curly Lambeau, has a rookie quarterback listed as LeBaron's back-up, but for some reason he keeps that youngster on the sidelines. Maybe the kid hasn't had time to learn the playbook, or maybe Lambeau just doesn't trust rookies. Whatever the reason, Lambeau sends in Harry Gilmer, a regular at running back who has in past seasons played some quarterback for Washington. In fact, as a sophomore at the University of Alabama, Gilmer gained some fame with an unconventional throwing style called the "jump pass." He'd leap before he threw, twisting his hips and snapping his body like a whip to add force to his throw. Tonight, though, Harry doesn't have much whip or jump. He has played every defensive down for Washington and half of the offensive ones. Bob Oates, reporting from the press box for the *Examiner*, watches Gilmer and sees a man so exhausted he can hardly bend over to take the ball on the snap. Once, Gilmer even drops it.

Two plays after LeBaron's brain bruise, Washington punts. Awaiting the ball for the Rams is Woodley Lewis, a Los Angeles native said to have the fleetest foot speed on the team. At the Rams' twenty-one-yard line, Lewis catches the ball, then darts and dodges. One tackler nearly grabs him, then a second and a third, but Lewis evades each to find the edge of the field. From there, it's an all-out sprint along the sideline, and no one is faster. Touchdown, Rams! The Toeless Wonder kicks the extra point, and Los Angeles now leads, 17–7.

The clock shows that there's time left, but everyone knows the game is decided. The fans know it, the reporters know it, the players do, too. Washington and Gilmer try, but for the rest of the game they can't manage even a single first down. The visitors are impotent, finished. Because they can, the Rams add a field goal. Final score: 20–7.

Fans applaud and cheer as the last seconds tick off, but it's not a full-throated whoop and holler. What they witnessed was far from the Rams' best effort. Wanting to test his new guys, Coach Hamp Pool tried out two, three, sometimes four players at every position except quarterback. Dad played left guard, but so did two others. Trying to win that way is like trying to tune up a Chevy with parts from a Ford. And an Oldsmobile. Also a Buick. The fans know this, and they know the game was only an exhibition, more about charity and the Boys Club and a night of family entertainment than it was about top-notch football.

Nevertheless, the home team won, so the paying public shows its respect, then crowds the exits. For all the early hubbub, there's little reason to linger. It's late on a Wednesday night, after all. There's work tomorrow— at the factory, the office, the car dealership.

Outside the stadium, cars and charter buses inch from parking lots, drivers with feet tapping the brake pedal more often than the gas. Eventually, everyone will make it home—west to the valley, or northeast to Pasadena; a short drive to Echo Park, a long haul southeast to Orange County or directly south to Long Beach. As they go people will orient themselves, recalling the mountains that are north, and they'll know by the ancient grids of Los Angeles's streets, first mapped in 1781, how to get where they mean to go.

◆

"DRIVE FROM THE OCEAN to Los Angeles," writes D. J. Waldie in *Holy Land*, "and you'll stay on the same grid of streets. The drive passes through suburb after suburb without interruption."

Angelenos have mostly constructed their city as if it is a series of giant checkerboards with streets running north to south, east to west. Downtown is an exception, though a slight one: its grid is angled so on a map it looks like Xs. This street pattern helps drivers find their way. Keep in mind landmark roads—Wilshire Boulevard or Adams Boulevard, Vermont or Western Avenues—and you can't get lost. You can always find a road or an intersection that is familiar and from there trace the way home. There is nothing innovative about these grids, which have their origins in Spanish colonial history. They are utterly predictable, measured with precision. As an example, in Waldie's suburb of Lakewood:

"Every block is divided into the common grid of fifty-by-one-hundred-foot lots...

"The streets do not curve or offer vistas. The street grid always intersects at right angles...

"The sidewalk is four feet wide. The street is forty feet wide. The strip of lawn between the street and the sidewalk is seven feet. The setback from the curb to the house is twenty feet...

"This pattern—of asphalt, grass, concrete, grass—is as regular as any thought of God's...

"The necessary illusion is predictability."

For this generation of Angelenos, predictability is an asset. It is a virtue. It is a comfort. Thirty or forty years from now people of subsequent generations might call Los Angeles's map and its endless grids a monotonous sprawl, but in 1953 the grids offer a respite. The people who drive these roads have lived with economic uncertainty through the Depression. As soldiers during World War II, they island-hopped the Pacific from deadly beachhead to deadly beachhead. They've been warned that anyone might be a communist infiltrator— from government officials to the people who write screenplays for Hollywood films. Just today, they learned that the Soviets have the H-bomb, putting the world's future in doubt. For these people—including the eighty thousand driving home after tonight's Rams game, their cares lifted by Danny Kaye and the night's hero, Woodley Lewis—for them, the great Los Angeles grid is a boon, a simple way home.

Perhaps an affinity for what is simple and unambiguous offers another reason why these fans love football as they do, the tens of thousands who come to watch this sport played on a grid. Sportswriters call the football field a gridiron, a word with origins in a medieval torture device used to roast heretics—but really, it's a lovely field of green, neatly and precisely mapped. One hundred yards from end zone to end zone. Every three feet a new chalk line, every five yards a number—twenty-five, thirty, thirty-five—like addresses on a neighborhood block, clarifying the boundaries of what's allowed and what's not so that a player always knows where he is, where he needs to be (fans know, too). Teams must move ten yards for a first down, another try. The home team camps on one side of the field, the visitors on the opposite. This gridiron, flat as a valley floor, makes football predictable, defined and finite, limited in space. Here there are no H-bombs, and if there are Commie infiltrators, well, they're watching the game, too. On this field, the world is easily understood, and any surprise is a surprise on a human scale: Woodley Lewis dancing through tackles, a man without toes on one foot kicking field goals. These things seem grand, and they are, but only because so many people pay money to witness them. In football, the necessary illusion is significance, what the fans pay to watch is what only truly matters. Eighty thousand people gather, bound by an agreement that for these few hours, what happens on the gridiron is momentous, life's only essential thing.

◆

Now that the game has ended, let Hollywood's camera again find my dad. The view is as if from the stadium's seats, but near enough to the field that we can make out his face as he laughs at something Duane Putnam leans near to say—some wry line, perhaps, about those silly tear-away jerseys. Sweaty and grass-stained, his forearms bruised from blocking, my dad keeps his head up, his massive chin lifted. Putter spits, his lip swollen with chaw. Then, a cutaway, and the picture is a close-up of Van Brocklin who barks and cocks a thumb, the signal from the captain that the boys need to hit the locker room. Cutaway once more, as en masse the players shift, then the camera eye focuses again on my dad in their midst. Even now, after his long night, there's power in his movement, there's momentum. This early in the season his legs recover quickly, so he jogs with his teammates into the lit tunnel that leads into the stadium's depths, the men's cleats clackety-clacking across the concrete.

They've earned a shower, these Rams, and maybe ice bags on sore shoulders and knees, and afterward a cold bottle of beer. Soon enough they'll be back to Redlands, that oven in the desert.

Tomorrow, though, at my grandparents' house, Dad can sleep late. No coach will wake him with some prerecorded *ready-set-hut*, and he's past the age when an early tap on his bedroom window summoned him to serve the Mass. Should one of St. Brigid's priests stop by, he'll want only coffee and conversation about the game. Dad will say he's grateful for the win, but that the Rams know they can play better. He can play better, too. If pressed, he'll admit he got a few licks in, and he took a few. He'll offer brief answers to the priest's questions, hoping the subject will change. He'll have no complaints, though he knows why Van Brocklin had so little time to throw. Van Brocklin's linemen couldn't protect him because an offensive line needs machine-like teamwork and that's impossible to develop when coaches are switching players at a dizzying pace. Against Washington, the Rams tried out sixteen fellows at the five offensive line positions. No one found a rhythm, because there was no rhythm. No linemen could practice teamwork, because who were your teammates? But that's the exhibition season for you. Once the coaches could settle on a roster, once my dad lines up regularly with the Putter and Charlie Toogood and Leon McLaughlin—the starters—to play an entire game, maybe then the offense will become the scoring machine Coach Pool says he wants.

But he won't tell the priest any of that.

What he will say, if the priest stops by, is that this was only an exhibition. It's a long season, and yes, Father, you're right, who knows what might happen. A championship?

We've got as good a chance as any. You like cream with your coffee, Father, isn't that right?

◆

IN THE LOCKER ROOM, Rams players know that they have escaped something, and they know which players rescued them: Paul "Tank" Younger, whose pile driving runs kept the Rams advancing when nothing else worked; and Woodley Lewis, who scored the game-clinching touchdown. Rightly, the newspapers will laud the pair the next day. What the *Times* and the *Examiner* will not mention, though, is the irony that the Rams won, and the Redskins were beaten, because of two men not welcome on Washington's roster.

Nowhere in the NFL rule book does it prohibit black players like Younger or Lewis from suiting up for an NFL team. In the league's earliest years, rosters included players both white and black (and Native American, including Jim Thorpe with the New York Giants and Chicago Cardinals, among others). But in 1933, for reasons that are murky and may have been different for each team, NFL owners adopted an unwritten edict: no black players on the field.

In 1953, Washington's owner, George Preston Marshall, still lives by that rule.

Six seasons earlier, the Rams were the first to break it.

Throughout the 1940s and '50s, the Rams and President Dan Reeves proved themselves innovators in many ways—the move west from Cleveland, the execution of a high-scoring passing game like never before, the marketing of a brand when Fred Gehrke painted gold horns on the team's helmets—but none of those ground-breaking changes involved questions of justice, morality, or human dignity. Welcoming black players to their roster could be called another Rams' innovation; it changed the established way of fielding an NFL team. But for Reeves and the Rams, breaking the league's unwritten rule against black players was foremost a matter of political expedience, integration as a means rather than an end in itself. Presented with an opportunity to integrate their team and thus reintegrate the league, the Rams took it—not to make history or because it was the right thing to do, but to guarantee themselves a chance to play in Los Angeles's Memorial Coliseum.

◆

ON TUESDAY, JANUARY 15, 1946, a meeting happened at the coliseum offices that would change the course of professional football history.

To that meeting came Charles Walsh, nicknamed "Chile" (sometimes spelled "Chili"), a football alum and graduate of LA's Hollywood High School, who had decades earlier moved to the Midwest but who still called Los Angeles his hometown. Just shy of forty-three years old, he was also general manager of what had been, until a few days earlier, the Cleveland Rams. And he was at the pinnacle of his football career.

A month and a day ago he'd been in Cleveland, bundled up in below-zero temperatures, watching rookie Bob Waterfield lead the Rams past the Washington Redskins, 15–14, to win their first NFL championship. And three days before this trip to Los Angeles, Walsh had been at the Commodore Hotel in New York City cajoling NFL owners into letting their now league-champion Rams scamper off to the West Coast.

When that vote went the Rams' way, it meant the team had bested the league twice in one month: once on the field, once in owners' meetings, and Walsh had been central to both efforts. Now a third challenge awaited him here in Los Angeles. His assignment: to secure a lease so the team could play its games at the Los Angeles Memorial Coliseum, the city's crown jewel of sports venues.

Walsh's boss, Rams president Dan Reeves, wanted to call the coliseum home, and it's easy to understand why.

Consider its size. Built of reinforced concrete and expanded when Los Angeles hosted the 1932 Olympics, the coliseum could hold more than one hundred thousand people. One hundred thousand ticket-paying, program-buying, hot-dog-eating fans.

A crowd of forty-six thousand had been considered impressive in Cleveland.

Then, consider the coliseum's aesthetics. Modeled on the one built in ancient Rome, the elliptical stadium featured at its east end a series of columns and arches, topped by a triumphal arch upon which the Olympic

Torch had once burned. The trappings gave any sport played in the coliseum the grand, legendary quality of an epic.

Then, understand its exclusivity. USC's mighty Trojans called the coliseum home, and UCLA played some football games there, too. The nine-man commission that governed the coliseum's use was known to favor its hometown college heroes and had never opened the stadium to any of the small-time professional football teams that in the 1940s and 1950s called Los Angeles home. The Trojans and the Bruins liked it that way.

To play in such a local landmark would confer immediate legitimacy. It would say: Behold, our new champions! Our *Los Angeles* Rams!

But both Reeves and Walsh knew it wouldn't be easy to win a lease, not with opposition from USC and UCLA. So Walsh, accompanied by the team's attorney, had come to his hometown bearing a gift for the commission and the city.

If granted the lease, Walsh promised, the Rams' first game in the stadium would be a headline-grabbing exhibition matchup: a replay of that winter's NFL championship against the Redskins. Moreover, the profits would go to charity. They'd call it the *Times* Charities Game, and if it was successful, the Rams and Redskins would play it every year. The offer was politically savvy given the power wielded in Los Angeles by the *Times'* owners, the Chandler family, and given patriarch Harry Chandler's influential role in the coliseum's financing and construction in the early 1920s.

How could the commission say no?

◆

THEY NUMBERED THREE, THE men—all African-American, all journalists writing for newspapers that served black communities—who came to the coliseum commission meeting that Tuesday in January 1946 to take on Chile Walsh and the Rams and through them the entire National Football League.

Herman Hill, who had played basketball at USC, worked as the West Coast editor of the *Pittsburgh Courier*, one of the nation's most prominent African-American newspapers. Abie Robinson oversaw the sports section at the *Los Angeles Sentinel*. And William Claire "Halley" Harding was a columnist for the *Los Angeles Tribune*, a man whose college career included football, basketball, and baseball—but who also boxed, acted, and fought with all his being against prejudiced whites (ofays, he called them) to create fair opportunities for black Americans. "God bless him," Herman Hill wrote years later in a letter to *Ebony* magazine, excerpts of which were published in 1970. "Halley used to tell ofays he got up every morning and proceeded to put his *boxing gloves* on as soon as he shaved and showered, to get ready to battle them and their prejudices!"

Hill, Robinson, and Harding sat together that day the coliseum commission considered the Rams' request for a lease. They were the only African-American men in the room—there to demand justice, to change history, to integrate professional football.

Professional football because it was not the Rams alone that day who wanted a lease to play pro football in the coliseum. An upstart league—the All-American Football Conference—had formed, and it included a Los Angeles franchise called the Dons, owned in part by Hollywood stars Don Ameche and Bing Crosby. Hill, Robinson, and Harding wanted to guarantee an integrated Dons, too.

The three sat listening while the teams made their pitches. Then, Commission Chairman Leonard Roach asked whether anyone else would like to speak regarding the teams' requests.

"That was our cue," Hill wrote in his letter to *Ebony.* "As a matter of fact, we had contacted Roach earlier and told him what we had planned to do—and he said, 'This will be your cue.'"

Halley Harding rose, metaphoric boxing gloves laced.

He spoke only a few minutes, and no record exists of his precise words. But those in the room remembered, and through their accounts published in books and magazines, the spirit of what Harding said survives.

Harding combined a journalist's brevity with a boxer's pugnacity to remind the commissioners—and Chile Walsh—that sports had long been integrated in California. Recall, he said, the UCLA team that featured future Rams quarterback Bob Waterfield playing alongside Kenny Washington and Woodrow Wilson Strode, both African-American and native to Los Angeles. Do not forget, he said, that the NFL was integrated at its start. He invoked the spirits of Fritz Pollard, who had coached an NFL team, and the famous Paul Robeson, who went from the Akron Pros and Milwaukee Badgers to a career in movies and theater. How can opportunity be denied to black players, Harding asked, when in the great war just won, black troops fought and died equally with their white fellows? Finally, he said, no public facility in Los Angeles ought to be leased to an organization that practices segregation. No organization that denies opportunities to people because of their race ought to be welcome in the City of Angels.

Chile Walsh hadn't expected this welcome home.

"He turned pale," Hill wrote, "and started to stutter."

Walsh denied that the Rams practiced discrimination. There's nothing in the rule book, he said, that bans black athletes.

Unwritten is not the same as nonexistent, said Harding. Look at the proof: no black man had played in the NFL in thirteen years. Kenny Washington, he noted, had been, arguably, the best football player in the country when he finished at UCLA, yet no NFL team drafted him or invited him to try out. Instead, he'd played football in Los Angeles for a team in a small regional league.

When Harding gave up the floor, the coliseum's commissioners began throwing their own punches. One asked whether the Rams would dare to bar Kenny Washington.

The Rams' attorney, according to Hill's letter, announced that "any qualified Negro could play with the Rams." Added Walsh: "Kenny Washington is invited by me at this moment to try out for the Los Angeles Rams."

Though the meeting ended without the commission granting a lease, Harding, Hill, and other African-American sportswriters kept pressure on Rams officials, even meeting with them at the Last Word Club on South Central Avenue at the heart of Los Angeles's black community. Negotiations continued, and the commission did eventually give both the Rams and Dons permission to use the coliseum.

The Rams then signed Kenny Washington to a contract, announced on March 21 at a press conference from the team's temporary headquarters, downtown's elegant Alexandria Hotel. A short while later, the team signed Woody Strode, Washington's friend and former UCLA teammate, in part to provide a roommate for Washington on road trips. When the Rams at last kicked off against the Redskins in the inaugural *Times* Charities Game—on the gridiron in Los Angeles's Memorial Coliseum—for the first time since 1933 black men wore the uniform of an NFL team in a game between NFL teams.

But wear the uniform is about all they did.

In his book, *Goal Dust*, written with Sam Young, Woody Strode notes that Rams coaches sent Washington into that first exhibition game for only one play in the first half, then for a few more in the game's final minutes. Strode himself watched from the sidelines.

That pattern foretold their careers. Washington, a running back who relied as much on quickness as strength, had joined the Rams already having endured multiple knee surgeries. With number thirteen on his jersey, his weary expression suggested a man who had worked hard for too long a time, whose body had aged too fast. He carried the ball only twenty-three times in his first season, and his time in the NFL lasted a mere three years. As for Strode, the Rams cut him in his second season, just after the *Times* Charities Game. Believing he had the skill and athleticism to succeed in the NFL and that the Rams coaches intentionally misused him, Strode ended his historic career embarrassed and angry. Famously, he told a reporter from *Sports Illustrated*, "If I have to integrate heaven, I don't want to go."

As if to prove that signing Washington and Strode was a token gesture to win the coliseum lease and sell tickets to LA's black community—less an innovation in how NFL teams could be built, and more a gimmick to make money—a Rams assistant coach once said, "I doubt we would have been interested in Washington if we had stayed in Cleveland."

So if the reintegration of the NFL was a victory, it hardly belonged to the Rams, who did the right thing out of political expedience and with little gusto. No, the victory belonged to Los Angeles itself, its culture of integration in sports, its public officials who were willing to push for change, and especially to Harding, Robinson, and Hill. Without ever playing a down of NFL football, they changed the league forever.

◆

BY 1953, WHEN MY dad had joined the Rams and the team played its ninth *Times* Charities Game against Washington, black players had not only been integrated, for the Rams, they had become integral.

Dick "Night Train" Lane's fourteen interceptions in 1952—his rookie season—set a league record that still stands more than sixty years later. What remains untallied were the number of players he knocked out of games. His hits were feral and feared, top-speed collisions pitting Night Train's forearm and shoulder against a receiver's head and neck. The Night Train Necktie, players called it, with equal parts admiration and apprehension—even after the league outlawed it.

Harry Thompson had started at right guard for the Rams in 1951, when they won the NFL championship by beating the Cleveland Browns. Now he was a substitute, suiting up in case any starting offensive lineman was ever hurt. Decades later, sportswriter Bob Oates would remember him in the pages of the *Times* as self-sacrificing, a man who almost always got cut, but somehow stayed on the roster.

Fleet-footed Woodley Lewis played halfback and defensive back, but he was most dangerous when awaiting a kick-off or punt. In an open field, he dazzled.

"Deacon" Dan Towler and Paul "Tank" Younger rumbled as part of what sportswriters had dubbed "The Bull Elephant Backfield." Each weighed nearly 230 pounds, making them as big—or bigger—than the linemen blocking for them.

But that was only five. Verdese Carter, my dad's teammate at Camp Drake in Japan, would be cut before the start of 1953's regular season.

Five out of thirty-five. The Rams were still majority white, like the county in which they played, which had about one black and one Hispanic resident for every fifteen Caucasians—less integrated even than the Rams locker room.

In 1953, there were grids on the city's map that white people wanted to keep for themselves—bright white lines across which black people couldn't buy homes without incident or penalty. That June, even as the Rams entered training camp, the United States Supreme Court handed down a decision that declared it unconstitutional for white Los Angeles homeowners to sue Leola Jackson, their white neighbor, who violated her development's covenants by selling her house to a "non-Caucasian" family. That spring, the *California Eagle*, perhaps LA's most prominent African-American newspaper, reported that threats and attempts at intimidation greeted black families moving into then working-class-white Compton. White and black youths clashed in school yards. Black families armed themselves against crowds of whites gathering outside their homes chanting "protect our children." Black players who were welcome in the Rams' locker room and cheered by fans would likely have been shunned in majority white neighborhoods no matter how well they tackled or ran.

On the road, players still found themselves segregated. When they couldn't stay in a hotel with the rest of the team—as they couldn't in Pennsylvania, or for exhibition games in Arkansas and Alabama, or in Chicago where they stayed in Southside hotels while white players bedded down on the Gold Coast—black players stayed with people who opened their homes, or they bunked in separate hotels.

Back home was better. A little.

In a group photograph of the Rams Kick-Off Banquet at the Los Angeles Biltmore Hotel in 1954, there is a sea of white faces in the hall, hundreds of revelers, including players, smiling up toward the camera. One needs a magnifying glass to find faces that might be African-American. Way in the back there are two. Maybe.

The Rams, the NFL, and Los Angeles still had much work to do.

"I think every athlete had to be embarrassed in those times," said Sam Huff. "Bobby Mitchell was the first black [player] to come to the Washington Redskins and the team was the last to have a black player. I know it's part of history, but it's a part of history I don't like."

◆

WAS IT A TWIST? A blow? Both?

Whichever, in his first season with the Rams, Dad's knee had gotten wonky during one of the last exhibition games, and now he needed to give it ice and rest. It wasn't just pain. Pain, he could ignore. It was swelling, stiffness, the way the knee didn't quite work right.

He needed the joint for those quick side cuts—the Rams offense called for linemen who could shift side-to-side quick as a finger-snap. And he needed the knee to plant, to make a foundation that allowed him to hold his blocks. Rules kept offensive linemen from using their hands against a defender—no grabbing, no shoving, no nothing. Get caught with your palms out and you might cost your team a five-yard penalty. So technique called for linemen to raise their arms like chicken wings, hands near each other at the center of the chest, and push from the shoulders. As linemen go, my dad didn't have the strongest legs. His weren't ever going to be compared to coliseum pillars. No, his work depended on his upper body—shoulders, chest, abdomen, back. But he still needed to plant those knees, to brace his powerful torso. Knees were the cornerstones. If one wobbled, the building swayed.

Though not one to fret, my dad must have felt a twinge of concern. The team hadn't yet made its final cuts, and other players had been let go during exhibition seasons because of injuries. Coaches always sought reasons to trim the roster. And Dad was no Van Brocklin or Tank Younger, not a player who over several seasons had earned the right to be carried through injuries. With the Rams, my dad was a rookie. Worse, he was a lineman—the most interchangeable position in the sport.

So you never know.

But when the Rams finished their exhibition season in 1953 and began the regular season—the part of the schedule when games counted in the standings and players at last got paid—my dad's name was on the roster. Even though his knee kept him out of that opener against the New York Giants and Harry Thompson lined up in his spot, he had made the team. Of the final thirty-five, he was one.

Had he doubted? After two seasons away from pro football, he had reason to wonder whether he still had the speed, the skill, the strength, the know-how to play. But if he had doubts, those were gone. Dad had earned a spot with one of the best teams in football—even with his cranky knee.

So when the Rams played the Green Bay Packers in front of some twenty-three thousand people in Milwaukee's County Stadium, my dad was on the field, throwing blocks for Van Brocklin, Younger, and the others. The Rams won that day, and then they won the next week, beating their old nemesis Detroit, the team that had defeated them three times the previous season, including in a game to determine which team would move on to the NFL championship.

By midseason in 1953, the Rams had won five of their first six games and led in the NFL's Western Conference standings. They'd beaten Detroit twice, the last time at the Los Angeles Memorial Coliseum in front of ninety-four thousand fans—only eight thousand shy of filling the coliseum.

A championship? The priest from St. Brigid's might ask again, his coffee black, a ritual repeated.

Sure, Father, my dad would say. *We've got as good a chance as any.*

CHAPTER 5

Safety

THE 1953 SEASON PROVED cruel to the Rams. At midpoint, they looked like world-beaters. If the NFL was a mountain, the Rams were like their big-horned namesakes, balanced powerfully on the tallest crag. They led the Western Conference standings with five victories against one defeat—and that loss had been only by one point. Twice, the Rams had beaten their chief nemesis, the defending NFL champions, the Detroit Lions.

Then they lost their footing.

A loss to San Francisco—the Rams' in-state rival since the 49ers joined the NFL in, coincidentally, 1949.

A tie with the Chicago Cardinals, perhaps the league's worst team.

Too late, the Rams finally won again, beating the Colts at Baltimore. Detroit had seized the conference lead, and the reigning champs weren't yielding the top spot. A third Rams loss, this time to the lowly Chicago Bears at Wrigley Field, had Rams fans and the team's owners looking toward the next season. The press blamed Van Brocklin, saying he was "struggling through the worst slump of his pro career." Recalling the speed with which Team President Dan Reeves had fired past coaches, sportswriters printed rumors that Hamp Pool's job was in jeopardy. The atmosphere mirrored that of the year's beginning, with players and coaches working to justify their jobs, but with one significant difference. In training camp, that need was coupled with optimism and hope for a season that shone with potential. Now, the work was spiced with disappointment and dissatisfaction over a bungled year.

Into that cauldron, the Baltimore Colts arrived for a game in Los Angeles.

Those poor Baltimore Colts.

A year before, they had been the hapless Dallas Texans, a team with only one victory to its name, so badly run that its owner ended the year having lost nearly a quarter million dollars. Now, as the Baltimore Colts, the players had a city that cared about them and a more successful owner in Carroll Rosenbloom, who would later own the Rams. But on the field, "hapless" still described them. Their starting quarterback had suffered a season-ending shoulder injury a few games before, and they'd already lost seven games, including that one to the Rams in Baltimore, 21–13.

Now, the two teams were to meet again in a game scheduled for a national television broadcast. The Los Angeles Almost-Was's against the Baltimore Never-Had-A-Chances.

Los Angeles fans couldn't generate much enthusiasm. Though ninety-four thousand had shown up to watch the Rams beat Detroit on November 1, that was when their team looked championship bound. Plus, that opponent was a rival and maybe the NFL's best team, a marquee draw in its own right.

Now, a month later, with almost no shot at the playoffs, and facing a lousy opponent with little name recognition, the Rams could muster only twenty-seven thousand fans on that beautiful, seventy-nine-degree afternoon.

That's about seven empty seats for every three taken. That's Rams coming out of the tunnel and being greeted by a vast emptiness, fans scattered here and there like beach sand blown across a Malibu parking lot.

Perhaps the small crowd embarrassed the Rams. Perhaps it angered them.

Because what those fans saw at the coliseum on December 5, 1953, was a one-sided butt-kicking. What those fans saw was a furious and proud Rams team, venting its frustration with a season turned sour. What those fans saw was Dutch Van Brocklin, on the first play of the game, throwing fifty yards to Skeet Quinlan, and only two plays later tossing a touchdown pass to Vitamin Smith.

What they saw was perfectly executed Rams football, just as Coach Hamp Pool had envisioned in training camp.

By the end of the first quarter, the Rams led, 14–0. The Colts' only opportunity to score in that quarter had been a field goal attempt, but Night Train Lane crashed through the Colts' linemen and sprang high to block the kick. And the Rams kept coming. Whatever adjustments Colts coach Keith Molesworth made to his game plan at halftime didn't matter. By the end of the third quarter, the Rams led, 45–0.

Forty-five to zip.

It was the most points the Rams had scored in a game all season. It doubled the scores of their previous two games.

But the afternoon wouldn't end perfectly. The Colts did eventually find some points, and the Hooker, my dad—in the last game of his first season with his hometown team—played an unwitting role.

◆

LATE IN THE GAME, Hamp Pool decided to give Van Brocklin—and the Colts—a break. He brought Dutch to the bench and sent in a rookie back-up from USC named Rudy Bukich who promptly found himself running a play deep on the Rams' side of the field, so deep that when he dropped back to pass he was standing in his own end zone. Unable to find an open receiver and desperate with the knowledge that the Colts were about to grind him into the grass, Bukich cocked his arm and tossed what one report called a "throw-away."

If the Colts had tackled Bukich in the end zone, they would have been awarded two points—a safety. Embarrassing. A safety would mean Bukich and the Rams offense couldn't take care of business and move the ball forward. It would mean the defense had pushed them right off the field.

So Bukich threw the ball away. He tossed it to my dad.

My dad was himself still in the end zone as Bukich's "throw-away" pass arrived. He had not practiced for this moment. In fact, if my dad had ever caught a ball in a game, it had probably been years ago. Catching passes had never been his job.

But he caught this one. My dad reached out, grabbed the ball, nestled it against his body. Now he needed to run and get the ball the heck out of the end zone.

Art Donovan meant to stop him.

Art Donovan: a future Hall of Famer, a crew-cut mass of fat and muscle some thirty pounds heavier than my dad, a man who famously joked in his Brooklyn accent that the only exercise he ever did was to "lift a twenty-four-ounce can of Schlitz" or "thirteen pushups in thirteen years" and who still managed to crush offensive linemen. He said to me, "I told [then-coach] Weeb Ewbanks, do you want a gymnast or a football player?"

Donovan plowed into my dad. Another Colt piled on, and together they crumpled my dad in the end zone for the safety.

And that was how the game ended, a few minutes later, with the score, 45–2.

It's easy to picture Dad chuckling after Donovan clambered up off of him. As a lineman, he was used to nobody paying any attention to what he did, except the quarterback, and maybe my grandpa in section eight, or a few friends and the coaches. But here, for one moment, all eyes in the stadium had been on number sixty-three. And in a game with no tension, with the season's smallest crowd, he gave everyone a final pratfall, a *hoop-de-doo* bit of comic relief. And that's the show, folks! Thanks for coming!

It's fun to imagine, too, what a laughing Van Brocklin had to say when ol' Lantern Jaw made it back to the sidelines.

Hey, Hooker! Maybe the Colts will give you their game ball!

◆

THE RAMS WON THEIR next game, too, the last of the season, beating Green Bay, 33–17. Maybe that, combined with the victory over the Colts, saved Hamp Pool's job, because the season ended, and he didn't get fired. His innovations—including that fast snap count—hadn't led to a championship, and Pool would need to come back with something new and better if the Rams were going to improve the results of this season.

In the NFL national championship game, Detroit beat the Cleveland Browns, 17–16. Shortly after, the *Associated Press* named its all-pro team and about half the first-team players were from those two franchises. But there were also a few Rams, including Elroy "Crazylegs" Hirsch and defensive players Andy Robustelli and Don Paul. Several Rams earned Honorable Mention, including Dan Towler, Skeet Quinlan, Norm Van Brocklin, Woodley Lewis, Charlie Toogood, and Night Train Lane. Right up there with them was the Hooker, my dad.

So, yes, the Rams still had the pieces. They still had the belief. They just needed another try. They needed 1954 to hurry up and arrive.

◆

BUT BEFORE 1954 BEGINS, step back once more to August 1953 and to that *Times* Charities Game featuring Danny Kaye at halftime, the game that put my dad in the Memorial Coliseum for the first time as a Ram.

The next day in Los Angeles, newspaper sports sections were almost entirely taken up by the Rams, except for an important piece of newspaper real estate, the column written by the *Examiner*'s Vincent X. Flaherty. For most sportswriters, the biggest story the day before had been football, but Flaherty had baseball on his mind.

Flaherty, a Los Angeles transplant, had left a sportswriting job in Washington, DC to follow his older brother who had headed west to pursue an acting career. The younger Flaherty, a fan of the Washington Senators, was also zealous in his belief that Los Angeles needed major league baseball. Bringing baseball to LA had become for him a personal crusade.

And baseball is what he was writing about the morning after my dad made his debut with the Rams at Memorial Coliseum.

"Del E. Webb," wrote Flaherty, "co-owner of the New York Yankees, is puzzled by the failure of Los Angeles to step up and make a strong organized bid for a major league baseball franchise."

Webb, a California native and famous real estate developer who would one day build Sun City, Arizona, was in Los Angeles overseeing construction of the $14 million Beverly Hilton Hotel on Wilshire Boulevard. He had been a principal owner of the Yankees for nearly a decade. Flaherty dedicated that day's column to Webb's thoughts about Los Angeles and the major leagues.

Webb told Flaherty that "Baltimore, Montreal, and Toronto also have pledged themselves ready to do anything to get a major league team, but Los Angeles has absolutely nothing. Los Angeles had better get a move on fast.

"If Los Angeles doesn't wake up and do something quick," he said, "this town just won't get a team."

That quote must have put Flaherty into a tizzy. In his book about O'Malley and the Dodgers, author Michael D'Antonio describes Flaherty as a "newspaperman, civic booster, and raconteur" who had "poured enormous amounts of time and energy into the cause of bringing the major leagues to Los Angeles" and who had become "a volunteer staff man for the self-appointed Los Angeles Citizens Committee for Major League Baseball. The leaders of this group included Howard Hughes, Conrad Hilton, Louis B. Mayer, and Reese Taylor, the president of Union Oil."

In fact, D'Antonio noted, Flaherty's efforts to consummate deals between the likes of major league owners, financiers from Texas, and Los Angeles's uber-wealthy citizens, drove him to exhaustion and a hospital bed that very August.

The next month, when major league baseball's owners gathered at the Commodore Hotel in New York City for their annual meeting, they listened to proposals from cities interested in winning a baseball team. In particular, the owners wanted to find a new home for the struggling St. Louis Browns. "Baltimore's presentation was the most complete," D'Antonio writes. "The LA group, headed by newly elected mayor Norris Poulson, said they could not put forward a specific ownership group but could raise the money to buy the club within a week." To prove this, Howard Hughes sent a $1 million check.

But Los Angeles's sketchy plans couldn't compete with Baltimore's careful proposal. The owners voted to let Baltimore have the Browns. The next season introduced a new city and team to major league baseball: the Baltimore Orioles.

In Los Angeles, Poulson, Flaherty, and others had to start again. They knew they had allies in both money and politics, including the young and energetic new city councilwoman Roz Wiener. Poulson was conservative, and liberal Wiener had opposed his appointment of a fellow to the library board because the man was a proponent of book burning. But it was clear she wanted Los Angeles to be a great city, and on that the mayor and she might find common ground.

There'd be other opportunities, after all. Los Angeles would have to be united in its effort. And better prepared.

But for now there was no major league baseball in Los Angeles, and the Rams remained safely atop the city's professional sporting world, unrivaled for the mantle of Hollywood's Team.

PART II

PART II

CHAPTER 6

The Weights

M R. AND MRS. JOHN Patrick Costello—
my maternal grandparents—planned
their daughter's wedding reception
for the backyard. Card tables and
folding chairs and a bar, and, because the Costellos had
generous neighbors and expected plenty of guests, a
second bar behind the house next door. The head table
and wedding cake would go in the garage, which was
a double garage, set toward the back of the lot, with
enough room. That it was a garage didn't really matter.
This was south central Los Angeles in June of 1955,
and if Hollywood could turn a scrub brush stage set
into a jungle or medieval castle for its cameras, then
certainly the Costellos could transform their garage for

a wedding. Build their own magic kingdom right there at Fourth Avenue and Forty-Eighth Street.

So my mom's uncle and aunt got to work. They lined the interior walls of the garage with vast sheets of pink paper, covering rough-cut two-by-four studs and oil cans. They unrolled strips of crepe paper, letting it sag from the ceiling like ribbon. They hung lacy paper wedding bells that unfolded like accordions. On the tables they arranged plastic daisies and tall tapered candles.

If Los Angeles taught any lesson, it was that a person with imagination could fool a camera, trick the eye. In years to come, when people looked back on photographs of my parents posing by their wedding cake, no one would guess that the happy couple toasting with champagne saucers could be anywhere but a pleasant supper club in the valley or a Knights of Columbus banquet hall.

Los Angeles and Southern California kept you guessing that way, even in 1955. You might, for example, stroll down a street and into a gunfight between police and mobsters, only to learn the bullets were blanks and the blood fake. A Chinese temple rising along Hollywood Boulevard, you would come to understand, was only a movie house. The TV show, *Dragnet*, insisted that every episode's story of crime was true; the actor who portrayed the show's hero, Sergeant Joe Friday, was called in by the LAPD to help interview police academy applicants. In Los Angeles of 1955, fantasies and illusions and artifice offered a relentless challenge to reality, so much so that the nature of reality needed to be reconsidered. Even as Bernadette Costello and my dad pledged on June 25, 1955, "I do," the animation impresario Walt Disney was overseeing the final touches on a $17 million 160-acre fantasy land, perhaps the world's greatest—if not most expensive—illusion, featuring moon trips and Mississippi River rides and a castle—all right there just over thirty miles away in Anaheim.

In such a place as Los Angeles in 1955, a short man becomes tall, a brunette becomes a blonde, a cartoon mouse dances with a snow-white princess. One day on a blind date, you might even step through a door for a St. Patrick's Day dance, as John Patrick Costello's daughter, Bernadette, did in 1954, and glimpse a fellow at the bar, an old friend. You wave to him with enthusiasm—the way you wave to a friend—and that's when you realize you don't recognize that man *at all*, and you just behaved in a very forward way with a stranger.

But a short while later, when that fellow at the bar looks at you again and stands, you aren't so troubled by your mistake. Because he stands and stands—he's so tall and broad-shouldered. Blond, too, with skin so Irish-fair it's pink. His eyes are bright-bright blue, visible from even over there—and what a jaw.

With a slight limp and a warm smile, he walks to meet you. Your blind date is about to not work out.

So much in Los Angeles depends on a trick of the eye.

◆

BERNADETTE WAS HER GIVEN name, same as my grandma's, but the Costellos called her Micki. Born in 1930, she arrived in this world—so the story goes—with red hair and blue eyes, inspiring her Irish uncle Ray Heinen to say, "If that's not a Mick, I've never seen one."

That hair color changed through the years, sometimes more red, sometimes more blonde (and sometimes *nudged* toward the blonde). She had a small mouth and a small chin and mischief in her smile. "Bubbly," a friend would call her, years later. She grew up working-class Roman Catholic near South LA's Leimert Park neighborhood not far from my dad's childhood home, in a craftsman-style bungalow that, for the area, was good-sized. Its second story and four bedrooms made it a rarity, though its one bathroom proved it still fit the neighborhood's working-class backdrop.

My mom's education began at St. Brigid's Catholic School, but a new parish opened in 1937 to accommodate the population boom. From then on, Mom switched school to where her family went to Mass, at the Church of the Transfiguration. For high school, she joined other Catholic girls at St. Mary's Academy, while her brothers attended the same all-boys Mount Carmel High as my dad, where they played football. (She didn't much care for the sport except that her brothers played.) Wanting to be a schoolteacher, she studied education at Los Angeles State College, and by 1954, when she was twenty-three years old, she had responsibility for a classroom of kids at Woodcrest Elementary School.

That was when she, unmarried and living still with her parents, agreed to a blind date with a friend's cousin for St. Patrick's Day.

All three hit the town—Mom, her friend, Beverly, and Beverly's cousin, the Blind Date. The gals wanted to dance. So they found their way downtown to the Roger Young Auditorium where outside they could hear big band tunes, peppy stuff to make your feet tap and kick. Just inside the entrance, a crowd of twenty-somethings wearing green milled around, talking loud over the band's blaring horns. Our trio pushed through, hoping to find a table somewhere, and that's when my mom glanced at the bar and saw two fellas talking, and she recognized the one and waved.

He waved back. And that's the moment she knew she'd just been forward with a stranger.

"Oh, God," she told Beverley. "I didn't even really know him."

They found a table, ordered, and the Blind Date asked my mom to dance. A few songs later, he still hadn't generated much enthusiasm in her.

But that fellow at the bar, the stranger who had looked familiar, his eyes kept finding her through all the St. Paddy's green, through all the cigarette smoke and noise. A nice looking man, that's for sure. And then he rose from his stool and strolled to their table, blue eyes and shoulders, and now she knew she'd never met him before.

My mom, at five foot five, felt dwarfed. Even his hands were outsized. She explained her mistake. He smiled some more. They chatted a bit. He'd grown up in St. Brigid's Parish and still lived there. She knew that church; it wasn't far from her own house. That's where she'd started elementary school.

No, he said, he wasn't planning to dance. Hurt my leg at work. But tell me your last name again. Costello? Did your brothers go to Mount Carmel? Yes, I knew them.

He telephoned a few days later and invited her out. When he came to my grandparents' home to pick her up for the date, her father—a man who'd once worked as a boxing promoter—took his daughter aside.

"Well," my grandfather told her, "this time you brought me a man."

That night, my mom and the man enjoyed a movie. Of course it would be a movie. This was Los Angeles, after all. But a movie would also serve as a conversation dodge, a way her date could avoid talking about himself. Though my mom didn't yet realize it, the familiar stranger didn't much like himself as a subject. So a movie was perfect: they could sit quietly for two hours, then afterward talk about the film, or he could ask about her, and bubbly as she was, they'd pass the night without him having to say much. In fact, after he dropped her off, she realized she didn't know much about him—except that he'd delivered her family's newspaper years before and that he would take her out again.

When later she told her oldest brother his name—John Hock—her brother said, "From Mount Carmel? You know he plays for the Rams?"

She did not. How could she have? Dad had never mentioned it.

◆

SHE COULD FILL A catalogue with all that he didn't say. He never said, for example, that he preferred red meat cooked well done. Instead, when my grandma served him a medium rare hamburger, he ate it up as if it were the world's only food and he a starving man. But later, when my mom asked privately how he had enjoyed the hamburger, he said:

"I'm accustomed to eating meat well done, but medium rare is growing on me."

Another time—the two of them on a date with people she knew—she began to introduce him by saying, "He plays for—" but she stopped mid-sentence when he nudged her gently. And without him saying, she understood that he'd rather be known as a guy from the neighborhood who had delivered her newspaper rather than as a man who spent his Sundays cheered by tens of thousands.

He also kept to himself about the extent of his knee troubles. But they, too, eventually became clear.

Dad seldom wanted to walk far when on dates. Very few long, romantic strolls. No hikes into nearby mountain canyons. Not much, if any, dancing.

His right knee worked all right, but she knew it was also his weak spot. If the Greek hero, Achilles, was vulnerable at the heel, Dad could be undone by his knee. That's why he babied it, made few requests of it in day-to-day life—because he knew the demands he asked of it on the field. She learned to share his concern; they weren't a couple to fox-trot or Lindy Hop.

They became beach people, Dad and Mom, often taking afternoons at Santa Monica. There, the only long walk involved traversing the vast California beach—sometimes as long as a football field—to the water's edge. Once arrived, Dad and Mom could arrange towels and lie in the sun from afternoon into evening if they wanted, sip sodas from a cooler, eat a sandwich or two. If the sun beat too hard, they could step out past the breakers and let the buoyant ocean lift them. There, in cool water up to his chest, Dad walked as if he weighed no more than a teenager. The ocean pushed and pulled him, but its great gift was how it relieved his knee of its burden. The Pacific carried him.

Then, he'd come out of the water and towel off, the California sun high and bright above him, its light caught by water drops on those broad shoulders. My mom might not have given words to her thoughts, because she wouldn't have wanted him to feel self-conscious, but she must have thought the same thing other women did—and men, too—seeing my dad shirtless.

What those others thought?

Adonis. Greek god.

But that would describe a man stepped right out of a library's classics section. For an Irish-American kid growing up during the Depression, maybe the more accurate reference would be to a man who stepped out of a comic book advertisement.

Maybe the more accurate reference would be Atlas.

◆

CHARLES ATLAS MADE A fortune convincing American boys that to be the perfect man required the perfect physique—and that he knew how to build one. His iconic ads told over and over again the story of a skinny, pitiable man at the beach getting sand kicked in his face by a bully. But after "Mac" adopted Charles Atlas's system and built his brawn, he returned to the beach, smacked the bully's jaw, and became a man who could stride the world. And win the company of bikini-clad lookers.

Dad tried what Atlas peddled—a system like isometrics. But my dad went far beyond that. He also pumped iron, lifted dumbbells and barbells. The results were Herculean.

It would have been blasphemous for my dad to say that he experienced something holy in the weight room. What he found, though, was familiar to what church provided. If not spiritual, lifting weights at least offered a particular kind of peace—or maybe calmness. Through the Mass, those qualities came from the repetition of words and motions, of kneeling and standing, counting the beads of a rosary, making the sign of the cross, humbling the self before the Father, Son, and Holy Ghost. In the weight room there was also ritual: the chalk on the hands, the measuring of weight, the lift, the drop, the squat, the curl, the counting of repetitions and sets. And if the weight room lacked as a spiritual place, it did make space for a quality in my dad that Mass could not accommodate. In the weight room, he could be both meditative and fiercely physical. He could calm his mind while forcing his muscles to the point of pain, then through and past that point. The weights would always win in the end—he could never lift them all forever. What mattered was that with weights he could bring himself to a single teeth-gritting, jaw-clenching, muscle-popping moment—be ferocious and conquer. This toil touched in him what was old and elemental. Men had slung weight for centuries, and in a place like Los Angeles, where so much attention focused on the newest and the latest, the most dazzling and the falsest, the weight room took my dad deeply into true, old ways, to the beginning of things—not to their future.

It was also for many years a thing not to share with his coaches, an activity best practiced underground. Even by 1954, most NFL coaches disapproved of weightlifting. They still subscribed to a myth that pumping iron was bad for a player.

The coaches, though wrong, had reasons to think as they did. The game, and how it was played—even its rules—rewarded a balance of speed and brawn. Offensive linemen, in particular, needed quickness balanced with strength. That blocking technique that kept the arms tight in front of a player's body meant linemen couldn't reach out to shove someone. A block had to be made with the body—so the body had to react quickly to a defender's feints and dodges. Fat, slow men, no matter how powerful, got cut from the team. Mobility and endurance mattered. In the NFL of the 1950s, the ideal offensive lineman was less an unmovable mountain than he was a galloping bull, deft and solid—strength and speed in careful balance.

Too much strength, coaches feared, would upset that delicate equilibrium; thus the wariness regarding weightlifting. They looked at a fellow like Charles Atlas and saw someone "muscle-bound," that is, tied up by his own muscles.

So if a coach caught a player in a gym doing a clean-and-jerk, that player could get a chewing out or maybe worse.

That risk—especially for my dad and his fellow lineman Duane Putnam—was necessary.

◆

THEY TALKED, THE LINEMEN did. Shared secrets. They talked about Frank Gifford. Gifford talked about his regimen, "what I did was run. I just ran everywhere. It was apples and oranges and nothing like they do today." The linemen were different. Through the 1953 season, the Putter had watched my dad and noticed the advantages my dad gained from lifting weights. They'd both started the year listed at around 230 pounds, but by the season's end the Putter had dropped to a skinny 207. He feared the Rams would cut him if he returned the next year at that weight. No matter how nimble, a 207-pound Putter would get brushed aside by defensive linemen like Art Donovan and Leo Nomellini, future Hall of Famers with the Colts and 49ers, who each carried fifty more pounds than Putnam.

Not only in Charles Atlas' advertisements would big guys bully smaller men.

But look at my dad. By the end of the season he still came in around 230 pounds. And my dad, Putnam knew, lifted weights. You couldn't look like Adonis if you didn't.

So Putnam filed that information away until a day that spring on the UCLA campus where he was taking graduate courses in physical education. This was 1954 and the same spring when Dad and Mom started to date.

Putnam met a familiar face on campus: UCLA shot-putter Clyde Wetter. The Putter had put the shot himself for a few years in college and had come to know Wetter that way.

Wetter had heaved a sixteen-pound shot as far as fifty-four feet. He was one of the strongest men Putnam had ever seen. As the man chatted, Putnam explained his weight loss, his lack of strength. "Putter," Wetter said, "I guarantee you I can put twenty pounds on you if you'll work with the weights."

Let's give it a go, Putter said. Maybe coaches would chew him out if they discovered he was lifting weights, but if he didn't gain weight the coaches would cut him anyway. And if weightlifting gave him a body like my dad's—or sort of like his—the Putter couldn't imagine coaches complaining at all.

Working with Wetter twice a week through that spring, Putnam bulked up to 240 pounds. By the start of the Rams training camp, he could dead lift 400 pounds and curl 135. Now, like his buddy Dad, he was ready for those Donovans and Nomellinis.

And just to make sure he was still quick, the Putter dropped ten pounds. He felt stronger, quicker, faster.

No defensive linemen would kick sand in Duane Putnam or my dad's faces.

◆

BUT THAT KNEE. DAD's danged knee. He could add power to his chest and shoulders, strengthen his quadriceps and calves, stretch his hamstrings…

The right knee still wobbled.

Through the 1954 training camp, he massaged it. Iced it. Sat in whirlpool baths. The team's athletic trainer rubbed and wrapped the knee. Yet if anything, it was getting worse, looser.

That August, when the time came for the 1954 *Times* Charities Game, my dad's second such, he gave his two complimentary tickets to a cousin and asked the cousin to bring my mom. My mom and Charles Grimes sat in section eight, near the thirty-five-yard line toward the southwest end of the stadium, where the guests of Rams players always sat—and for this game, so did Bob Hope, who now owned a small share of the team and was just a few seats away from my mom. The event proved festive, as the *Times* Charities Game always did, and the field play went well for Los Angeles, which beat Washington, 27–7. But the evening didn't go so well for Dad. Mom would always remember that in this, the first game she ever watched him play, he got hurt.

It was the knee, of course. The injury kept him out of the next exhibition game against the Cleveland Browns while doctors looked him over. A tendon in his right knee—likely the patellar, connecting the kneecap to the shin bone—wouldn't heal by itself, they said. If the knee were to be repaired, it would need surgery. The prognosis for recovery must have covered a range of possibilities—from a few weeks to much, much longer— because there was some hope and even an expectation among coaches and players that my dad could recover and return to the team in a few games.

He didn't. The knee met the knife in August, and that cost him all of 1954.

◆

"FRESH FLESH."

Decades after his NFL career ended, that's how Art Hauser described the attitude of coaches and management toward players. One player goes down, gets tired, gets old, the team finds fresh flesh. A new body.

In that summer of 1954, his rookie year, Hauser wanted little else than to be a body the Rams could use. With a flat-nosed and flat-browed face that looked tough enough to break a brick, Hauser came into camp as a recent graduate from Xavier University in Cincinnati. He brought what he had: a Midwestern work ethic, a quick and powerful body, a suitcase, a few pairs of socks, and not much else. Rams coaches listed him third on their depth chart, behind the starters and the reserves. A third-string linemen, Hauser knew, seldom made the team. So his investment of time with the Rams carried a big risk. Players, after all, didn't get paid for training camp—not a penny—and Hauser's wife, Joanie, was eight months pregnant.

Each day he learned by his failures. In practice, across the line of scrimmage, crouched Duane Putnam and my dad. Hauser had been a pass rusher in college. His job had been to tackle the quarterback. But now he'd try to headfake Putnam and my dad and they'd still get in his way. He'd spin, and they'd know where he was going. Maybe he was as strong as them, but these guys, they had technique.

He must have done something right, though. Cut after cut, the coaches kept Hauser around. But as the last exhibition game approached—the final cut to follow—he believed he was done. He counted, studied the line-up, figured which veterans the Rams would keep, and the calculations always ended with the same result: Art Hauser wouldn't make the team. There just wasn't room. Even when Rams coaches let him start in that last exhibition game against the Eagles, he figured his time was done.

The Rams had played that last exhibition game in San Antonio, then boarded a plane for Washington, DC where they would open the regular season. They brought Hauser along, but he knew the inevitable was coming. And in the nation's capital, in a meeting room at a hotel on Dupont Circle, Hauser gathered with the rest of the players, and prepared himself for the final word. Coach Hamp Pool stood before the group, looked around at the faces, and announced, "This is the Rams team for 1954."

Hauser looked around the room. Veterans stared back at him. Who was cut? What veteran was let go?

Later, everyone heard the explanation. No one got cut. But my dad's knee surgery would keep him out for the season. Hauser, that fresh rookie flesh, won my dad's spot.

◆

If there had been any Rams season Dad would do well to have missed while convalescing, 1954 was the best choice. No one could blame him for the mess.

The Rams finished 6–5–1, their worst record since 1948. That 6–5–1 record gave them fourth place in the

NFL's six-team Western Conference. Given regular Rams' expectations, the 1954 season was a disaster.

The problems were myriad, though Coach Hampton Pool received the blame for many. He was in his third season as Rams coach and never under him had the team improved. He'd begun the 1954 season by making questionable trades—sending away Night Train Lane, for example—but once the season began, the "Ramanian Empire" (as one journalist called it) crumbled. Pool changed the offense every week to suit each new opponent, then raged against players who couldn't master a new system in time for Sunday. Players publicly complained after he railed against them during halftime of a game against the Lions in October, and several assistant coaches pledged to quit. Pool, chastened, apologized and said he would adopt a new attitude, that of a "Happy Warrior." He even brought Norman Vincent Peale's *The Power of Positive Thinking* to a team meeting and read aloud from it for an hour.

That didn't get a positive reaction.

But his ever-changing game plans remained, and it became clear that "Happy Warrior" wasn't Pool's style. He was a twenty-hours-a-day kind of worker, and what he demanded of himself he also demanded of his players and assistants. After a loss to the Chicago Bears on November 29, Pool again unleashed his temper.

During a film session in which he and players reviewed the previous game, he lambasted all-pro running back "Deacon" Dan Towler and berated as "a loafer" Tom Fears—a player on his way to the Hall of Fame. He warned everyone that the next two games would decide who was called back for the '55 season and how much money they'd earn. "I've been too easy on you guys," Pool reportedly said. "We're going to play this my way, again."

Players rebelled. "If Pool stays," one veteran star anonymously told the *Los Angeles Times*, "there are going to be some very good players who won't be back next year. All we want to do is win the championship, but we've gotten to the point where we don't think we can do it with Hamp Pool." Added a lineman: "That blow-up Wednesday was the worst I've ever seen in all my years of pro football. Players expect to get chewed out, but not when they haven't got it coming to them."

Through the public feuding, Rams president Dan Reeves insisted Pool would be his coach again in 1955. Then the 1954 season ended, and Rams assistant coaches resigned en masse—or maybe they were fired. Stories say both happened. A few days later, Pool was out, too. "I should have spent less time on the field, held fewer team meetings, kept everything simpler," Pool is quoted saying years later in Mickey Herskowitz's book, *The Golden Age of Pro Football: A Remembrance of Pro Football in the 1950s*. "I would change the offense every week to fit the opponent. I was a stickler for detail. Football should be a simple game, really."

Yet football isn't a simple game. It wasn't so in 1954, and it was becoming more complicated every season.

A game can't really be simple when it involves precise technique and timing between eleven men, while another eleven wearing different color jerseys try to violently disrupt that timing. In such a game, details do matter; sticklers are welcome. Of the three aspects Pool considered to be at the root of his failure with the Rams, the one that rings most true is that he shouldn't have changed the offense every week.

The Rams' culture since the move west had been akin to Los Angeles's culture: one that encouraged the next new, best thing. Reeves hired men who could invent, innovate. He seemed to like the mad-scientist model of coach. But Pool had become less inventor and more nonstop tinkerer. An example: he'd brought back an innovation—the two-headed quarterback— introduced by his old mentor, "Jumbo" Joe Stydahar, except that tactic wasn't a surprise anymore. Worse, it angered Norm Van Brocklin who again had to share his job. If Dutch had endured that arrangement when the other quarterback was Mr. Ram, Bob Waterfield, now he was flat-out insulted that he had to share the ball with a *rookie*: Vanderbilt's Billy Wade.

What Pool did by changing the offense every week wasn't innovative, it was week-to-week problem-solving. He didn't create a surprising way to play football that would force other teams to react to the Rams. That's what had happened in the 1940s, when Rams coach Clark Shaughnessy moved a halfback to the line of scrimmage and introduced the position people now call a wide receiver. That change surprised teams, made the way they played defense irrelevant. Something similar happened when Stydahar put three two-hundred-plus-pound "bull elephant" fullbacks in the game at the same time, so they could rumble over opponents.

What Pool did was to react—weekly—to the Rams' opponents. In a way, he paid more attention to other teams than he did to the Rams or to football itself.

That pattern didn't appeal to players. They needed a playbook they could rely on, one to master. The playbook could offer something new; it just couldn't keep changing. As Pool kept awake into the wee hours devising his gambits and stratagems, he'd forgotten that a person could tinker so much with a car that it would never, ever drive right.

So Pool was out.

And Reeves started a nationwide search for his next new mad scientist.

◆

DAD, MEANWHILE, HAD SPENT that lost 1954 season in pursuits other than learning Hamp Pool's playbook. When the cast came off, his leg was stiff and the muscles atrophied, so he began to stretch and exercise. Sometimes my mom helped, massaging the joint, rubbing the muscles around it. He kept the rest of his body in shape as best he could, lifting weights while taking care not to strain the knee. He lifted books, too, because he'd begun to take graduate courses in education at the University of Southern California.

He missed football, my mom could tell, though he seldom gave voice to how or why, and he never complained. He put himself to work, because missing the 1954 season was a reminder that he needed a plan for life after football. Even next season, when he rejoined the team, one good shot at his knee could end his career. Guys got hurt all the time, especially linemen. Broken noses and jaws and fingers and legs. Night Train Lane, after his trade to the Chicago Cardinals, suffered a fractured skull—in practice. In a game that fall against San Francisco, Bob Carey, a Rams offensive end, ran out to set a block for Skeet Quinlan and had his leg snapped for his troubles. His season ended at Queen of the Angels Hospital, and who knew whether he'd be back? And Stan West, a Rams defensive lineman, once got smashed in the face so hard his front teeth drove straight through his lip. Football hurt people, sometimes for good. The smart player had a back-up plan. Dad's was to teach history to high school students. The salary would be about the same, and maybe he could coach a high school team for a little extra money. Get summers off, so he and my mom could spend them together at the beach.

◆

EIGHT DAYS AFTER HAMP Pool was fired, My dad came to my mom's house with a little box in his pocket.

With my grandparents busy in the kitchen preparing Christmas Eve dinner, and my mom seated on the couch in her parents' living room, Dad presented her with the engagement ring, her Christmas gift.

◆

DAD FELT PLAYFUL THE day of the wedding, posing for a photograph with his best man—my mom's older brother, Jack—as if the two were late to the church. Jack gripped my dad's wrist with one hand and with the other pointed at his watch. "*We have to go!*" Dad, gape-mouthed, raised his free hand to his forehead. "*Oh no! My wife will kill me—and we're not even married!*"

He wore a tuxedo with striped pants and an ascot, with a carnation as his boutonniere. When he met his bride that morning at Transfiguration Church, she wore a simple crown to hold her veil, a scoop-neck gown with a poofy skirt, and she carried a bouquet of roses. Inside the sanctuary, Mom and Dad stood under a dark, mahogany-stained ceiling, before the church's altar, white-washed walls aglow with light that filtered through rose-shaped stained glass windows on the church's eastern wall. Ahead and above them, depicted in a mural and atop a mountain, a transfigured and radiant Jesus spread his arms, accompanied by prophets: Moses with God's commandments to the bride's side, Elijah on the groom's.

That day—June 25—was unseasonably cool, a day when gentlemen didn't mind keeping their suit coats buttoned and ties knotted tight: a good day for a wedding. In fact, that day three Rams were "deserting the bachelor ranks," as the *Times* put it. Along with my dad, Les Richter, a first-year linebacker, married Miss Marilyn Shaw. Tom Dahms, a tackle from San Diego State, married Miss Diane Ewing.

At the Costellos' house, the wedding was small and simple, friends and family. The only NFL players to attend were men who had played with my dad in high school at Mount Carmel: Jerry Hennessy, who had suited up with Washington, and John Helwig who was with the Chicago Bears. Helwig served as a groomsman. Guests mingled in the garage and in the backyard, and when my mom tried to go to the one bathroom in the house, she found a line snaking down the stairs. Naturally, she was given priority.

"Get through this," my dad whispered to my mom in the midst of the toasts and the hubbub, "and then we're all right."

The party ended that afternoon. My mom and dad changed into traveling clothes, then met in the driveway. Her car, a fire-red Chevy convertible coupe, was packed and ready for their honeymoon. Plastered to the trunk were two signs reading "Just Married." My parents planned a few days up north, in the tiny beach town of Carpinteria, just south of Santa Barbara. Dad, after all, had been out of football for the past year. They couldn't pay for much more than that.

Nor were they rich in time. Training camp would begin in a few weeks, probably why so many Rams had scheduled their wedding days for June 25. Dad planned to report early. After having missed an entire season, he wanted to arrive in Redlands by July 12, get a jump on things. There was a new coach to learn, with a new system. The Rams had hired a college fellow from the Midwest, someone with no professional football coaching experience. The scuttlebutt said Sid Gillman was a kind of genius—a fellow who played jazz piano, wore a bow tie on the sidelines, and had come up with new ways of studying game films. Certainly he'd won plenty at the University of Cincinnati. But you never knew with a new man at the top how things would go. Dad wasn't the sort who liked too many surprises.

Two weeks and three days until then. Hardly much time at all. Just enough for that Carpinteria honeymoon. Just enough to move out of their parents' houses and into their new home (a small second-story two-bedroom apartment on Slauson Avenue; my mom's aunt lived underneath, but she owned the building and gave the newlyweds a deal). Just enough time for my mom to feed her husband chocolate cake, and steak cooked the way he liked it, and potatoes, and bring him coffee in a small cup, because he always liked to drink from the smallest cup in the cabinet. Just enough time to figure out how to share the bathroom, and for her to enjoy riding in the car's passenger seat, and to decide who gets what side of the bed. Just two weeks and three days to learn everything she would miss after he left for Redlands.

CHAPTER 7

Tomorrowland

THE SUMMER OF 1955 brought lots of news to Los Angeles, news that would usually grab people's imagination—but not this year. What people wanted to talk about was the opening in Anaheim, on July 17, of a magic kingdom built over land that a year earlier had been orange groves.

The Rams' training camp had opened with a new coach and new hope after the dismal 6–5–1 season, but so what? Roz Wiener Wyman, the now-married, young city councilwoman, was appointed by her colleagues to pursue the New York's Giants or Brooklyn's Dodgers—but who cared? Louise Brough of Beverly Hills won Wimbledon, but…

And it wasn't just people in Los Angeles excited about Disneyland. The whole nation had turned its eyes to Southern California.

The Washington Post: "22,000 Guests Attend Disneyland Premiere"

The Baltimore Sun: "CROWDS JAM DISNEYLAND OPENING DAY"

The New York Times: "Disneyland Is a Child's World of Fantasy Come True"

Hedda Hopper, the gossip column queen, wrote that there weren't "enough adjectives in Mr. Webster's book to describe the wonders of this playground."

Adjectives, perhaps not. But there were facts aplenty:

- From groundbreaking to grand opening took one year and a day
- The park cost $17 million to build and, with parking lots, covered 160 acres
- The King Arthur carousel was the world's largest with more than seventy horses
- To guarantee authenticity along Disneyland's jungle river, Walt Disney had arranged for trees from thirty to fifty years old to be shipped from Africa, South America, and southeast Asia, including Australia, New Zealand, and China
- The parking lots combined to cover three million square feet, all paved
- Construction required 3.5 million board feet of lumber

- Fifteen thousand people stood in line for the opening, four abreast, snaking a mile from the gate. Thirty thousand visited that day
- On opening day, the Santa Ana freeway leading to Disneyland was jammed for five miles—adding to skies already smoggy—until Disney officials opened their parking lots that morning
- Tickets were one dollar for adults, fifty cents for children
- Dishwashing machines broke down in one restaurant and a gas leak closed part of Fantasyland's castle, but both repairs were made in a short time

In the weeks before the opening, Walt Disney himself had overseen the final details of construction, flying by helicopter from his offices in Burbank so as to avoid the Santa Ana, which clogged with construction and supply trucks on their way to Disneyland. One problem he'd had to solve was the loss of construction workers.

Many had been drawn away from building Disneyland by the promise of bonuses to help construct nearby tract housing—part of Anaheim's Disneyland-fueled growth spurt. This was part of a new phenomenon in Southern California. Most growth in previous decades stemmed from manufacturing and wartime spending. Hollywood and the entertainment industry had helped to create an identity for the region and to bolster the economy and population, but the most powerful engines of economic expansion had come from those other sources. Now, with the nation out of wartime, Walt Disney was turning entertainment and tourism into major economic forces. If Hughes Aircraft had helped remake physical landscapes in past decades, now it was Mickey Mouse and Dumbo driving backhoes.

Or, more specifically, Peter Pan and Captain Nemo and Davy Crockett. Those had been Disney's biggest hits the previous three years, the latter appearing on a Wednesday night TV show on ABC and dominating that night's ratings. The TV show had debuted for the 1954–55 season, keeping the Disney brand in front of audiences year-round, and it had provided a weekly advertisement for the park, then under construction in Anaheim.

As a concept, Disneyland itself was like nothing the world had ever seen. It was not an amusement park like Coney Island. It was not a fair. People groped to describe it. Some called it a new wonder for the world. "An integrated juvenile world's fair of fantasy," *The New York Times* decided. "A juvenile fairyland," said *The Boston Globe.*

Though the park itself contained five "lands"— Main Street, USA; Fantasyland; Adventureland; Frontierland; and Tomorrowland—visitors could opt for only two experiences of time: the past or the future. At Disneyland, there was no present.

The park's backward glance took visitors to gas-lit streets (Main Street, USA), paddle-wheel riverboats

(Frontierland), and colonial jungles in Africa (Adventureland). For future dreams, Tomorrowland launched visitors on a rocket bound for the moon and drove them through a four-wheeled paradise called "Autopia." There, children steered while parents, as passengers, relaxed—an idealized view of a world with roads far less cluttered than the Santa Ana Freeway.

In his book, *The Hollywood Sign*, historian Leo Braudy notes that a characteristic of Hollywood has been to juxtapose the future with a sentimental past— and Disneyland did exactly that. Visitors could choose from two narratives. In one, the distant past was fun and thrilling, and safe and clean—and romanticized. In the other, the future promised technological achievement and societal perfection. In promoting Tomorrowland, the company line was that designers had been given the task of theorizing what the decades would bring— from the types of chairs to how people would dress. In actuality, they'd been given the task of creating an idealized future—a sentimental hope to equal a sentimental past.

Disneyland's concept of time was perhaps the greatest difference between this park and what Americans had known as "amusement parks." Places such as Coney Island, with their Tilt-A-Whirls and the Ferris wheels, were neither past nor future. They were about thrills, right now, relentlessly in the present.

The present lay outside Disneyland's walls. The present—its smog and traffic jams, its racial tensions, its Cold War enemies with their hammer and sickle, its sex symbols, its litter, its crime—was what people escaped at the gates of that fairytale kingdom, that national time machine, as seen each week on TV. The promise Disneyland made was that the present would one day vanish and make way for a perfect world where kids could drive safely. Perhaps even across the surface of the moon.

◆

To ACCOMPANY ITS STORY headlining the news that the Rams had hired Sid Gillman as head coach, the *Los Angeles Times* chose a photograph of Gillman sitting beside a film projector. In the photo, his eyes are wide, as if he's been too long in the dark. His straightforward look suggests that he's focused on whatever that projector projects. Lacking the stereotypical football coach's square jaw or thick neck, Gillman in the photograph most resembles a Hollywood director reviewing a final cut. More Elia Kazan or Joseph Mankiewicz than Curly Lambeau or Jumbo Joe Stydahar.

Clearly, he's been posed by the photog. There's no light emanating from the projector. Gillman's probably looking at a blank screen. Nevertheless, the *Times* couldn't have chosen a better image.

David Gillman, Sid's father, had run movie theaters in Minneapolis when Sid was a boy. As a college football coach, Sid found a competitive edge in the film room, using the technology to see the game in new ways.

While other coaches studied game films from kickoff to final tick of the clock, Gillman cut them up, spliced them. With scissors and tape, he edited films by play or by player. He could then watch a dozen versions of the same trap or counter play over and over again, and by comparison discover what worked best and what didn't. He could isolate a quarterback and see under what circumstances the quarterback made accurate throws and when he didn't.

Then, he could take that information and teach.

Films helped him design his game plans, showed him his team's strengths and opponents' weaknesses. Films allowed him to "grade" his college players on their performance and to show them—right on the screen—what they'd goofed up and what they'd done right.

The nickname Van Brocklin gave his new coach—"the Rabbi"—was a poke at Gillman, who was Jewish. But from another angle the title fit, given that Gillman really was a teacher, though more interested in the lessons of football than of Judaism.

His football heritage had its roots in Ohio. He'd played and served as an assistant coach at Ohio State University under Francis Schmidt, an early adopter of the forward pass. Gillman eventually also coached at Denison University east of Columbus, and at Miami University on the state's western boundary, before he took the job at Cincinnati. Even his brief flirtation with professional football had been an Ohio affair. In 1936, a friend asked him to play for a fledgling team in an upstart league trying to challenge the NFL. Gillman agreed and played just that one season in Cleveland. That league would eventually fold, but the team, called the Rams, proved successful enough to be absorbed by the NFL.

Then those same Rams won the league championship in 1945. And then they moved to the West Coast.

Nearly twenty years later, in this different league and different city, and under different owners, Gillman had found his way back to the Rams.

Coming into training camp with them, he had already studied the films.

◆

A YEAR BEFORE, IN the summer of 1954, the summer before Disneyland opened, Joanie Hauser had been the young, eight-months pregnant wife of a Rams rookie, and the team seemed to her like a wonderful family. Kind and caring, the players and their wives: my mom and dad. Patty and Duane Putnam. Jean and Andy Robustelli. Lu and Tom Fears. Gloria and Dutch Van Brocklin. Everyone was so nice.

Coming to Los Angeles from Xavier University in Ohio, Joanie and Art Hauser didn't know what they'd find. *God kissed this place*, Joanie thought, as she and Art explored the mountains, the ocean, the Pacific Coast Highway. All the buildings seemed to be either white or pink or blue. It was all so exotic and beautiful.

What impressed her most, though, was the welcome she and Art received, how the Rams took in a young couple, especially when her husband had only just made the team because of my dad's season-ending injury. Joanie had the impression that rookies received no special treatment, especially rookies who had made the team by a margin no bigger than a knee tendon.

And especially not the wives of rookies.

That's why she was so surprised when the team, which had been in the Midwest playing road games, offered to provide her a seat on their charter plane early in the season to bring her from Ohio to Los Angeles. Pregnant and sitting alone by a window, she was even more surprised when Elroy Hirsch came and asked to sit beside her. Here was a football player who was also a movie star—in 1953 he'd starred as himself in a biopic called *Crazylegs*. He was a Ram veteran, entering his ninth year in the NFL. A movie star and a star athlete! So why would he even talk to her, she who considered herself a "little rookie wife"?

But he did. Hirsch, like her husband, had grown up in Wisconsin, a fellow Midwesterner. He asked if she was excited to be going to games.

"Oh, I won't be going to the games," she said. She motioned toward her pregnant belly. She told him she'd need to care for the baby.

He protested. His wife, Ruthie, had come to games when she had a baby at home. The answer was as easy as having a great babysitter. "Let me have Ruthie call you," he said. "You can trust her sitter."

Other players and their wives were just as nice. Gloria and Norm Van Brocklin, for example, gave the Hausers' baby clothes their kids had grown out of. So Joanie, who had never lived anywhere but Cincinnati, felt welcomed and cared for. And she was able to attend games. Even better, the coaches gave Art lots of playing time, and he received a game ball for his work as a pass rusher in the season's final game.

Then all that Hamp Pool stuff came on like a big family squabble. Though some players had complained about Hamp, others took his side. "The man does a week's work every day," said Don Paul, the linebacker and a team captain. "It seems some of the Rams will never mature." Paul was one of Pool's drinking buddies. They'd get together with Bob Waterfield and Bob Kelley, the team's radio and TV announcer, and have a raucous time playing practical jokes on each other, like when Pool secretly delivered dozens of Christmas trees to Waterfield's house, or the time the others smeared Limburger cheese over Kelley's car engine before he took a long drive through 102-degree weather. Kelley kept having to pull to the side of the road to throw up.

Then Pool was fired and Gillman hired, so there wasn't a side to take.

So, in Redlands that summer when Disneyland opened, today was a better place than yesterday. Players could be easy with each other again. Play cards at night;

drink down at Ed and Mary's Tavern where the beer was so cold. Line up in practice, listen to the new coach's instructions. Behave like a family again and wait to see what tomorrow might hold.

◆

WHAT GILLMAN HAD SEEN as he studied his carefully edited films was a team too smitten with the grand gesture. What he'd seen was a passing game that a Hollywood critic would call melodramatic.

Norm Van Brocklin was the star of this picture show. There he was, in black and white on the screen, over and over again, cocking back his arm and chucking the ball as if wanting to throw it over the goal posts and out of the coliseum. Streaking wide receivers—Elroy Hirsch, Tom Fears, and especially Bob Boyd—scrambled to get under those passes. The ball flew from Van Brocklin's hand, spiraling without a hint of wobble, tracing an elegant arc from Van Brocklin to...

Well, that was the problem.

Opponents had figured out that Hamp Pool and the Rams liked to sling that ball as far downfield as often as they could. So, opposing coaches positioned their defensive backs far from the line of scrimmage, and when Dutch hefted those long passes the opponents had almost as good a chance of catching them as the Rams.

What Gillman was seeing were the downsides to Hamp Pool's "READY-SET-*HUT*-TWO-THREE-FOUR!" score-fast-so-you-can-score-again football. No matter the result of those long passes—a touchdown, an interception, a catch, a dropped ball—the plays lasted scant seconds and robbed the Rams defensive players of any time to rest. If the Rams threw such a pass on first or second down and the result was an interception—and too often it was—the Rams defense might have just reached the benches when it was time to get up and trudge right back onto the gridiron.

So, one of the first things Gillman changed in training camp: fewer long passes. Let's use the whole field, he told Van Brocklin. Throw to the sidelines. Throw shorter.

The next thing he changed? The defense. He emphasized its necessity and made a trade with San Francisco to help recapture what the team had lost with the departure of Night Train Lane. He moved Don Paul, known as a tough, nasty linebacker, up into the center of the defensive line, a position *Sports Illustrated*'s Jim Murray equated to serving as the defense's shock absorber.

Then he made endless hours of film part of training camp life. He even invited Bob Waterfield back to training camp as a special consultant. In addition to his work as quarterback, Waterfield had been the best placekicker in Rams history and still held several NFL kicking records. So Gillman put Waterfield in a dark room with four hundred feet of slow-motion footage showing the current Rams kicker, Les Richter, at work. *Study his technique*, Gillman said. *Let's make him better.*

Finally, he ran a different sort of training camp. Players found it to be rigorous, but more relaxed, better organized. They could offer suggestions and believe they were heard. "We're not asked to do something that can't be accomplished," Skeet Quinlan told the *Los Angeles Times*. "Just because it looks good on paper doesn't mean it will work in a game. Before we try anything in play it has to weather the test of trial and error."

When the exhibition season began, Gillman offered another surprise. Though the Rams had, in the last decade, fired at least one head coach after exhibition losses, Gillman argued that victories and losses in those games shouldn't matter. Why beat up your best players for games that didn't count toward the championship? An exhibition game was a learning tool, a classroom exercise. The score? Immaterial.

For the first time in years, the Rams lost to Washington in the *Times* Charities Game. Next, they faced the Cleveland Browns and Coach Paul Brown, who treated exhibition games in the same manner as Gillman. Brown usually played rookies and was reputed never to look at the scoreboard. So here was a game that neither coach cared to win. At the coliseum, though, were some thirty-five-thousand fans who wanted a victory, so the Rams mustered enough touchdowns to keep those paying customers happy.

But as the Rams left the coliseum field, Brown awaited them in the tunnel to the locker rooms. His teams had played in the last five NFL championship games, winning two, and he wanted to make sure these Rams understood that a victory over Cleveland's Browns in August meant as much as banking Monopoly money.

"Okay, okay," he shouted at Van Brocklin and my dad and bow-tied Sid Gillman as the Rams jogged past him toward the locker room. "But what about December?"

◆

DEAR MR. O'MALLEY...

The day before the Rams' non-game against Cleveland, Roz Wyman had written to Walter O'Malley, the president of the Brooklyn Dodgers. In her letter, the city councilwoman asked to meet with him. Later that month, it so happened, she'd be in New York with Councilman Edward R. Roybal on other LA-city business. They'd be happy to talk about the ways Los Angeles could accommodate the Dodgers, should the Dodgers like to move their operation west.

In writing to O'Malley, Wyman was following up on a telegram the city council had recently wired at Wyman's urging to let O'Malley know of the council's resolution, which read in part that "Los Angeles is seriously interested in making a home for a major league club and it would be appreciated if the gentlemen could come here for a serious conference and 'look-see' at our facilities." The council had also sent a similar telegram to O'Malley's opposite number with the New York Giants. Knowing that Wyman and Roybal had a trip east scheduled, the council agreed with her that it should empower Wyman and Roybal to meet with either owner.

O'Malley read Wyman's letter and wrote back. No, he couldn't meet. He was busy, his team was in a pennant race. And, he added—because that telegram the council had sent appeared in newspapers before he'd even received it—"I assumed it was part of a publicity stunt."

Thus, once again New York brushed off Los Angeles. Second-class LA. Kid brother LA.

"I was really mad, to put it mildly," Wyman said in an interview years later. "I thought it was pretty rude, to tell you the truth, the way you answer two elected officials. 'I thought this was a publicity stunt or something.' I felt O'Malley had dealt too long with New York politicians, and we were a little different out here. There were no Tammany bosses, and there was none of that in LA."

If O'Malley's letter stung with a kind of East Coast smugness, the prick may have felt worse, because East had just competed with West in one of the year's most-watched sporting events, a winner-take-all horse race pitting the nation's two best: Southern California's Swaps against Maryland-bred Nashua. The race on the last day of August had carried all the tensions and imagery of the East-West dichotomy. The western horse, Swaps, was owned and trained by cowboys, his jockey a young Willie Shoemaker from Texas. The eastern horse was owned by an heir to a banking fortune, his jockey a man who had won his first Derby nearly twenty years earlier. Prior to the match race meeting in Chicago, the two horses had met only once—at the Kentucky Derby, which Swaps had won. Nashua won the Preakness and Belmont Stakes that followed, but Swaps hadn't run in those, likely because his owner couldn't afford the fees. Yet, out west, Swaps continued to race undefeated, and it was clear to the country that these were the nation's top two horses. Their one-on-one rematch pitted western aspirations against eastern eminence.

A national television audience of some fifty million watched. It had rained in Chicago the night before, and Nashua's jockey, with years of experience on young Shoemaker, forced the western horse to the outside and into a muddy path where the run was troublesome and tiring. Nashua won by 6.5 lengths.

In its quest for major league baseball, though, the west would not be so easily pushed aside. Walter O'Malley, after all, had written back. Perhaps his tone was prickly, but he hadn't ignored Roz Wyman's letter.

Now, they were correspondents. Now, he knew who she was.

Very truly yours,
ROSALIND WIENER WYMAN
Councilwoman—5th District

◆

It's a Sunday morning, autumn, in any NFL city that's not Los Angeles. Maybe the Rams are in Detroit or Milwaukee. Maybe Chicago or Baltimore. This happened in all those places. So let's say Baltimore. Let's say it's November 20, 1955, a clear, windy, and cold day, with yesterday's snow blown into piles like dust against curbs and across lawns. Later this afternoon the Rams, with five victories against three losses, will play the Colts at Baltimore's Memorial Stadium.

But this morning, we'll station Hollywood's cameras inside a church sanctuary, the primary shot focused on the church's entry. There, framed by the doors and silhouetted by morning sunlight, a quartet of burly men cross the threshold, removing gloves to dip their fingertips in marble pedestal fonts filled with Holy Water, making the sign of the cross.

In real life, in any NFL city, this scene would likely be whatever church was within walking distance of whatever hotel houses the Rams. And my dad could have rounded up more to attend Mass—or fewer. But for this scene in Baltimore, our Hollywood director has decided on four players, and he's chosen Baltimore's Basilica, in the heart of the city. Less well-known by its full name—the Basilica of the National Shrine of the Assumption of the Blessed Virgin Mary—the site is historic. It's the United States' first Cathedral, and it's the site where bishops created the Baltimore Catechism— so any visiting Roman Catholic would want to attend Mass there—and it's within walking distance of several hotels where the Rams might have stayed. But the primary reason for the director's choice is the interior of the Basilica—with high stained glass windows and two saucer dome ceilings, each decorated by pink rosettes, and at the highest point of the largest dome: a white dove sculpted and suspended below a golden radiance as if the bird flies from the heart of the sun.

(Later, the director will order establishing shots from outside, show the church's columns, its neoclassical style, then add those frames in the editing room.)

For now, though, the camera follows our burly quartet—the Pope's Rams. These are men used to space and speed and collisions, long strides across one hundred yards of open grass. But here? In this Sunday-morning church crowd? They shuffle. They "pardon me." They teeter and tilt and try not to bump other parishioners or step on their feet. They are especially wary near the older ladies. People stare, they know these robust, shy strangers who draw attention to themselves by trying not to draw attention to themselves.

It's comical as the four squeeze into a pew, shoulder-to-shoulder, rump-to-rump.

By now we recognize them: Andy Robustelli, the defensive all-pro with his Italian-olive complexion and that off-kilter look to his face, the left eye sitting a little lower than the right; Art Hauser, the Midwesterner in his second year, with his flat face that looks tough enough to break a brick; and my dad.

The fourth, on the end, is Duane Putnam, and it's clear from his actions that he's the outlier, the non-Catholic in the bunch. He fidgets. He looks around too much. He studies his teammates, tries to imitate what they do. At the threshold, when they dipped fingers, he dipped fingers. When they genuflected at the pew, he genuflected. When they picked up a book, he peered over my dad's shoulder for the page number.

When the times comes for them to drop cash in a plate, he drops cash in a plate. A pipe organ blares, and in a minute or so, another plate passes. The teammates drop cash. The Putter drops cash.

"How many times is that coming around?" he whispers to my dad, his roommate on the road.

Dad grins.

And when they kneel, Putnam kneels, too. Four big guys and not nearly enough space for all the ways their legs want to go. Mo, Larry, Schemp, and Curly would do it funnier, but only just.

Putter whispers, "Playing for the pope is pretty hard on those stumps. And all this time you've been blaming football."

Dad grins at that, too. "Might have been part of it," he says. But the camera, focusing on his face, can't detect a grimace or a twitch. He'll kneel or rise as the Mass requires, and he'll carry that soreness, that twinge. Behind them, on a wall, is a portrait of Christ's descent from the cross, his side pierced, his feet broken. If a man can't take a little pain for God, well, how can he share a holy space like this one, with his Son?

The four stand, they kneel, they stand again. The Putter says, "We don't even have to warm up for the game, we're getting up and down so many times."

◆

SOMETIMES, DUANE PUTNAM COULD hear a grinding come from Dad's knees, probably the kneecap grinding on the bones behind it, the cartilage all worn down. Sometimes, Dad couldn't hide the pain the knees caused him, and he winced as he moved. Putnam probably knew my dad's knees better than anybody outside of the sawbones and my mom. On the road, they were roommates. At home, their lockers sat near each other. After games, Dad would set plastic bags filled with ice on his knees to check the swelling. Before games, though, that's when you had to admire him. He kept a box of bottles, and in each bottle was a red liniment of some sort. He'd rub that stuff into his knees, say, "I'll get it. Don't worry. I'll be there."

"John's knees," Putnam recalled years later, "were so bad."

◆

IN 1955, THE ICE and the liniment and the surgery held those knees together. And with them, my dad started every game. The Rams, under their new coach with his new philosophy, won their first three games, then went on a win-loss yo-yo until that cold, cold day in Baltimore. That one was a tie, 17–17. Then, the Rams won in Philadelphia and headed home to Los Angeles with two games to go, a 6–3–1 record, and good odds to win the Western Division champion.

Awaiting them on the schedule were two rematches with teams that had gotten the better of the Rams. First, they'd face Baltimore again. Then, the Green Bay Packers would come into the coliseum, having beaten Los Angeles earlier that season by scoring a game-winning field goal in the last minute.

Avenge themselves on both teams, and the Rams would secure a spot in the NFL championship game.

"We should never have been beaten by the Packers nor tied by the Colts," Van Brocklin told a reporter. "We owe both Baltimore and Green Bay real good whippings."

CHAPTER 8

The Sweep

IN 1955, NO STUNTMEN played for Hollywood's Team. But there were actors—and one self-proclaimed villain.

Like many villains, he presented an appealing smile (dimpled!) and a friendly manner. He proved loyal to friends. Probably he was kind to dogs and children. His new restaurant, the Ram's Horn, had just opened that November on Ventura Boulevard in Encino, and he greeted patrons like there was no one else he'd rather have visit. He'd happily fetch the menu's newest cocktail, the "Middle Guard." *Give it a taste*, was the joke. *You'll want to tackle and block.*

But not hurt anyone. The Rams' Don Paul said he never intentionally hurt players from other teams. He acknowledged that the NFL did include some really awful human beings who tried to hurt other players. *Vipers*, he called them. He knew of one who stomped the hands of men who, having been tackled, lay helpless on the grass.

Villains (like him), said Paul, only want to harass, frustrate, intimidate, bully, and bedevil. Villains, he said, want to be hated. Specifically, he, Don Paul, wanted players—be they Lions or 49ers or Browns or Bears—to hate him with such blood-red fury that they would forget everything but their hatred. He wanted their hatred to swell until it pressed from inside against their skulls and the backs of their eyes and made them forget whether it was first down or fourth, or that they were supposed to run a post pattern, or that punching someone (say, Don Paul) leads to a fifteen-yard penalty.

Many in the league did not seem to appreciate Paul's carefully considered distinction between a viper and a villain. Many just called Don Paul "dirty." In *TIME* magazine the previous season, several Detroit Lions were quoted saying that nobody in football played dirtier than Don.

The 1955 season was Paul's eighth with the Rams, and he had played for no other team. He'd played linebacker and middle guard, and he admitted to throwing an elbow here and there when referees weren't looking. Yes, he baited other players into shoving him— after he warned a ref that so-and-so was giving poor Don the business. He studied, and when possible, adopted the techniques of other villains he admired. In a *Sports Illustrated* article, published just as the Rams returned home for their last two games of the 1955 season, Paul spoke of his admiration for Art Donovan of the Colts. It happened that the Colts were coming to Los Angeles for a rematch of that that 17–17 tie in November. Donovan's specialty, Paul said, was to crush any running back playing the role of decoy—that is, any back pretending to have the ball when he doesn't. After the decoy got accordioned two or three times by Donovan and his 260-something pounds—without even carrying the ball!—the decoy tended to get timid, no longer faking with gusto. Then it was easy for every Colt to recognize who really carried the ball.

Another villain Paul cited was George Connor of the Chicago Bears, nicknamed "The Foot" because of the regularity with which other team's receivers tripped over George's feet. Once, Connor combined with a fellow Bear to harass Paul's teammate, Elroy "Crazylegs" Hirsch, until Hirsch made the wrong move and got sandwiched by the two Bears. As Hirsch picked himself up off the turf, Connor turned with mock disapproval to his teammate and said of the movie star at their feet, "Don't go messing up Hollywood like that."

All those villains, and Paul himself, specialized in defense. Offensive players—running backs, wide receivers, quarterbacks—had to master techniques to counter villainous antics. Among them:

1. Never show that a villain has rattled you; never show you are hurt

2. Make the villains look like fools. Send a fleet-footed decoy so far away from the real play that Art Donovan will look like a fat beagle chasing a rabbit

3. "Bumstead." Or, as Norm Van Brocklin puts it, "ham it up good"

No stuntmen played for the Rams in 1955, but there were actors, and Dutch Van Brocklin was one. Not a student of method acting, he instead learned his thespian craft at the Funny Pages School of Drama, particularly from the cartoon strip, *Blondie*. Whenever Blondie's husband, Dagwood Bumstead, tumbled or fell (often downstairs), he gyrated and his feet scrambled and his arms windmilled. Van Brocklin learned that whenever a villain so much as breathed on him, it was time to "Bumstead." Once, he Bumstead-ed after being brushed by George Connor, that Bear who called Hirsch, "Hollywood." When Dutch spilled, the ref called Connor for a penalty. Van Brocklin winked at Connor, who snarled, "Get up, you bum. You're not hurt." And Connor was penalized again—this time for unsportsmanlike conduct.

A lot of this theater, however, came with a real price. There were no stuntmen, after all. Part of football's allure—likely one reason for its popularity in Southern California where Davy Crockett and the Indians, no matter how many times they fight at Disneyland, always live to fight again—is that real bodies are at stake. If

Disneyland and Hollywood tell stories of adventure without risk, football reminds its fans that life is a struggle, that people are built to be hurt and to heal and get hurt again. Flesh-and-blood men risk bruises and ruptures of their own flesh, risk gashes and scrapes that draw their own blood. Everyone in the NFL knows that some pain is necessary, even sanctioned. But anything extra—anything dirty—in 1955 made players grumble. So, Otto Graham, a future Hall of Fame quarterback for the Browns, claimed dirty play that season after he suffered a concussion against the Giants. A growing number of players wore face guards with their helmets to keep from being punched or having their eyes poked. Said Detroit Lion halfback Doak Walker: "They're chiefly interested in protecting themselves against dirty football."

That term, "dirty football," was spit out by more coaches and players through the 1954–55 seasons than probably through all other NFL seasons combined. In Hamp Pool's last season, the 49ers' coach publicly accused the Rams of "dirty football." Pool said no, it was the 49ers who played dirty. Then Pool accused the Chicago Cardinals, led by his one-time boss, Jumbo Joe Stydahar, of dirty play. The managing director of the Cardinals shot back that Pool was "nothing but a crybaby." Et cetera, et cetera. Coaches throughout the league studied their own game films and made lists of fouls that no official had noticed and then complained to Bert Bell, the NFL's commissioner.

The problem wouldn't go away. That facemask designed to keep players from getting eyes gouged or noses smacked? Villains figured out that it was easy to grab the facemask and yank a runner to the ground. In another year, fearing broken necks, the NFL would make that technique illegal.

And in January 1957, Bert Bell would still hear so many gripes about dirty football that he'd have to defend the league, declaring in *Sports Illustrated*, "I don't believe there is dirty football... I don't believe there are any maliciously dirty players in the National Football League."

◆

NORM VAN BROCKLIN PLAYED several games of the 1955 season with a broken bone in his throwing hand. Andy Robustelli, a defensive all-pro, twisted a knee. Don Burroughs, a defensive back, suffered bruised ribs. Lineman Paul Miller *sprained his neck*. Other players knocked out for a game or more included Deacon Dan Towler, Bob Boyd, and Crazylegs Hirsch.

The Rams in 1955 suffered more injuries than in any other year the team's veterans could recall.

"Maybe twice as many as last year," Van Brocklin told a newspaper reporter that December, just before the Rams' late season rematch with Baltimore. "And yet, we've thought about it less." Gillman, he said, was not one to moan about injuries, "like some other coaches

I've known. He just keeps putting someone else in there to fill the gap and that player comes through."

But in the midst of this injury-riddled season, in this era of dirty football, three Rams at least never missed a game. And together the trio gave the Rams perhaps their most potent weapon.

One of them was my dad. Given the tenuousness of my dad's knees, it must have seemed a miracle that game in, game out, he found his way onto the field. Another who never missed a kickoff was Duane Putnam. The third was a rookie halfback named Ron Waller, a slippery kid from a farming town in the mid-Atlantic.

Think of my dad and Putnam as Waller's bodyguards. Each game they led the way, running first into the fists and fury of the defense, throwing blocks, with Waller steps behind, scurrying his way to an all-pro season as a rookie.

"They helped me out a lot, I know that," Waller recalled decades later from his home in Delaware. "They were great guards, man. They were great pulling guards… It was Putnam leading and my dad behind him. They did a hell of a job."

◆

TOM FEARS, A VETERAN receiver for the Rams who had given Night Train Lane his nickname, decided Ron Waller would be called "the Rat."

"I don't know why he gave me that name," Waller said. "I guess because I scampered… I was a rookie. I didn't ask any questions."

Four years before, the Rat had been Delaware's high school athlete of the year, coming out of the tiny town of Laurel, known for sweet potatoes until a blight in the 1940s. The Rat's high school graduating class numbered forty-four. Waller didn't travel far for college, just across the Chesapeake Bay to the University of Maryland. Then the Rams used their second draft pick in 1955 to select him, and suddenly, the young halfback was Los Angeles–bound.

"The first time I walked into camp," he said, "there were about twenty-five halfbacks, and they were looking to replace one guy. I said, 'Shit, I'll never make this team.'"

That summer, the Rams coaches excused him from training camp to play in the national college all-star game, where he ended up on defense. Back in camp, the coaches tried him out at wide receiver, and he proved he could play there, too. Wide receiver, defensive back, halfback—that versatility worked in his favor. "In those days, they looked for guys who could play more than one position," he recalled. So the Rams offered him an $8,000 salary with a $1,000 bonus for signing his name to a contract. Waller signed. By the second game that season, a 17–10 victory over Detroit, the *Los Angeles Times* was calling him "one of the most graceful runners in Rams' annals." Later, the paper wrote that Waller "has about five different gaits. He minces, he drives, he sprints…" The other two gaits must have been indescribable; the reporter never named them.

Game in, game out, no Ram carried the ball more often. None gained more yards. None scored more touchdowns. No one benefited more from having my dad and Duane Putnam as teammates.

◆

IMAGINE MATCHING PILLARS OR bookends, jersey numbers sixty-three and sixty-one, my dad taller and Putnam thicker, one at right guard and the other at left, the Hooker and the Putter, with flecks of grass sticking to the sweat on their forearms and faces. Waller remembers the pair as quiet men, reserved, neither a seeker of attention. That both were fierce on the field, and tough, is a given—they played offensive line in the NFL. But to distinguish them, Waller gives the edge to Putnam. "I wouldn't ever want to get in a fight with him," he says. "He was really tough. John,"—the former altar boy who led Sunday morning visits to Mass—"was more mild-mannered."

That the two were great pulling guards, Waller says, means that they excelled at the play called the sweep. Rather than require my dad and Putnam to smash into whatever defender faced them across the line of scrimmage, the sweep required them to sprint—or *pull*—away from the line, out either to the right or the left. While running, they needed to make split-second decisions about who to hit in order to *sweep* clear an alleyway for Waller.

If the play went left, "Putnam would look to seal and start that alleyway," Waller says. "And then my dad would go downfield and take out a cornerback or a safety—anybody supporting. I would stay right behind them, and they would hopefully create an alleyway for me." If the play went to the right side, the men would reverse roles.

Against Detroit in the second game that season, Waller ran behind my dad and Putnam to gain ninety-eight yards, eight more than the entire Lions team. In a second game against Detroit, he gained 132 yards, averaging nearly eight yards per carry—and, again, my dad and Putnam's blocking made it work. "Lions were flying all over the joint," the *Los Angeles Times* reported, "as Ron's interference lowered the boom."

Waller's talents included not only his speed, but an ability to slide between tacklers without losing speed. His new coach, Sid Gillman, compared him to "a piece of wire." An assistant coach noted that tacklers could seldom hit Waller head-on, and that probably saved the rookie from injuries. "Tacklers never get a square shot at him," the assistant coach said. "When they catch him, he's turned sideways."

By the time the Colts came to Los Angeles that December for a rematch after that 17–17 tie, Waller had established himself as the Rams' top running threat. The teams met on a soggy, drizzly December 4, the kind of day that surprises Angelenos so accustomed to reliable sunshine. Perhaps because of a lack of umbrellas or raincoats, only about thirty-seven thousand fans showed, the year's smallest crowd by some ten thousand souls. Those hardy fans watched, according to *The Baltimore Sun*, as a mud-splashed Waller "squirted around the Colts' flank" to gain 138 yards. Tank Younger scored two touchdowns, and the Rams won, 20–14.

Exactly a year before, the Rams had been in turmoil, arguing with their coach and suffering through one of the worst seasons in team history. Now, with a new coach emphasizing defense and a more patient offense, and with a knockout rookie running back, they had worked their way back to the top of the league. Maybe the victory over Baltimore wasn't the "good whipping" Van Brocklin had said the Rams owed the Colts, but it was the first of the two revenge victories Los Angeles needed to win the NFL's Western Conference title and a spot in the NFL championship game.

One remained. Beat Green Bay's Packers, and the Rams would play for the NFL's crown.

◆

THE RAMS AND PACKERS had first met that season in Wisconsin, a game waged in Milwaukee rain and mud and fifty-degree misery, the sort of day when players spent sideline time using wooden tongues to clean mud from between their cleats. The Packers won, 30–28, on a field goal with only twenty-four seconds left. The game had been, perhaps, Norm Van Brocklin's worst performance of the season, if not his career. The man who had once thrown for 544 yards in a single game managed only thirty-four. Three of his attempted passes were intercepted.

Dutch kept mum about it then, but that broken bone in his throwing hand troubled him. Already stubby-fingered for a quarterback, he found himself unable to grip the ball with his swollen mitt. He'd played anyway. That was the NFL code: play hurt. Show no pain. Stay on the field until the coach says you can't. After all, every player was hurt—all the time. "The only time you weren't hurt," Ron Waller recalled, "was at the beginning of the season." So, in Wisconsin rain, Van Brocklin tried to hold that ball and throw it where it needed to be. He tried until Gillman benched him for the second-string quarterback, Bill Wade. Gillman had known something was wrong with Van Brocklin's hand, because he was accustomed to hearing a sound—*zzt!*— when the ball left Dutch's fingertips. He hadn't heard that sound for a while.

For the second Packer-Rams game—this one in Los Angeles—the *zzt!* had returned. Weather forecasters called for the usual: clear and temperate, with a high around seventy. Oddsmakers gave the advantage to the Rams by 7.5 points. Based on pregame ticket sales, about fifty-thousand fans were expected for the 2:05 p.m. kickoff.

Then, the day of the game, people began lining up at the coliseum ticket windows. They lined up by the hundreds. They lined up by the thousands. Then tens of thousands. So many people wanted tickets that by the time the game began, hundreds of fans still waited to buy their way into the stadium.

In the end, some forty thousand tickets sold the day of the game. That brought the crowd to just over ninety thousand, about as many people as lived in Burbank and nearly a full house in the coliseum.

Through that 1955 season, there had never been a larger crowd to watch an NFL game.

"With gold and glory within their grasp," wrote the *Times'* Frank Finch, "I think we're going to see a top effort by the Rams today. They're long overdue."

CHAPTER 9

Game Ball

"Whatever LA is, it has a certain amount of entertainment sophistication."

—Melvin Durslag, legendary Los Angeles sportswriter

I T'S NEVER EASY TO perform for the performers.

Take any Los Angeles crowd arriving at the coliseum to watch the Rams. Among them are film critics and publicists, makeup artists and lighting technicians, musicians and dancers, directors and animators. Be they award-winning or aspiring or merely adequate, many of those taking their seats are people accustomed to being in front of an audience, so being part of one presents less of a thrill. Their business is entertainment, and entertainment is their business.

They react to a performance—appreciate its virtues and failures—differently than people who build cars on assembly lines or run Laundromats or diagnose cancer.

Melvin Durslag is in a good position to explain the nature of Los Angeles fans. What others call fun and thrills—watching sports—was for him a job spanning six decades at Los Angeles newspapers including the *Herald-Examiner* and the *Times*. He knows what it means to appraise entertainment with a cool, professional detachment. He understands that it is in the character of an Angeleno to hold part of the self in reserve when watching a movie in a darkened theater, or when hearing a symphony at the Hollywood Bowl, or attending a football game at the coliseum.

What this means—when talking sports—is that LA's fans don't tend to paint their faces and scream until their jugular veins bulge, and they don't wear hog snouts over their noses or cheese wedges on their heads. They are not likely to rattle cowbells as if a cowbell may mean the difference between their team winning or losing. What is true today was true in 1955. Rams fans, no matter how many tens of thousands, never—in Durslag's memory—deafened a visiting quarterback with their roar.

To impress sophisticated Los Angeles, to bring it to its feet in an ecstasy of shouting and cheering, requires a performance that is rare, an occasion that overwhelms.

◆

IT WAS A COMPLICATED affair, the city's with the Rams during their first decade together.

By 1955, Los Angeles—in the person of Councilwoman Roz Wyman and columnist Vincent Flaherty, among others—courted baseball's Brooklyn Dodgers: flattered, proffered gifts, argued and flirted, cajoled.

But in 1946 when the Rams had arrived from Cleveland, they came—as did so much of Southern California's immigrant population boom—uninvited. Perhaps in some corners of Los Angeles the Rams were even unwelcome. The city already had two minor league football teams, and it had the Dons, a team from a league challenging the NFL: the All-American Football Conference. And what did the NFL matter anyway? If, in 1946, major league baseball was the national pastime, pro football was the national "maybe-we'll-care-if-we-have-the-time." On the gridiron, college football held the nation's affection, and that was especially true for longtime Angelenos who lined up to cheer USC's Trojans and UCLA's Bruins.

When Dan Reeves brought his team from Cleveland, it wasn't because Los Angeles wanted the Rams; it was because Reeves, the Rams president and owner, wanted Los Angeles.

Yet, eight seasons later, Rams players appeared in films and on TV shows; children and adults waited outside the locker room to get Crazylegs and Tank Younger and others to sign their names to photographs and game programs. The city and the Rams would set an NFL attendance record, drawing 93,751 to watch the home team play the Lions, more fans than had ever witnessed a single game. By 1955, they'd nearly match that number for their final regular season game against Green Bay.

What made the difference? How did the Rams attract headlines and popping flashbulbs and autograph-hungry crowds in a city where such attention was among the most valuable commodities?

It helped that the All-American Football Conference failed after four seasons and took the Dons with it. It helped that the Los Angeles sun shone more often than did the sun in Cleveland or Pittsburgh or Detroit and made a day at the game more inviting. It helped that when the Rams arrived from Cleveland, they were the reigning national champs and that their leader, Bob Waterfield, had prepped at Van Nuys High School, played for UCLA, and married a movie star. It helped that Los Angeles was in the midst of yet another population boom, the region growing annually by hundreds of thousands, so even a small percentage of Angelenos buying tickets meant *stacks and stacks* of tickets. It helped, too, that many of those immigrants—Sooners and Longhorns and Razorbacks—arrived with a love for football and no allegiance to either Trojan nor Bruin nor any pro team. Those folks might attend their first Rams game because they enjoyed football in general, not Rams football in particular. But maybe

they'd come back for a second game or a third, because—
man alive!—Tom Fears could run a great good-lord
pass route, and did you hear the "*whoof!*" from that
Packers running back when Andy Robustelli caught
him shoulder-to-midsection? And the touchdowns!
Who could keep track with the Rams scoring fifty-one
points, or sixty-five…even seventy! That was just plain
fun. That would get people through the turnstiles.

But Reeves seemed to understand that for the Rams
to last in Los Angeles he needed more than people
in the seats. He needed to make professional football
part of the city's culture, to transform the Rams into an
LA institution as significant as Sid Grauman's theaters
or traffic jams or the Hollywood Bowl. He needed
Angelenos to wake up during football season thinking
about the Rams, to chat at lunch about that week's game,
to schedule their lives around Sundays.

This was bigger thinking. Reeves was no Walt
Disney, but what he wanted to build would require
Disney–esque inventiveness and optimism and risk-
taking. It would require a spirit and ambition to match
that of Los Angeles itself.

Thus, his efforts to collaborate with the coliseum
and the *Times*—because how better to become an
institution than to affiliate with other institutions?
The resulting *Times* Charities Game drew some eighty
thousand fans to the coliseum each year. Then, Reeves
took a risk and gave away seats—sometimes as many
as twenty thousand—to children under twelve years

old whose parents bought a ticket, calling the program "Free Football for Kids." Not only would this lead to children bothering their parents about the Rams, but in ten or fifteen years, Reeves figured, those kids would be back on their own. Fred Gehrke's idea to paint the Ram's horn logo onto helmets fit Reeves strategy, too, providing a way to brand the team.

Then there was television.

In 1947, people had yet to embrace TV. The nation's television manufacturers built only 178,000 sets. But that number grew to three million two years later. Those manufacturers had learned that sets sold faster if there was more and better content broadcast on TV. Sports—especially boxing—were popular. Football, with the rectangular shape of its field, its right-to-left and left-to-right action, appeared to be a sport well suited for the tube. So it made sense to Reeves when the Admiral Television Company offered to sponsor broadcasts of Rams home games to an LA audience. This was a groundbreaking idea; no NFL teams had ever broadcast home games. The upside? The Rams would work their way into the lives of more and more people. The risk? Reeves and his staff recognized it immediately. Why would fans pay for a ticket when they could watch a game at home for free? Given that, Reeves agreed to the deal with a condition: Admiral would subsidize ticket revenue lost during the season. Admiral agreed, and in 1950, Angelenos became the first in the country to watch their NFL team play home games on TV.

Attendance did fall. The Rams' previous average of nearly fifty-two thousand fans per game dropped to about thirty-one thousand. Admiral paid the shortfall, about $307,000.

But Reeves had the benefit of people watching from home in Pasadena or Pomona, perhaps even some who would never have come to a game. The broadcasts reminded Angelenos that Waterfield and Crazylegs and Tank and Dutch worked magic on the gridiron right down the highway from those houses in Pasadena and Pomona. These football players? They were neighbors.

With the Rams on TV every week, some people became accustomed to having the Rams in the living room or den. Maybe they even looked forward to a Sunday with the team, just as every week they looked forward to *Meet the Press* and Ed Sullivan and *Kukla, Fran and Ollie*—growing institutions, all.

The next year, the Admiral deal ended. The Rams again blacked out home game broadcasts, and attendance rose. By midway through 1953, Dad's first season with the team, the Rams drew their record-setting crowd, those ninety-three thousand–plus.

That was a high. There were still lows. Later that same season only twenty-three thousand showed for a game against the Packers. Maybe they stayed away because it was cold that day, a high of forty-five degrees. Or maybe smog hung low, and few people wanted to spend hours outdoors, risking that telltale burn at the back of the throat. Maybe LA's fans didn't want to give much time to a team that was out of contention for a title, as the Rams were that year.

Any and all of those reasons.

Attendance continued to rise and ebb like the coastal tide, fluctuations that could doom a short-term endeavor like a movie or a television show. But institutions survive such shifts, and by 1955 the Rams had become an institution, had become part of the fabric of Southern California life. At banquets to honor the team, people paid ten dollars a plate. The "Ye Old Rams" fan club offered weekly luncheons. Bob Oates of the *Times* published a book chronicling "the story of the Rams...the finest book on professional football ever published." The Rams even sold Christmas gifts out of their game day programs. "Rooter caps" were two dollars each. For $1.50 you could drop a lapel pin in your husband's stocking, and for $8.50 a cuff link. Big spenders could unload $21.50 for a Rams blanket, good for use at the stadium or the beach, and "attractive for the den."

And the team's away games were regularly broadcast on KABC-TV.

The Rams had become such an organic part of Los Angeles that nationwide, they were among those institutions—including Disneyland, Hollywood, smog, and beaches—that people associated with Los Angeles. Melvin Durslag was writing about the Rams for national magazines such as *Vanity Fair* and *Sports Illustrated*. People throughout the country—from

Maine to Mississippi—could watch Rams players star in movies. In the consciousness of the country, the Rams had become Los Angeles's team; there was no other. Perhaps the best indication was that derisive name George Connor of Chicago's Bears had spat that day he and a teammate knocked over Crazylegs Hirsch, the word that equated player with place:

Don't go messing up Hollywood like that.

◆

TWENTY-EIGHT DEGREES. THAT WAS the high in Chicago on December 11, 1955, the last day of the NFL's regular season, when George Connors and the Bears met Philadelphia's Eagles. So chilly and bright was the afternoon that the Bears' coach, George Halas, wore sunglasses along with his fedora and heavy overcoat as he worked the sidelines at Wrigley Field. Halas, called Papa Bear, was one of the NFL's founding coaches; as a player-coach he'd brought the Bears to Chicago in 1921. Earlier in the 1955 season, he'd announced his plans to retire. When the Bears played their last game of the year, it would be his last—period. Now, taking the field, the Bears knew, as did their fans, that this one might be Papa's finale. They trailed the Rams in the NFL's Western Division, and a loss to the Eagles would end their season. But a chance remained. With the right combination of events, including a victory over Philadelphia, the Bears and Halas might yet play once more—in the NFL's Championship game.

So, that afternoon carried with it a particular poignancy. Newspaper photographers stalked Halas, capturing his every move: kneeling on the sideline, applauding a successful pass play, shaking his fist, listening to information from his assistant coaches. On the field, running and tackling with a combination of hope and desperation, Halas's Bears did their part, beating the Eagles, 17–10.

What remained for them now was to wait.

After interviews with reporters and showers and clean clothes and combed hair and cologne, Bears players, some fans, and Halas himself gathered at the Edgewater Beach Hotel, north of Wrigley and near the lakeshore. WGN radio sounded over the hotel's south terrace. The station was broadcasting a game from two time zones away: the Rams versus Packers at LA's Memorial Coliseum. Because the Bears had beaten Philadelphia, they had one remaining chance to win the Western Division Title and go on to the NFL championship game. One outcome in Los Angeles would extend Halas's legendary career and give the Bears a shot at a storybook ending to Papa Bear's fabled career.

That's why every Bear and every Bear fan was rooting for Green Bay to win and for Los Angeles to lose.

◆

TAKE STOCK, FOR A moment, of my dad's life, that morning of December 11.

He's twenty-seven years old, an Army veteran, a devout Roman Catholic, educated in history by the Jesuits. Six months ago, he married a pixie of a girl who grew up a few blocks away from his boyhood house. Right-handed, he wears a college ring on his wedding-band finger. He is one of some 420 men in the entire country who play professional football for the NFL, and he is one of only 132 who start on offense. Only eleven other men start at right guard, his same position.

He's twenty-seven years old, and there are days his knees feel twice that age. Long scars run parallel along the outer edges of the right joint. He plays for the NFL team in his hometown, so his wife and mom and dad easily attend home games, like today's. He wears jersey number sixty-three. Teammates call him Lantern Jaw or the Hooker. The newspapers, when they mention him, often call him Johnny Hock as if he's still the teenager who impressed people while playing at Mount Carmel High School. He stands six foot two and 235 pounds, lifts weights, wears his blond hair neatly trimmed (when it needs the scissors he can tell because the tip of his widow's peak reveals a wave). He's no jabber mouth—sometimes he's quiet as stone—but he likes to laugh. A good time for him is watching other people have a good time. He does not like to draw attention to himself, though people notice when he enters a room. He and his wife, who is a schoolteacher, make their home in a small second-floor apartment owned by her aunt, who lives on the ground floor. The American city where they live—his hometown—is glamorous and dramatic, intoxicating. Even its seedy and scandalous sides—the affairs, the murders, the feuds—fascinate people. On its way to being the entertainment capital of the world, his hometown might be the American city that most craves *and* captures the nation's attention (but don't tell that to New York). Whether people here are TV and movie stars at a party or neighborhood folks around a charcoal grill, they have a good time. My dad, he enjoys watching them laugh, play pinochle or horseshoes.

In his twenty-seven years, he's faced many crucibles: the first Mass he ever served, the rabbit-skinning table in the backyard, the Orange Bowl while in college, basic training at Fort Ord, the Far East Bowl while serving in Japan, a season without football so his knee tendon might heal. In their ways, each of those made demands of him, put him under particular pressures. They required that he act with precision, that he practice patience, that he understand what he was called to do and put aside all other concerns. Those tests required him to focus on a single thing—when to ring a bell, where to cut with a knife, how to assemble pieces into a rifle, who to knock down—and only that thing.

He's twenty-seven, newly wed, and about to play the most important game of his career.

That day would start early, but not with an alarm clock. There'd be no reason. He and my mom were not people to stay up late or to sleep in; they'd wake early enough. Probably he'd have slept well. Seldom nervous, never overwrought, he would carry the weight of the coming game with an easy grace.

Maybe she'd make breakfast while he shaved. Bacon sizzling in a cast iron pan, eggs over-easy, toast patted with butter—and then more butter. A small glass of chilled juice, hot coffee from the percolator. At the table, with the Sunday paper, he'd set the sports section aside. What others had to say about his team's game held little interest for him.

Then, because it's Sunday morning, my parents would go to Mass, proclaim the mysteries of faith and share in the miracle of Christ's sacrifice. Soon after, he'd leave for the stadium. My mom would drop him off, so that later she could drive together with his dad and after the game they could all go home together. Or maybe she and Dad would come separately, because sometimes, after games, the Hocks and the Hausers, the Putnams and the Robustellis, would drive out to the valley for dinner at the Ram's Horn, Don Paul's restaurant. Today would be a nice day for that, especially if the Rams win. A festive way to celebrate.

Once at the stadium, my dad will join his teammates in stretching and light calisthenics. They'll practice a few formations. The trainers will tape players' ankles and knuckles and wrists. Players will screw cleats into the soles of their shoes. Today they'll wear their gold jerseys, the ones with blue numbers, and when they come onto the field, that gold will glow in the bright day's light. Ninety thousand people will rise to greet them.

A Los Angeles crowd, sure, so maybe less vocal than others in Pittsburgh or Baltimore—but when ninety thousand people whisper it's a loud whisper, and when they shout, that sound cascades to the field, envelops the players, comes like late day heat—from everywhere and nowhere in particular. The players spill over the field, west to east across the grass, toward fifteen arches that decorate that end of the coliseum. Through those, this morning, the sun glared. Now it sits overhead as if it, too, wants to watch the game. The stadium sinks below grade, and its top rows are so high that from the field, the city is hidden from the players' view. All that the Rams can see are people filling the seats, and those arches recalling ancient Rome, and the Southern California sky unfolding forever, and footballs that spin and spiral against the unending blue. What else is there in the world?

Then, the Packers and the Rams line up for the kick-off.

◆

UP IN HIS BOX, Dan Reeves watches. What a strange week it has been for him. Six days ago he met with his fellow Rams stockholders. Years back, when the Rams were losing money, he and his partner Frederick Levy Jr., had sold stakes in the team for a dollar to a few others willing to help absorb the financial losses with the promise of profits later. Now, with a stake in the team of 33 1/3 percent, Reeves needs to sign a contract

each year keeping him as president. This year, though—
six days ago—the other owners balked. They told him
he was spending too much time on his Beverly Hills
brokerage firm and not giving enough attention to the
Rams. Fred Levy, who owned 22.5 percent of the team,
said the owners wanted Reeves to work full time for
the Rams or not at all. Continue as an owner, yes, of
course, but if he couldn't give himself fully to the job of
president, they wanted him to give up the role.

This must have rankled.

Reeves had purchased the Rams with Levy in 1941,
with Reeves controlling the team's operations. He'd
come to football using money inherited from his father,
the owner of a New York–area grocery store chain, and
through the years he'd parlayed that wealth into even
more as principal owner of the Rams and of Daniel
Reeves & Company, his brokerage firm. Though he'd
been an athlete at Georgetown University, he was not a
big man. His nose came to a sharp point, and his oddly
shaped ears looked as if they'd been used too often
when he was a boy to yank him out of trouble. And
he seemed often to be in an argument with someone:
fellow NFL owners, his coaches, other owners of the
Rams. Those arguments were often about Reeves' ideas
for modernizing the NFL or his team.

A team about to play for the Western Division Title.
*The Western Division Title. In front of ninety
thousand people.*

And his fellow Rams owners believed he wasn't doing enough.

Said Reeves to the press: "After fifteen years as head of the Rams I have no intention of stepping out."

Answered Levy: "If he is able to devote enough time to the job, he may continue as president."

Levy, however, a man who had been Reeves' close friend since the Cleveland days, may have been speaking in a code only Rams insiders would understand. For years, Reeves had shown himself to be a binge drinker. Tex Schramm, who would go on to be the general manager of the Dallas Cowboys, and whose title with the team in 1955 was "assistant to the president," believed that Reeves had probably been drunk years before when he fired Hamp Pool. Sober and focused, Schramm knew, Reeves could solve any problem his team faced. Drunk, he became an unsolvable problem. Sometimes he would disappear for days at a time.

Years later, Melvin Durslag would remember the Rams' owners as a strange bunch, most of whom enjoyed parties, alcohol, and arguing—all a bit too much. He called Reeves "an alcoholic" who "fought it all his life."

"He was born on Fifth Avenue, and he got ill," Durslag said. "He was really a good guy, you see, but the guy had a drinking habit."

In other words, when the other owners said publicly that Reeves was spending too little time on the Rams, they may also have been saying to Reeves: "Sober up."

◆

ON THE GAME'S THIRD play, with only a minute and seven seconds elapsed and some late-arriving fans still clambering to their seats, Van Brocklin called for a sweep to the left. The Rams had reached their own forty-five-yard line, nearly midfield, and Waller was to receive the hand off.

On the snap, Putnam and my dad pulled left, Putnam leading the way, my dad a half-step behind. Van Brocklin tucked the ball into Waller's gut, and the Rat took off, chasing Putnam and my dad. The Putter rumbled into the first would-be tackler, and Waller deftly dodged that pileup. But another Packer loomed to grab him and keep him from a good gain. Dad, though, still charged ahead. He angled himself so he'd hit that Packer square on. He chicken-winged his arms, lowered his helmet, and—at precisely the right moment—uncoiled. The block was perfect, devastating. It raised the Packer player off his feet and my dad kept driving his legs, driving, driving, until the fellow went down, my dad rolling over him. It was the rare sort of block that even fans notice; teammates and coaches, too. Exquisite in its execution, timing, and result. "Crushing," the *Times* would call that block the next day.

Now Waller faced a mostly open field. A single player remained to beat: Doyle Nix, a defensive back who'd played college ball at Southern Methodist University and who, like Waller, was a rookie. Waller used Nix's momentum against him, cutting back to the right and twisting Nix's legs into such a knot that he tumbled to the turf. With Rams' lineman Charlie Toogood following a just-in-case half-step behind, Waller finished his run, covering fifty-five yards to the end zone. Les Richter kicked the extra point, and the Rams led, 7–0.

Green Bay kicked a field goal not long after to make it 7–3. The Rams came right back, driving all the way to the Packer one-yard line where they had a first down. One yard to go, with four tries to get it for a touchdown. Van Brocklin called on Tank Younger, the thick-muscled 226-pound back. Once, Tank rushed the Packer line, then twice. Neither time could my dad, Putnam, and the other Rams linemen budge the Packers, and Younger, plunging straight forward, was stopped with hardly an inch gained. On third down, Van Brocklin tried a pass play to Woodley Lewis, but a Packers linebacker knocked the ball to the turf.

That left fourth down. Van Brocklin was known to be a stubborn play-caller who had once insisted on the same play four straight times to prove it would work. This day, he must have believed in *Tank-straight-ahead*. Yet again, he called for a hand-off to Younger. Younger gripped the ball against his abdomen, lowered his shoulders and bulled toward the right side of the line.

Two men—270-pound Jerry Helluin and 240-pound Bill Forester—hit him. "Nailed Younger cold," reported the *Times*, "and shortened his neck a couple of inches, maybe." The series of downs was so impressive even Rams fans applauded Green Bay.

Dejected, the Rams' offense gave way to the defense. But the Packers, stuck back on their own one-yard line, weren't going to have an easy time of it, either. On their first play, quarterback Tobin Rote handed off to Breezy Reid who fumbled. Art Hauser of the Rams fell on the ball at the one-yard line. Rams ball! And Van Brocklin, my dad, Younger, and Co., came right back out on the field.

"We knew they were going to fumble as soon as they took over," Van Brocklin later quipped.

So here were the Rams, back where they'd started, on the one-yard line with four tries to score. Except this time Van Brocklin handed the ball to Waller, not Younger. And skinny, wiry Waller split two tacklers at the line of scrimmage and scampered into the end zone.

Now, with Les Richter's kick, the Rams led 14–3. A third Waller touchdown early in the second half made it 21–10, and at the Edgewater Hotel in Chicago, Bears fans began to despair. When Skeet Quinlan's fifty-five-yard punt return pushed the lead to 31–10, the outcome appeared certain.

In Chicago, Papa Bear Halas was shaking hands with myriad guests when someone mentioned to him the score. "Thirty-one to ten?" he said. "Is that what it is?"

◆

THOSE LOS ANGELES FANS. Those relaxed, detached observers of all things entertaining. When the gun cracked to end the game, and the Rams had won, 31–17, that sophisticated Los Angeles crowd gave up its whole self.

First came the roar, a resounding approval. And then came the fans themselves. Thousands spilled over the stadium walls onto the field. Wanting the euphoria to last, wanting to grip the joy the Rams had brought and not to let go, the fans tromped the grass, touched their champions, dry fingertips to sweaty shoulders and arms, patted their backs, engulfed them. If there had ever been any questions about Los Angeles's feelings for this uninvited team playing something less than the national sport, those were answered. The Rams belonged to Los Angeles, and Los Angeles belonged to the Rams.

In one section of the stadium, the team's band blew brass and thumped drums. Cheerleaders cheered. Gene Lipscomb, a Rams defensive tackle, and Don Paul, the Rams' villain, seized their bow-tied first-year coach, lifting Sid Gillman to their shoulders so awkwardly his pants legs rode up to his knees. They carried him that way, with other Rams gathered around as if they were Gillman's Praetorian guard and he their Caesar. They pushed through the mass of their own celebrating fans toward the edge of the field and into the tunnel, all the way to the locker room.

Dan Reeves was at the door to meet them. "Well done!" he said, and then again, "Well done!" shaking this player's hand, patting that one on the back. Then, with all the Rams safely tucked away in the locker room, they removed their helmets. Van Brocklin raised Gillman's arm, and my dad, right beside them, lifted his right fist, and all the Rams mirrored him, shouting their triumph as one.

When they'd quieted, Tom Fears stood to speak. A tall, powerful man, he was a cocaptain and one of the most respected players on the team, known as much for the ferocity of his blocking as the precision with which he ran pass routes. He'd scored the winning touchdown the last time the Rams had won the NFL championship—in 1951, against the Browns—when he snatched a Van Brocklin pass from the air and ran nearly fifty-five yards to break a 17–17 fourth-quarter tie. Even in this, his eighth season in the league, he'd caught forty-four passes, more than any other Ram.

Now, in the dank, warm locker room, its bright lights shining down out of the ceiling, Fears took a football in hand. This was the ceremonial game ball, the award given to the man who provided the day's greatest contributions, chosen by his peers.

Fears looked first at his coach. When Gillman had come to training camp, he'd promised more defense and a more patient offense. Then, he'd improved the defense with a trade, and maybe as a result of that the Rams' Will Sherman led the league that season with eleven interceptions, while Don Burroughs was tied for second with nine. On offense, Gillman had cut back on the long pass plays, using the run more often and the shorter pass. The Rams ended up passing more often than the season before, but the yards they gained per pass dropped from 10.1 to 6.9. Even with a broken hand through much of the season, Van Brocklin threw fewer interceptions under the new system. Finally, Gillman had dealt with injuries by assuming that every player off the bench could contribute equally. With these changes, the Rams had won their way all the way to the NFL title game.

Fears held the ball forward so all could see. "We thought of giving this ball to Coach Gillman," he said. "But there's an even more important game coming up."

Everyone in the room knew what that meant: The Rams would give Gillman the game ball after they beat the Eastern champions, the Cleveland Browns, and captured the NFL title. It was a challenge Fears and Don Paul, as team captains, were making to their teammates and to themselves and even to Gillman. It was as if they were saying, "Lead us to one more victory, Sid; do that, and this ball is yours."

Then Fears turned back to his teammates.

"So today's award," he said, turning toward the man who had delivered the day's most bone-shivering block, "goes to John Hock for his fine play in the line."

He offered the game ball, and my dad took it in his big hands. He held it shyly, nodding his gratitude to his teammates, who applauded and cheered him. He understood how rare a gift this was, only twelve given a year on a team of thirty-five players, and even more rarely did it come to offensive linemen, those players who neither tackled nor scored touchdowns. It was a gift that said, "We saw you today. We saw how you opened the field for the Rat, but also every trap and counter, every sweep right or left. We saw how you protected Dutch. We saw how you pitted yourself against Green Bay's best and beat them. We saw all that you did and how well."

Amid the cheers, my dad ducked away, back to his locker even as Putnam and Hauser and Robustelli and the others slapped his shoulders and back, grinned at him, shook his hand, recalled this play or that, how my dad dominated.

Then the players made their way to their own lockers or to George "Mother" Menefee, the athletic trainer, to grab a bag of ice for a shoulder or ankle. Reporters huddled around asking questions of Dutch and Gillman. Dad needed ice, too, for his knees. But in a quiet moment he looked at the ball. Someone, maybe Don Paul or Fears, had written across its face in indelible black ink, with a careful hand. "Western Division Champs, 1954" it read, just above the Rawlings stamp. And below that, "Green Bay Packers 17, LA Rams 31."

He rolled the ball over in his hand to read the other side: "Game Ball," it said, "to John J. Hock."

The attention attached to this prize was done, which was fine. What remained, what would last, was what the ball represented. A decade or so earlier, on the Mount Carmel High School football field a few miles south, my dad had discovered the work for which he was best suited. Since then, he'd wanted little more than to be steady in that work and to do it well. It was never easy on his body or his will—and that, in part, was the reward. The work suited him because it tested him, just as it tested every man who played. Fans might not always understand that, not in the rough bone and sinew and gut where such understanding lived. Perhaps even coaches had forgotten the pain and sacrifice their players renewed each day. That's why this football mattered, the one my dad held in his big hand. It came from the men who knew the work, who knew it today, who knew it now, who knew it in that place deeper than any bruise, past any broken part. They knew, and they had taken this moment to say, "Good job."

◆

As the Rams showered, reporters gathered around Gillman, who had pulled a cuff link from his pocket. The piece was big and new and shiny, with a gem like a diamond—maybe it was a diamond—at its center. Around the edge was an inscription:

"1955 World Champions" and "Chicago Bears".

A friend, Gillman said, had sent it from Chicago. "Someone back there jumped the gun," he said.

He was asked whether the Rams might order their own such.

"Let's wait until we get over the Cleveland Browns," Gillman said.

Practice, he added, would start again on Thursday.

CHAPTER 10

The Loser's Purse

R EMEMBER PAUL BROWN'S TAUNT? The Rams did. It came after they had beaten the Browns, 38–21, in that exhibition game back in September. Everybody knew the results didn't matter, didn't indicate a thing. But Cleveland's coach couldn't let it go. As my dad and Van Brocklin and Waller and the rest jogged past him, he had challenged them: "Okay, okay, but what about December?"

What *about* December?

December was the Browns' month. They owned it in a way no other NFL team did. The franchise had existed for only nine years, born the season after the Rams left Cleveland. But in those nine years the Browns had played in nine league championship games: four as part of the All-American Football Conference, and then five in a row after that league folded and the Browns joined the NFL. Cleveland had won all four AAFC title games, and they'd won two in the NFL.

Now here came December: the day before Christmas, in the midst of the lunch hour, a plane carrying Coach Brown and his team touched down at Burbank's airport. Clouds like gray wool dropped sprinkles, which landed on the suit coats of Browns players as they descended from the plane to the tarmac. They might have hoped for sun, but it had been raining for days, so much so that at the coliseum the grounds crew had spread a new $16,000 tarp across the field to keep it in good condition. Still, the greeting Los Angeles's climate offered to the Browns was better than the hard, frigid cruelty they'd left behind in northeast Ohio where icy fields made practice hazardous.

Otto Graham, the Browns' quarterback, looked up into the dreary sky and deadpanned to reporters: "Unless you guarantee that the temperature will be at least fifty degrees, we won't play."

The last time Graham had been in Los Angeles was almost a year before, in more pleasant weather, as the starting quarterback for the East's squad in the NFL's Pro Bowl. Graham had an easy smile when making jokes— but when he pulled on a helmet his face changed. He wore a dark intensity like a mask; his glare looked as if it could cut glass. Perhaps more than any other player, perhaps even more than Coach Brown, Graham was responsible for the Browns' success. He'd been their quarterback since the team's founding in 1946, running his coach's preferred offense—the T-formation—better than anyone in the league. On any play, Graham might hand off to one of three running backs lined up behind him, or he might pass, or he might run himself—and at six foot one, two hundred pounds, he was tough to tackle. In the previous year's title game—a 56–10 thrashing of Detroit's Lions—Graham had thrown three touchdown passes and run for another three. After that game, he announced his retirement, wanting to end his career with a championship. But without him, the Browns lost a string of exhibition games to start 1955—including that game when Paul Brown taunted the Rams. The taunt was bold, given that Brown knew the primary reason his team had lost. Without Graham, there might be no December. So, just after that loss to the Rams, Brown telephoned Graham and set up a meeting at a restaurant in Aurora, Ohio. There, he offered his old quarterback a $25,000 salary—the highest pay in the NFL—to draw him out of retirement. It worked, and with Graham back, the Browns regained their old form and finished with a 9–2–1 record. Now, both odds-makers and bettors favored them to beat the Rams for the title, the line running as high as six points.

The Browns headed from the airport straight to a field nearby for practice. The next day was Christmas, and Coach Brown—a no-nonsense disciplinarian—wanted his team to work right away. There wasn't time to waste. The day after Christmas, they'd meet the Rams.

And after that, no matter the outcome, Otto Graham planned to retire. For good this time.

◆

TWICE BEFORE, THE RAMS and Browns had clashed for the NFL title.

Each game had been decided in the final quarter. In 1950, the Rams had lost at Cleveland, 30–28, when Browns kicker, Lou "The Toe" Groza, kicked a field goal with twenty-eight seconds left.

The next year the Rams won at the coliseum, 24–17, on that long, fourth-quarter scoring pass that made a local legend of Tom Fears.

Four years had passed since Dutch-to-Fears won it all, and quite a few players from those days still wore Rams helmets: Tank Younger, Deacon Dan Towler, Don Paul, Andy Robustelli, Bob Boyd, and Crazylegs Hirsch, among them. All could remember what it meant to play a Cleveland Browns team at its best.

But most Rams, including my dad, had only played Cleveland three times—all exhibition games. Since my dad had joined the team, the Rams and Browns had never played each other in a game that mattered—and certainly not in the NFL's pinnacle game with all its attendant spectacle.

It couldn't match the opening of Disneyland for national attention and economic upswing, but NBC had paid the league $100,000 for the rights to broadcast the game nationally. The contract prevented the game from being shown in Los Angeles because the NFL wanted to encourage the hometown fans to pay the five-dollars-a-ticket price and head out to the coliseum. By Christmas Eve, sixty thousand tickets had been sold, and coliseum officials expected to blow up the record for attendance at a championship game. It was a safe prediction, given that the previous best was 58,346, the number who watched the 1946 championship at the Polo Grounds in New York, pitting the Giants against Chicago's Bears.

Tickets sales mattered to players, too, who would receive bonuses based on the league's revenue earned from the game, sometimes as much as a couple thousand dollars. Each player would get the same fixed amount; the winners would earn a bit more than the losers. For a player with Otto Graham's highest-in-the-league salary, the bonus might seem small, perhaps 10 percent of his annual take.

That amount going to an offensive lineman, say to my dad, might be half again his annual salary.

◆

THE X-RAYS SHOWED A hairline fracture cutting through a vertebrae bone in Tank Younger's neck, that same neck Frank Finch of the *Times* had described as "shortened" by all those failed one-yard runs against the Packers.

It was a smart-aleck comment—until it wasn't.

"This is not to be confused with a broken neck," said the Rams surgeon, Dr. Dan Fortmann, who himself had played offensive line for the Chicago Bears as he finished his medical degree. "The hairline fracture has started to knit. However, it is not deemed advisable to permit Younger to play."

In a season when the Rams had suffered more injuries than in recent memory, Sid Gillman had hoped that he could meet the mighty Browns with a team at full strength. Even Elroy Hirsch looked to return, who had limped through most of the season and spent about as much time in the team's whirlpool as he had on the field. To lose any starter, but especially to lose Younger, was disappointing news. That season, he had been the Rams' leading fullback and second-leading rusher after Ron Waller.

A mainstay of the Rams offense since 1949, he would spend his third NFL championship game on the sidelines in street clothes.

Younger had come to the Rams from Louisiana, raw and trim and tall, and already bearing the nickname, "Tank." He'd received the name while playing at tiny Grambling College, a school founded by black Louisianans as an agriculture and industry school for black students. When Paul Calhoun Younger signed his pro contract, he became the first player from an all-black college to sign with an NFL team. While the Rams had signed Kenny Washington and Woody Strode under pressure to integrate, the decision to sign Younger, while historic, was based entirely on his quality as a player. That the Rams signed him as a free agent rather than selecting him with a precious draft pick was less a statement about him than it was about the attitudes NFL players and coaches had toward players from "Negro colleges." The Rams knew no other team would want Younger—they might not even know about him. So why waste the draft pick?

That the Rams knew about Younger was indicative of their cutting-edge scouting system. In the postwar 1940s, they knew more about potential players than any team in the league. It was another way Reeves leapt ahead of the NFL's old-guard owners and coaches. Those other teams spent little, if any, money on scouting. Mostly, each relied on good-ol'-boy networks, informed gossip from buddies and former teammates, thought it was still only gossip. Reeves organized a methodology.

In 1946, as the team headed for Southern California, he hired Eddie Kotal, a one-time running back with Green Bay's Packers, as a full-time scout, the first in NFL history. Kotal's job was to drive all over the country—from Louisiana to Oregon to Wisconsin to Connecticut—evaluating talent at football powerhouses such as Ohio State University or Notre Dame, but also in hideaways such as Scottsdale Community College, Arnold College, or Grambling College. He'd visited Tank Younger a few times, including once after Younger and Grambling played in the Vulcan Bowl, a premiere bowl game for black colleges. "Have you ever considered playing pro football?" Kotal asked Younger. "I've never given it a thought," Younger told him. When the time came for him to sign with a team, Younger knew he wanted the Rams. "By showing personal interest in me," Younger told *Ebony* magazine years later, "Kotal impressed me."

Kotal, bushy-browed and dapper and happy to play a hand of gin rummy, was the face of the Rams scouting operations. But those operations involved many more people than Kotal. Tex Schramm, Reeves' assistant, explained the system in detail years later to Michael Mac-Cambridge, author of *America's Game*. Reeves had a network of some one hundred college coaches around the country whom he paid for twice-a-year reports. He paid honorariums to California high school coaches to visit the Rams headquarters in Beverly Hills and watch game films to evaluate potential players. Rams staff mailed questionnaires to players in their junior years and studied the responses. Reeves hung a wall map of the United States in his office and with pushpins marked the location of each four-year college that played football.

So, come draft day, when NFL owners and coaches would gather at a hotel, usually in New York City, the Rams would call out names of players no other owner or coach had heard of—or expected.

Andy Robustelli? Who? Where's Arnold College? Who have they played? The Sisters of Charity?

After a few years, though, chuckles gave way to something else. You can imagine the *oh-hell-not-again* dread. Soon, every team had hired its own Eddie Kotal with the hope of finding its own Tank Youngers.

In 1955, Curly Lambeau, the legendary Packers coach who had spilled cigarette ash on my dad's dormitory bed, gave credit to Kotal and Dan Reeves for the Rams' ascendence to the NFL championship game. "I'm not taking anything away from Sid Gillman—he's done a wonderful job," Lambeau told the *Los Angeles Times*, "but I think Dan Reeves and Eddie Kotal deserve a lot of credit for obtaining the high type of player that represents Los Angeles in the National Football League."

But now Younger was out for the championship game, and the Rams would turn to "Deacon" Dan Towler, another of those scouting system successes. Towler, a little-known running back when the Rams drafted him (in the *twenty-fifth round*) from Washington & Jefferson College south of Pittsburgh, arrived the year after Younger made the team. Together, the two joined with Dick Hoerner from Iowa to make that legendary trio nicknamed "The Bull Elephant Backfield," because all of them stood taller than six foot two and weighed more than 220 pounds. The Rams often played all three fullbacks at once, and they trampled other teams.

Hoerner was traded after the 1951 season, breaking up the herd. Of the two who remained, Towler was the more successful runner, gaining almost nine hundred yards in the 1952 and 1953 seasons. Younger gained less than half as much, but also played linebacker on defense. The two presented much different personalities, as their nicknames suggested. Younger, well-liked on the team, could curse with the best of them. His struggles through a brief and unhappy marriage led to a fourteen-day jail sentence after he was accused of hitting his mother-in-law. He said she'd been drinking a vodka cocktail called a "Moscow Mule," which she threw at him, and she called him a "bum football player," so he pushed her and she fell. The Rams paid his $1,000 bail. Later, when his wife sued for divorce, she accused him of drinking too much, staying out late, gambling, using vulgar language, and, on occasion, hitting her, too. Younger said nothing during the divorce hearing. The judge granted the separation with no alimony and gave custody of a keeshond puppy named Jolie to Younger's now ex-wife.

Towler, on the other hand, carried the nickname "Deacon" because even as he played for the Rams, he studied at USC toward a graduate degree in theology with the goal of becoming a minister. He had, on occasion, called the team together and led pregame prayers. By special arrangement with Reeves, he was allowed to miss practices or training camp when he deemed it necessary for his studies. And still he'd gained more than 5.7 yards per carry over three seasons.

But in 1955, Deacon suffered a leg injury in the season's third game. Since then, he'd only carried the ball four times. He'd gained all of eight yards.

In Tank's absence, the Rams would need every bit of power and grace left in Deacon's legs.

◆

IF ANY TWO TEAMS were known for visionary work in professional football through the postwar decade, it was the Rams and the Browns. With Los Angeles, innovation began with Dan Reeves. With Cleveland, it started with Paul Brown.

Reeves hired the first year-round scout; Brown hired the first year-round assistant coaches. Reeves popularized branding the team through its helmets; Brown was first to add a single-bar face mask (trying to protect Graham, who had suffered a mouth wound that required fifteen stitches); Reeves had integrated the NFL; Brown, back in the AAFC days, made Cleveland the first pro team in the modern era to draft African-American players. Reeves moved a team from Cleveland. Brown built a new one there. Both made NFL history and would one day be voted into the league's Hall of Fame.

The NFL they dominated was in many ways still young, its rules comparatively few. The game's past was flat, solid ground. Upon it, strong skilled men struggled against each other in familiar ways. The results were often predictable, because it was easy for coaches and owners to see who was the strongest and most skilled. But clever minds willing to explore and dare could discover ample other ways to win. What Reeves and Brown had done since 1946 was to open themselves to the future. The past asked who: Who was strongest? Who was best at this position? Who was the most motivational coach? Reeves and Brown asked "What if?" They imagined.

Because they did, each had won two NFL titles. Their teams were meeting for the third time in the league's top game. And that meeting would take place in Los Angeles, the city itself an engine of the imagination.

But some quality that had vaulted the Rams and Browns atop their peers had gone missing. Though they could claim to be the best of 1955, the teams lacked the snap and surprise of the forward-looking. The Rams had won through dependable, grind-it-out, blood-and-bone football. Gillman, the Rams coach, worked with film in new ways, but on the field he had turned his players back toward old ideas. Reeves, for so long an inventive and indulged autocrat, had slipped enough that there came a public rebellion from the rest of the Rams' ownership. As for Brown, he'd resuscitated his team's season not through anything new, but with a desperate and pricey plea to the past and what had worked before. And after this title game, the day after Christmas, that old quarterback, Otto Graham, who had transformed the Browns from losers to winners, would leave for good.

Maybe in a season to come Reeves and Paul Brown would rediscover that forward snap and surprise. Maybe they could find the creative energy to push not only beyond the way *things are done* but, more importantly, beyond the way the Rams and Browns had done them. Reeves was only forty-three years old; Brown only forty-seven.

Or maybe not. Each had built an institution; sustaining such a thing would require other skills, a different vision. Maybe the two men had become convinced that their way of winning was the only way, and the Rams and Browns would become as hidebound, stagnate, and entrenched in failed practices as musty as those of George Preston Marshall and his all-white Redskins.

Maybe the 1955 NFL championship was the great good end of the best their teams would ever be.

◆

WHEN HOLLYWOOD'S CAMERA NEXT finds my dad, he's got the meaty side of a fist smashed against his helmeted head.

Why?

"There's an old theory," says Bob Gain, who played defensive lineman for the 1955 Cleveland Browns. "Wherever the head goes, the rest of the body follows. We could head slap. It was legal. I didn't really head slap. I punched."

So that's why. And that fist upside My dad's head? Let's say it belongs to Bob Gain. Gain and my dad faced each other across the line of scrimmage in that 1955 championship game. The two men had history, though maybe even they didn't realize it. They'd lined up against each other nearly six years before, when Dad's Santa Clara Mustangs beat Gain's Kentucky Wildcats in the Orange Bowl.

So: Gain's fist. He's got huge hands, after all, maybe even bigger than my dad's. Hands like a grizzly's paws.

Hands big as a cast iron pan. Though he and my dad match height, Gain outweighs him by some twenty-five pounds.

It's a fist and then chaos that the camera and audio capture. A hand there, a jaw there, another fist, a helmet. Mostly, it's sound. A growl and a huff, a crack when helmets hit, a thud, a pop, a rip. After so many days of rain, there's mud mixed with sweat and spit and snot. The only colors are the burnt orange of the Browns helmets; the shiny blue of the Rams; some jumble of dirt-smeared white and yellow—the jerseys.

The men line up to do it again. The camera pulls back a bit, giving a less intimate view and more context. The Rams try a pass play. Dad and Putnam and the other linemen step backwards, trying to catch the stampeding Browns, trying to stop Gain and company from reaching Van Brocklin.

Another pass play, and the lineman back up again.

A third play, and again it's a pass. Dad, Putnam and the rest are playing—literally—on their heels.

Finally, Van Brocklin zips one, and the camera follows the ball's arc as it travels through a gray sky, the stadium floodlights burning against that gloom. A Brown reaches out and grabs the ball—interception—then collapses under a pile of Rams.

My dad and the rest jog to the sidelines, and if their heads aren't dipped, there's still something about their postures that suggests frustration. The interception's bad, sure, but worse is how the game is unfolding.

The linemen will fall back as often as is called for, but they'd like to pull away from the line, too, run into open field, hit someone. That'll be rare in this game, and that's part by design and part by circumstance. Coach Gillman thought the Browns might be vulnerable to a passing game, so his strategy gives Van Brocklin plenty of tosses. When the camera catches the scoreboard, the circumstance is apparent: Browns seventeen, Rams seven, with just a few seconds left in the first half. Los Angeles trails and the fastest way to get points is by passing.

Now the camera pans the Rams sideline, and there's Van Brocklin jawing with one of the Browns who has hurried by while showing four fingers, one for each of Dutch's interceptions. The camera keeps going until it catches my dad, and there it stops. He's lifted his helmet, so it sits high on his head, the single-bar guarding making a shadow on his forehead. His cheeks are flushed, fists at his hips, chest expanding with heavy breaths. But his mouth isn't open. He's not panting. That big jaw is set. His eyes show the reality; he'll go out there on the field again, and he'll fight and grip and hold and work to keep Dutch out of trouble. He's not beaten, and neither are the Rams—and they won't be, not until the final gun cracks. But any clear-eyed pro can already see that that the Browns are the much better team. The Rams aren't beaten, no, but they will lose this game.

◆

JUST ABOUT THE TIME the game ended, the rain, which had threatened all afternoon, began to fall, a fitting coda for the Rams and their fans.

"We got our butts kicked," recalls Ron Waller, then the Rams rookie halfback.

"We ended up winning it pretty good," says Cleveland's Bob Gain.

Thirty-eight to fourteen was the final score, and—as the sportswriters say—it wasn't that close.

Van Brocklin threw six interceptions to tie an NFL record no quarterback would ever want. After Gillman benched Dutch, his replacement, Bill Wade, threw another to make it seven for the game. Waller managed only forty-eight yards on eleven carries.

For the Browns, Otto Graham had run for two touchdowns and thrown for two others. When Graham left the field, the Los Angeles crowd of nearly eighty-eight thousand—larger than any to ever have watched an NFL title game—rose as one and offered a loud and long ovation. A similar spirit waited at the Browns' locker room, where Don Paul—the Rams' infamous villain and cocaptain—congratulated each of the winning players.

And some eighty-eight thousand disappointed fans, many hiding under umbrellas, headed for the parking lots. They hadn't been able to help their Rams to victory, but they had staked the NFL to its largest net profit for any championship game—$431,538.88.

The players, by contract, would receive seventy percent of that. The Browns players—as winners—would each cash a record championship paycheck of about $3,500.

The loser's purse to each Ram? About $2,300.

"Hell, you could buy a new car for that," recalls Bob Gain, then corrects himself.

"Not all new cars, but—like—a Chevy."

CHAPTER 11

Those Strange Things Yet To Come

HOW COULD MY DAD live in Los Angeles and not look forward to tomorrow? How could he, in that spring of 1956, be anything but optimistic? He'd always risen early, which served him well in the military and as an altar boy and at training camp with the Rams. Night scrubbed dust and grit from the world, and what had been tomorrow came quiet and fresh, rich with potential, so rich that if it carried a price tag no one could afford it, not even Howard Hughes. Yet those mornings belonged to him: a kid selling rabbit skins during the Depression, a GI in Japan, a football player making schoolteacher wages. Wake early, open his senses—that's all it took. So he'd rouse himself from sleep and listen to the day gather its energy: the sizzle and smokiness of bacon in a pan; a Western swing tune, staticky and thin on a radio; the surprise of a car backfiring; then the growing thrum as engines heated and people drove to work. It didn't matter whether his joints ached or his nose or a finger was broken. He would push through that, because pain mattered less than astonishment. Out there life waited, and it promised to thrill, because every day was all so new.

Los Angeles was like that, too, crisp and bright as his favorite minutes of morning, promising each day to astound him. All he had to do was venture from home, drive out to the beach, or to Rams headquarters on Beverly Boulevard, or up to Granada Hills with my mom, to visit the Putnams—Duane and Patty—for a cookout in the backyard of their tract home.

Drive. That's all he had to do.

Past that new Capitol Records building, built like a cylinder of stacked thirty-threes, and shake his head and marvel. First circular office building in the world, the newspapers said. Stop at a traffic light on Santa Monica Boulevard and stare at that massive new church the Mormons built and called a temple, that religion's largest in the world. Gawk at a donut shop with a giant donut on its roof, bigger even than Art Donovan and Big Daddy Lipscomb combined. Such sights made my dad a tourist in his own hometown. He didn't have to pay for a ticket at Disneyland to be amazed. Every day it seemed the city offered something else to make him smile: a coffee shop that looked like it had been built on

Venus, with arches bent over its roofline like comet tails of steel and plastic; a drive-in diner with enough angles to confuse a billiards whiz; a bowling alley just opened in Covina but straight out of Egypt by way of Polynesia (or Polynesia by way of Egypt, who knew?). And the colors! No one would call them subtle. Yellows and reds and blues, flat and bright and hot. Strange, those buildings, sure, but so danged cheerful and whimsical and surprising. Like morning every day.

He'd marvel for years, my dad would, the astonishment present and palpable as in 1956. "It was all so new," he'd tell people again and again.

◆

"'WE CALL IT GOOGIE architecture,' said Professor Thrugg, 'named after a remarkable restaurant in Los Angeles called Googie's.'"

There actually was no Professor Thrugg. But there was a clever architecture critic from the East Coast named Douglas Haskell. And there was a Googie's. Haskell, driving through Los Angeles, came across a diner with a bright red roof that tilted upward, as if a giant red wafer cookie had been glued to the corner. A neon sign added eye-pupils into the Os in Googie's. The crassness of the design seemed to represent everything Haskell disdained in a new, popular style that, as yet, had no name.

So Haskell named it. His stand-in, Professor Thrugg, appeared in *House and Home* magazine's February 1952 issue, lecturing on the new architectural direction. Haskell transcribed an imagined conversation between Thrugg and a horrified student.

"'Do you mean then,' asked the student, 'that Googie is an art in which anything and everything goes?'"

"'So long as it's modern,' came back the Prof."

What Thrugg and Haskell were describing was the architecture that so overtook Los Angeles after World War II, what my dad saw popping into view, new, it seemed, day after day. Alternately described as space age, uninhibited, incoherent, whimsical, dynamic, cartoonish, outlandish, and, as one journalist wrote in *Smithsonian Magazine*, so exaggerated and flamboyant that it is "almost beyond parody."

And it was inherently optimistic. It brought the promise of the future to Los Angeles's working and middle classes, to anyone who could afford a cup of coffee or ten frames of ten pin. The future, Googie said, is fun. The future can do anything! It tilts walls and turns triangles into birds and birds into triangles. It puts flagstone together with plastic and massive glass plates.

"It's too bad our taste is so horrible," Professor Thrugg concluded. The only benefit he acknowledged might come of Googie was that its jarring strangeness could someday prepare people "for those strange things yet to come which will truly make good sense."

Googie, from an East Coast point-of-view, was nonsense.

◆

HOW COULD DAD DRIVE around the palm trees and neon of Los Angeles in the spring of 1956 and feel anything but optimism? My mom was pregnant and expected their first child—my brother Jay—in June. Dad's knees had held up through an entire football season; the Rams had reached the title game; he had received two grand for the privilege. Seven of his teammates had been voted to the Pro Bowl, including the Putter, my dad's best friend on the roster, and he couldn't be happier.

All over the league, people were calling Duane Putnam one of the NFL's best guards. "If you'd take a 'toughest guy' poll among the [Rams]," wrote Frank Finch in the *Times*, "he'd win in a walk." How tough? Years later, Rams lineman John Houser would tell of a time when Putnam jumped off-sides on the first play of the game and head-butted Baltimore's Gene Lipscomb and bloodied his nose. Lipscomb, the man called "Big Daddy," was not only six inches taller and fifty pounds heavier than Putnam, he was a former teammate, who had helped carry Sid Gillman from the field after the Rams won 1955's Western Division title. "Aw shit, Putter, what'd you do that for?" Lipscomb said, according to the tale. Putnam didn't answer, just smiled, and according to Houser's story, "Lipscomb was putty in Putter's hands from then on."

Some said it was that toughness—what Ron Waller had called "feisty," the reason he'd never want to fight Putnam—that made Putnam one of the league's top guards. Some cited the Putter's greater power since he'd started weight lifting, the beef added to his legs and shoulders. Others gave credit to Gillman and the new coaches. "He was good last year but he's absolutely great this season," said Skeet Quinlan. "The coaches studied him in films, changed him around a bit and capitalized on his potential. The result is that his blocking has been terrific." Feistiness, strength, or technique—Putnam's play had improved since he and my dad had first paired as tandem guards back in 1953. That year, my dad was named honorable mention all-pro by the *Associated Press*. In seasons since, though, he had struggled with his knees, and he'd missed 1954, and, maybe because of all that he'd lost a step or two. Or maybe it was just that Putnam had improved so much. Regardless, near the end of the 1955 season, Gillman called Putnam, "the perfect guard."

That assessment would come into play the next season when Gillman changed how he used the Rams' offensive line and—consequently—threatened my dad's career.

◆

How COULD ANY LOS Angeles sports fan not be optimistic early in 1956? The city kept climbing in the sports world, and if it wasn't on top, it was close. From Swaps the summer before to the Rams finishing second in the NFL to the city hosting the annual NFL Pro Bowl game, LA was making an argument for itself as a sports capital. Roz Wyman felt the momentum and kept it going by offering resolutions to the council— one congratulating Sid Gillman on his success with the Rams and another welcoming the NFL's East and West squads to the Pro Bowl, including the seven gentlemen from the hometown Rams.

Among those was young Ron Waller, who had also finished second in the league's Rookie of the Year voting to another running back, Baltimore's Alan Ameche.

After such a fine season, Waller decided he ought to be making more money. The Rams had signed him the summer before for $8,000, plus a $1,000 bonus. He asked to meet with Tex Schramm, and then Waller asked for a contract worth nearly double what he'd made the year before.

Fifteen thousand? asked Schramm.

Fifteen thousand, said Waller.

"Son," Schramm said, "you've got be in this league a long time before you make fifteen thousand."

So Waller signed for much less. But in reality, his pay no longer mattered much to his day-to-day life. Since his move to Los Angeles, he'd met and become engaged to a woman some five years his senior—a competitive swimmer, an aspiring actress and granddaughter to one of the country's wealthiest women.

A kid from Laurel, Delaware, where a sweet potato blight had a decade earlier devastated the local economy, was about to join the highest of societies.

◆

Won't you marry me, marry me, off to the altar please
carry me?
Give me combs for my curls, made of silver and pearls,
and a two-penny bridal bouquet...say!
Hurry up, hurry up, hitch that old horse to the surrey-up,
and I'll vow to be true to no one but you,
so marry me, marry me, do.
> —The Hudspeth sisters, including Pearl, played by
> Marjorie Durant, off-key and serenading Anthony
> Perkins in the film, *Friendly Persuasion*

IN HER FIRST FILM, in her first scene, she's splitting wood on a farm somewhere in what's supposed to be the rural Midwest, nearly one hundred years ago (but is really California in 1955). Her character lives with two sisters and her widowed mother, all four of them desperate for the company of men, which we'll learn shortly, because Gary Cooper and Anthony Perkins, playing father and son, rumble toward her in a wagon. Marjorie Merriweather Durant swings the axe like a pro, her long blonde braid flailing with it. When the blade sticks in a hunk of wood, she kicks it free like she's been splitting wood her whole life.

"HEY, MAW!" she bellows toward the farmhouse. "A COUPLE-A MEN TO SEE YA!"

It's a comic role lasting only ten minutes in a movie that stretches over two hours. She's physical in it, wielding that axe like Paul Bunyan, shoving Anthony

Perkins here and there as she ogles him, her inbred leer saying, "I will violate you in every way and enjoy it."

"Wanna smoke?" she later asks Perkins, who plays a thoughtful Quaker lad. When he demurs, she asks, "Wanna drink?"

Filming took place over autumn in 1955, even as the Rams worked their way toward the Western Division title and a date with Cleveland's Browns. The next April—seven months before the film's release—Marjorie Merriweather Durant, granddaughter and namesake of Marjorie Merriweather Post, heiress to a cereal fortune, married Ronald Bowles Waller at St. Thomas Episcopal Church in Washington, DC, near where the bride's mother raised thoroughbreds in Maryland. *The New York Times* gave the wedding eight inches on its society page. The article lists ten attendants in addition to the matron of honor. Among them was Mrs. Bud McFadin, whose husband played lineman and linebacker for the Rams.

Marjorie was no Jane Russell. She was more starlet than star. But her family wealth gave her social standing and celebrity, and her family history—her father had worked as a personal assistant to Charlie Chaplin—gave her Hollywood connections. She was represented by Allied Artists, the studio that produced *Friendly Persuasion*. That movie had done well, meaning Durant had a bit role in a picture that competed with *Giant*, *The Ten Commandments*, and *The King and I* for Best Picture at the Academy Awards. It won the Palme D'Or at the Cannes Film Festival. Altogether, Durant had enough of a resumé to reassert the Rams' connections to glamorous Hollywood.

She'd host parties at the home she and Ron shared in the Santa Monica mountains near the water. At the Wallers' home, Rams players could mingle with Hollywood actors the likes of Richard Boone, Tab Hunter, and Ty Harden, aka, Bronco Layne of the Western TV series *Bronco*. The Rams and their wives called their hostess Marge, and sometimes she was just as brash and sassy as Pearl Hudspeth from *Friendly Persuasion*.

When my mom, pregnant with her first child and nauseated, decided to skip a Durant social event, Marge sought her out saying, "Micki! Why the heck aren't you coming to my party?" Once, at a game, sitting behind my grandpa, Harry, Marge couldn't control her enthusiasm and kept kicking him in the back. When he finally turned to object, she teased him: "Old man, if I'm kicking you, well, you need to have your coat cleaned once in a while."

Not all Rams and their wives were comfortable sharing in that Hollywood life. For some it was too fast, too loud, too inebriated, too many ex-husbands and ex-wives, too many dramas. After a couple of seasons trying to live in Los Angeles, for example, Art and Joanie Hauser decided to live in the off-season back home near Cincinnati. "It was just really wild for us," Joanie Hauser recalled, years later. "We just weren't from that wild background… It was different, the Hollywood part."

It was different for Ron Waller, too. Less than a year before he'd been a rookie at training camp, worried that he'd get cut and be heading back to tiny Laurel, Delaware. Now he found himself visiting with his wife's grandmother at Mar-a-Lago, her mansion estate in Palm Beach, Florida. Mar-a-Lago, had well over 100 rooms, 20,000 roof tiles, and 2,200 black and white marble floor blocks in only the entrance hall, living and dining rooms. Laurel High School, with forty-four students in Waller's graduating class, was smaller.

"It was a big jump," he recalled. "I tell you…"

◆

THAT SAME SPRING, THE Rams signed Ron Miller, who had played end for USC. Also, he was Walt Disney's son-in-law. During the 1956 season, Diane Disney Miller sat with the other Rams' wives in the coliseum, and once Walt Disney joined them outside the locker room as they waited for their husbands to emerge. Diane and Ron were older—the military had kept him out of pro football for a while—and already had children. Now and then, my mom babysat for Walt Disney's grandchildren.

But Ron Miller's football career didn't last long. Against Detroit at the coliseum during the 1956 season, he took a vicious hit across the face from Night Train Lane, now playing for the Lions. That collision broke Miller's nose and knocked him unconscious. Walt Disney watched horrified from a seat in the stadium. It's easy to imagine Disney, with his visionary foresight, dreaming of a nightmare future in which Miller became crippled or worse. Later Disney demanded his son-in-law accept a prominent job in the family business, a chance to build a company and provide for his family rather than suffer broken bones. Miller accepted.

As a parting gift to his teammates, though, he arranged a deal for all those with whom he shared the locker room: bring the families through the gates of the Magic Kingdom in Anaheim—anytime, gratis.

◆

SOMETIMES, PLAYING FOR THE Rams in the 1950s, you said hello. Oftentimes you said goodbye. Sometimes, though, there wasn't much chance to say anything.

Dad didn't get to say goodbye to Andy Robustelli that summer of 1956. Robustelli was one of my dad's best friends on the team—two soft-spoken and Roman Catholic men who surprised people with their ferocity. Robustelli, a stalwart on defense, hailed from a small college in Connecticut and seemed to be one of those necessary pieces for the Rams' success. He seemed one of those fellas Sid Gillman especially had in mind when he'd filled the locker room with praise after the Rams beat the Packers for the division title, saying: "You not only are the greatest players I've ever been with, but as a group, you're the greatest bunch of men."

So when Dad and the Rams left to go their separate off-season ways, they shook hands and my dad knew that when Andy returned he'd get to meet my parent's firstborn, my brother Jay, expected in June. The men believed the next time they'd see Robustelli would be out in dry, dusty Redlands for training camp. Robustelli had been a regular Pro Bowler, and he was good for team morale. Ma Robustelli's spaghetti had stuffed more than a few Ram bellies. The team even announced in February that Robustelli, Norm Van Brocklin, and Bob Boyd had all signed new contracts. That was good news for Robustelli and his growing family. His wife, Jeanne, was pregnant with the couple's fourth child.

The baby was born on the eve of training camp, and Robustelli placed a long-distance call to Gillman to explain that he'd be late to report. He was needed at home. Three kids and a new baby and all.

It was not an unreasonable request given that, since Robustelli had joined the team, Dan Towler had been able to skip parts of training camp for his theology studies and Elroy Hirsch had missed days to finish up movie acting jobs. But Gillman, whose own children were often football orphans, reacted harshly. He ordered Robustelli to report, ASAP.

In his memoir *Once a Giant, Always...: My Two Lives with the New York Giants*, Robustelli recalled saying "Sid, I'll be out there as soon as my home situation is settled."

Soon after, Robustelli received a phone call from Wellington Mara, a co-owner of the Giants and the man in charge of their personnel. "I've been talking to the Rams about you," Mara said, "and they're willing to trade you. I know you're thirty years old, but do you think you could play two or three more years?"

Betrayals happen that fast in the NFL. One minute you're with a team, the next you learn that the team doesn't want you. But playing for the Giants would mean Robustelli could stay with his family in southwestern Connecticut year-round. Strange as it seemed, maybe Gillman was doing him a favor. Robustelli answered Mara honestly and quickly.

"I'll try to play as long as I can," he said. "But I don't know how long that will be."

"If you tell me you can play," Mara said, "or at least will try to play for that long, then I think I can make a trade for you."

Robustelli said, "Make the deal."

The announcement came on July 27. In return, the Rams received a high draft pick they could use after the 1956 season. Robustelli would go on to be the general manager of the Giants and my dad would relish reconnecting with him when we moved to New Jersey.

◆

SOME FOOTBALL JOURNALISTS HAVE speculated that the Rams let Robustelli go because Gillman believed a player lost zip after age thirty. Robustelli had celebrated the big three-oh that past December, and his dedication to his family gave Gillman a pretext for a decision Gillman already wanted to make. But maybe it wasn't Gillman who believed that age thirty was bad news.

After all, this was only his second season working with pros. As a college coach, his players were seldom older than twenty-one. Mara's concern about Robustelli's age suggests that in the NFL of the 1950s it was the practice to treat thirty as the beginning of the end. Otto Graham had retired for the first time at age thirty-three. Bob Waterfield quit when he was thirty-two. It makes sense that what Gillman believed about players at age thirty was only what others had told him.

In the spring of 1956, on March 15, Norm Van Brocklin blew out thirty candles on his cake.

It's easy to make the connection between that fact and what Gillman decided, going into training camp, involving Van Brocklin and my dad. Gillman's plan was a dramatic shift in how the Rams operated and in who called the shots. Certainly his decision about Robustelli had hurt team morale, but this other decision—the one that threatened my dad's career—angered Van Brocklin.

And when had pissing off Dutch ever helped anything?

CHAPTER 12

Shuttle Guard

C ALL THIS SID GILLMAN's perfect dream:
At the coliseum, the day sparkles as only
a Los Angeles day can—clear and dry, warm
but not too, a breeze clearing the smog,
making way for the blue. Across the field, let's say, are
Philadelphia's Eagles: a good matchup for the Rams, but
nothing worthy of a ticker-tape parade. Because of that
and the blue-breeze day, the crowd's only half strength,
some fifty-five thousand. It's summer, after all, in Los
Angeles. With a whole season to go, there's plenty of
weekends to come when casual fans might catch a
Rams' game. Sid, bow-tied as usual, doesn't mind the
sparser crowd. It's not his job to put people in the seats.

It's his job to win ball games, and to that end he's got this new idea he's trying out today.

The Eagles start with the ball, but the Rams' defense holds, so Philadelphia punts. Now's Sid's moment: As the Rams' offense readies itself to take the field, Sid instructs his starting quarterback, Norm Van Brocklin. He's telling Dutch which play to run to start the game.

Though this has never ever happened before, though Dutch has *always* called his own plays, Van Brocklin nods. Maybe he even says, "Great call, Sid! I hadn't thought of that." (Remember, this is Sid's dream.)

Then Van Brocklin and the offense trot onto the field. The Rams run the play their coach wants, and perfectly—a twelve-yard gain, first down! Sid, straining to stretch his arm across the big shoulders of a second-string offensive lineman, tells him the next play. Then he gives the lineman a gentle shove toward the field. The substitute sprints to the huddle even as a starting lineman sprints out, his place taken by the man with Gillman's message. In the huddle, Van Brocklin listens as the lineman conveys the next play. Then Dutch glances to the sidelines, gives Gillman the thumbs up. Another first down for sure!

That's the dream version.

◆

GILLMAN BORROWED THE IDEA from Paul Brown who'd pioneered it and used it in the 1955 championship game when his quarterback took instructions from his coach on the sidelines via a steady rotation of linemen. Though stripped of the authority to call his own plays, quarterback Otto Graham threw two touchdown passes and ran for two more.

Gillman, across the field, watched helplessly as Van Brocklin decided which plays the Rams would run—and threw six interceptions.

The convention in the NFL had always been that coaches drew up the plays and crafted the strategies, but quarterbacks decided which plays to call, and when. This was often a practical matter. There had never been a foolproof method to get a message from the sidelines to the quarterback without the other team figuring it out. Then the NFL changed its substitution rules, allowing coaches to shuttle players in and out of games, and Paul Brown had his epiphany. He could choose the plays and send them via a substitute. He opted to use offensive linemen as his messengers, perhaps because offensive linemen were less specialized than players at other positions. They were necessary but interchangeable. Light bulbs on a movie set.

There were good reasons for a quarterback to call plays. He had the best view of the field. He knew what player might have been hurt on the last play. He could listen to guys in the huddle and adapt. But Brown had arguments for giving himself the job. Unlike the quarterback, he had a telephone line to the press box where assistant coaches with a bird's-eye view saw what no one on the field could see. He'd been the one to study game films and the opponents' tendencies, and he possessed decades more experience and insight into the game than his quarterback.

Gillman could claim several of those reasons, too—though Van Brocklin had played seven seasons in the NFL—so he understood the league in ways Gillman, a longtime college coach in his second season with the pros, was only just learning.

For example, unlike in college, an experienced NFL quarterback might get caught up in shenanigans. He might get annoyed at a defensive lineman's cheap shot, so call a play in which his blockers stepped aside so that lineman could charge unimpeded and the quarterback could throw the ball hard at the lineman's face.

Not that Van Brocklin ever did that, except for that time when he did. Hit the lineman right between the eyes.

Van Brocklin's way of choosing plays was not always cerebral, so Gillman—a professor of football, a teacher, a "rabbi" in Van Brocklin's lingo—decided to follow Brown's model. The big difference would be that Brown had assumed the role of play-caller from Otto Graham. Graham hadn't wanted to surrender the responsibility, but he—this future head coach at the Coast Guard Academy—respected authority. He followed Brown's orders.

Van Brocklin, since his first year in the league, had never shied from disagreeing with a coach—often via a creative and robust heaping of Anglo-Saxon invective.

For Dutch, calling plays wasn't just a responsibility he'd prefer to have. It was part of his natural self. His wife, Gloria, more than once woke to hear him in bed beside her mumbling and yipping. "Even at three a.m.," she says in the book, *The Golden Age of Pro Football*, "he was calling plays."

To take that role away from Dutch would be like cutting out his brain. The message would be, "You're an arm; leave the thinking to me." To insult Van Brocklin that way carried a risk, but Gillman wasn't going to get himself fired because his quarterback chose the wrong plays and the Rams lost. If Dutch didn't like this new reality, well, Gillman had an option other than a thirty-year-old who had thrown six interceptions in the one game when his play counted most. The Rams' backup quarterback, Bill Wade, had been named the most valuable player in the football-devoted Southeastern Conference while he played at Vanderbilt University. Tall, strong, talented, and young, he'd sat on the sidelines most of two seasons with the Rams. In some ways, he was the anti–Van Brocklin: polite while Dutch was crude, soft-spoken while Dutch was loud and profane. Dutch skipped optional Monday night meetings at Gillman's house; Wade always attended. Van Brocklin "would cuss and all that," recalled lineman Art Hauser. "Bill Wade, he was my roommate when we were rookies. At training camp in Redlands he'd sit down on the john and read quotes from the Bible."

Wade believed himself to be just as worthy to start as Van Brocklin and in better playing condition, and he thought he'd performed well enough in training camp to win the job outright. Sitting on the bench frustrated him, and he began to wonder whether there might be other reasons—even conspiratorial forces—that kept him off the field.

"It seemed like to me that there were certain elements in Los Angeles that did not want me to be the quarterback," said Wade, years later. "I hated it. Every minute of it. I mean, I wanted to play football. I was in good condition and better condition than my competitor. I could throw the ball eighty yards in the air. I didn't know how far he could throw it, and I didn't really care."

Wade had worked to be a good team player on the bench and wait for his chance. If running Gillman's plays meant he'd take the snaps, well, yes sir, he'd run those plays.

◆

WHAT WORKED IN CLEVELAND turned out to be disastrous in Los Angeles. Imagine it this way: a guy in the backseat tells one of the best drivers in the country when to turn, when to brake, when to merge into traffic. Sometimes the driver roars back that the directions are as useful as a "how to wipe your ass" manual written in Russian. Then, with the car stopped at a pumping station, the passenger pockets the keys and hands them to a fellow who'd spent two years changing the oil.

The worst part? No matter who drove, the car kept smashing—into donut shops and office buildings and other cars' big-finned rear ends.

By the first week of November, the Rams—the defending Western Conference champs—had played six games. They'd lost five.

Van Brocklin kept throwing too many interceptions. He threw his first in the season's opening game, with less than two minutes ticked away, and *zip!* Gillman benched him for Wade. Wade threw interceptions, too. In fact, he and Van Brocklin were each throwing more interceptions than touchdown passes. But Wade ran the plays Gillman wanted. Van Brocklin spent games fuming that Gillman sat him—or, when he played, scorning whatever plays Gillman wanted. That Van Brocklin sometimes ignored Gillman's calls frustrated the coach.

At Rams' weekly luncheons, fans complained—loudly. Some argued Gillman should return the play-calling responsibility to Van Brocklin—or Wade, whoever. Gillman sometimes snapped back his answers. The newspapers wrote regularly about the controversy. The locker room split.

Decades after, it was clear who Duane Putnam wanted in charge during the game.

"Sid wanted to be in control, to control everything, control the play," Putnam said one summer afternoon, sitting with his wife Patty at the dining room table in his home outside Los Angeles. "It was just his way of doing it."

"You mean he wouldn't let Dutch call his plays?" Patty asked.

"No." Putnam had a small pouch of tobacco in his lip and spit discreetly. "Quarterbacks knew what was going on more than the coach knew."

Then he praised Van Brocklin. "He was honest," Putnam said, "and he was a man about everything. He wasn't against anything or anybody. He was just out to get the game won. You like to be around people like that. They shoot straight."

During that dreadful 1956 season, insiders like Putnam knew the offense wasn't the only problem. The defense missed its captain, Don Paul, who had retired to run his restaurant. And it really missed Robustelli, whom Gillman had traded to the Giants. Robustelli's replacement, Frank Fuller, had suffered a broken leg during the exhibition season against the 49ers, leaving the Rams with what amounted to a third-stringer in Robustelli's spot. Meanwhile, the Giants, with Robustelli starting at defensive end, were 5–1 at midseason.

Play-calling, play-calling, play-calling! The fans, the press, Van Brocklin and Gillman, the Rams talking among themselves—it was a lot of noise. It was so loud, filling so much of every head that cared, hardly anyone could give a thought to the messengers, the shuttle guards who now carried the plays from Gillman to the quarterback.

In particular, hardly anyone gave a thought to the effect all this had on my dad.

◆

WHY MY DAD, OF all five starting offensive linemen?

Paul Brown had used guards, not tackles, and Gillman followed that lead. That gave him two guards from which to choose: Putnam or my dad. Putnam was all-pro. "A perfect guard," Gillman had said.

My dad was a good, high-quality guard. Excellent, even. But Putnam was a shade better. If a coach is always working percentages to give himself and his team the best chance to win, he needs his best guard on the field as often as possible. That was Putnam.

Dad became the messenger.

◆

MAYBE IT DOESN'T SEEM like such a bad thing, to deliver a coach's plays from the sideline. Leave the field after a tough play, take the next one off. Sip water. For thirty seconds or so, no one hits you in the head.

But consider this: my dad had only a few seconds to rumble on and off the field. He had to sprint. Usually, as a lineman, the most he'd run on a play is six or ten yards before he smashed somebody. As a shuttle guard he had to run from Gillman's side to the line of scrimmage wherever the heck that happened to be on the field. If it was at the five-yard line, my dad had to gallop thirty-five yards to get there. Then, he ran a play. And if the team gained no yards? He galloped thirty-five yards back. A short gain? Thirty yards to carry the next play. That's one hundred yards over two plays instead of the twenty to which my dad was accustomed. Hitting and being hit, that's what my dad expected—it's what he practiced. If he hadn't liked collisions, he would never have become an offensive lineman. Sprinting a hundred yards? That was for track and field guys, skinny fellas with batons and flimsy shorts. My dad wore cleats, not winged Mercury's sandals.

Something else bothered him about being a shuttle guard. It wasn't anything easy to explain, but through years as an offensive lineman, my dad had come to know and value the game's rhythms, how to pair his actions and reactions to its flows. A game was, what?, waves and tides?, and to live in its violence required a routine, a practiced sense of timing built over years snap-by-snap, block-by-block, so that when it became part of him it felt as if it has always been part of him. Then it wasn't thinking that told him how long to hold a block or when to let it go. It wasn't counting the seconds. He could just tell. The game—or its rhythms— lived in him, and he lived in them, and that gave him comfort, satisfaction.

Now, Paul Brown's innovation and Sid Gillman's imitation had broken that routine to pieces. Now it was in, then out. In, then out. A long sprint, a short sprint, a somewhere-in-the-middle sprint. Where does anybody find a routine in all that? My dad had become a yo-yo, one moment in hand, the next spinning uselessly in space.

◆

EACH DAY OF HIS football life—and with special care during the season—Dad calibrated how he used his legs. It was as if he knew his knees had only a finite number of strides before they'd quit on him.

So, he wasn't much for walking. He didn't climb stairs if he could press an elevator button. He drove to the grocery store, even if it was only a few blocks. Better to use whatever was left of his knees on those sweeps and traps. Better to use them for football.

Not to play Western Union.

"He didn't like to take any extra steps, I remember that," Duane Putnam said, recalling those days. "He just didn't have the good pins under him. His stumps would get clanked every week. He'd have to rub them and put ice on them. They weren't skinny. They just weren't structurally strong to handle what he had on top."

Dad didn't grumble in the locker room or at the bars where players gathered to drink Schlitz. But playing shuttle guard took some of the joy away, and those who knew him could tell. At home, he'd sit in a chair with his feet up, or lie on the couch, my brother Jay, then an infant, in his lap, a light from a table lamp falling across the boy's astonished face. Or maybe, Jay asleep and my mom sitting nearby, he'd have a magazine in his hand, the glow of the television flickering across his face. He'd find reasons to stay put, and though my mom could see that his knees hurt him, he'd never acknowledge it, even if she asked.

"I suppose," my mom wondered aloud so many years after, "he didn't want you to say, 'If it hurts, don't play.'"

◆

A FEW DAYS BEFORE the Rams' fifth loss that 1956 season, news broke in New York that Walter O'Malley, president of the Brooklyn Dodgers, had sold Ebbets Field, the team's home stadium, to a real estate developer for an undisclosed price "in seven figures."

O'Malley had long and loudly and publicly complained that Ebbets Field was "outmoded, dirty, and inadequate" and said his baseball team wouldn't play there after the 1958 season. Even so, the sale of the ballpark contained a provision that allowed the Dodgers to lease it back until the end of the 1961 season. And Marvin Krattner, the developer who bought the stadium, said he'd extend that lease as long as necessary if it meant the Dodgers would stay in the borough. "I would never do anything to keep the Dodgers from playing in Brooklyn," he said.

So far, though, O'Malley's efforts to arrange for a new home in Brooklyn had whiffed so badly, some people suspected a sham, that he didn't want New York at all. That season, O'Malley had scheduled more than half a dozen of the Dodgers' home games in Jersey City,

New Jersey, and declared that the team would do the same the next season. Were the "Jersey City Dodgers," as some journalists called them, a trial separation for life away from Brooklyn, perhaps a gauge of how things might work even farther west?

Replied O'Malley: "Would you make a move to Los Angeles with a stop in Jersey City on the way?"

◆

IN JERSEY CITY, THE fans booed the Dodgers. Razzed 'em. Heckled. When a public address announcer mentioned that fans could buy a Dodgers yearbook, they booed the yearbook.

"They wouldn't applaud if you gave them free hot dogs," a Dodgers rep told William Conklin of *The New York Times.*

Players were flummoxed. Journalists scribbled stories. The reasons given most often for the Jersey cheer? Loyalty elsewhere. The Giants had kept a farm team in Jersey City for years, which cultivated a following for that Big League team. Jersey Citizens would buy tickets to Dodgers games just for the opportunity to boo the Giants' archrival: those bum carpetbaggers from Brooklyn. That's how much Jersey City loved its Giants.

Out in Los Angeles, a rivalry with San Francisco meant that Rams games against the 49ers regularly drew more fans than those against the Chicago Cardinals or Pittsburgh Steelers. Sports teams do unite the people of a city or region in ways little else does, and they often engender a fierce loyalty that makes a city seem inseparable from its team, and vice versa. So John Lardner, a sportswriter and son of the more famous Ring Lardner, asked in *The New York Times* in 1956, "Would it still be Brooklyn? Without the Dodgers?" (The answer was no.)

A city comes to see in its team the qualities its people believe make them exceptional. Teams embody fans' aspirations and the narrative they tell about themselves. A team may even seem to take on the personality of its city. To watch their team play, Green Bay Packer fans in the 1950s proudly endured asphalt-cracking cold, frigid temperatures that would keep Rams fans home. But because the players also endured that cold, the shared suffering gave Packers fans the sense that they too were in games with the players, struggling with them. The fans' identities so melded with the guys wearing green and gold, they used plural personal pronouns to talk about the team: what "we" had to do to salvage the season, how the Bears always gave "us" trouble.

Likewise, Los Angeles fans could embrace "Crazylegs" Hirsch, who came from Wisconsin, and who was movie-star handsome with sculptured hair, who found his way into the pictures, and called the boys who crowded around for his autograph "Little Rams." ("A prima donna," Duane Putnam recalled. "He had LA in his fist.") And Ron Waller had married a high society starlet. And Bob Waterfield had wed a bombshell. And didn't all that combine to make the Rams, like Los

Angeles, exceptional? Because what other city could claim Hollywood?

It's a selective identification, though. It neglects the foul-mouthed genius of a quarterback with a face for radio. Or the devout thinker from outside Pittsburgh, who is black, and who is studying to become a minister. Or the intensely private offensive lineman with bad knees who marries a schoolteacher. Which Los Angeles are they?

When it's there, and when it's fierce, the identification of a city with its professional team is always blind. It's a manufactured illusion, a communal willingness to believe in something that's not real. Yet that fierce belief, that loyalty and identification, is itself a true, verifiable thing. The passions, the enthusiasms, the shared irrationality—they exist. And when that identification is broken, when a team like the Dodgers leave Brooklyn, it can rend hearts.

It's like love that way. Or the movies.

◆

NEVER HAD THE RAMS suffered a losing season in Los Angeles. But here they were, 4–8, the 1956 season over, last place in the Western Division. From top to bottom in twelve months. That they won their final two games seemed not to matter.

Too many fumbles, too many interceptions. Wade threw thirteen; Van Brocklin, playing less often, added twelve. Even the third string quarterback, Rudy Bukich, who once in a panic had tossed the ball to my dad for a safety, threw three interceptions. That's twenty-eight altogether. Those three quarterbacks combined for only eighteen touchdown passes.

And the absence of Paul and Robustelli? With them in 1955, the Rams defense allowed opponents to score only 231 points. Without them? Opponents scored 307 points—an extra touchdown every game.

Just before the season ended, a reporter from the *Los Angeles Times* visited Gillman's wife, Esther, at the Gillmans' new house on Mulholland Drive in Sherman Oaks, in mountains above the city. The Rams then had lost eight games with one more to play. Esther admitted to the reporter that her husband wasn't accustomed to losing, so neither was his family. "Why, it's his first losing season!" she said. "Losing is something new. It's not pleasant."

But then she looked out the living room's bay windows to the surrounding slopes leading down to the city. Nearby was acreage graded level, ready for foundations and frames, and nearby were frames ready for walls. People were coming, more and more people. Esther's disposition tended toward optimism, and here she was, living in that most forward-looking of cities, in a hopeful country, during what may have been its most optimistic decade.

Losing isn't easy, but this was Los Angeles. It was all so new, each day so full of promise.

"Every morning," she told the reporter, "we wake up to the sound of bulldozers carving new lots out of the mountains. 'It's sounds of progress,' I say to Sid. 'Everything is all right as long as those bulldozers keep moving.'"

PART III

PART III

CHAPTER 13

A Special Invocation Honoring the Mothers

THE SEASON NEAR ITS end, there'd be a banquet. There was always an end-of-the-season awards banquet at the Ambassador Hotel's famous Cocoanut Grove or at the Biltmore or other such places, always presented by the Ye Olde Rams club. There'd be white tablecloths and waitstaff in uniforms. There'd be beer and cocktails, cigarettes and ash trays. My parents and Duane and Patty Putnam and all the others would sit before plates of chicken ("Got to get all dressed up and eat that chicken again," Patty Putnam recalls saying to her husband). Depending on the year, Jerry Lewis would take the stage, or Bob Hope, or Milton Berle. The comedian would make a joke at the expense of each player—get the laughs going, comedy as social lubricant. As many as a thousand fans bought seats or tables, and old-timers like Bob Waterfield would present awards for best rookie or best lineman or most inspirational player.

Some banquets proved happier affairs than others. When the team in 1956 finished 4–8? Less happy.

When in 1956 the team finished 4–8 and players selected five veterans to make demands of management? With those veterans insisting on salaries and expenses during preseason games, and threatening a player protest—maybe even a strike?

Less happy, much more tense.

Van Brocklin, who had led the players' committee that met with Rams owners near the end of the 1956 season, also happened to be his team's representative to a new league-wide players' association. Its purpose was to provide a united voice for the guys in helmets and pads as they called for changes similar to those the Rams had made of their own owners. The players' association had even picked Van Brocklin as one of two players to bring the new group's demands to the NFL commissioner, Bert Bell. Rams players had each ponied up twenty-five dollars to pay for the trip.

◆

WITH THE AWARDS BANQUET and season over, the Rams management would issue to players their final paychecks. These last were larger than the others, because they included the 25 percent that front office folks had held back all season, saying they didn't want players to be broke at the end of the year and asking to borrow money from the team for travel expenses home.

Then the players would head for their off-season lives—jobs, reunions with family, rest, healing. The better players, though, still had a bit of football to go: games like the Hula Bowl in Hawaii, pitting the pros against some college all-stars, or the NFL's Pro Bowl right there in Los Angeles, in which the best from the Western Division played the best from the East. "The sixty greatest football players in the world," promoters called the game.

After that disastrous 1956 season, only a few Rams got picked up for either game. But Duane Putnam was invited to both.

Putnam accepted—Hula and Pro. In particular, he appreciated the invitation to Hawaii, because it would be a way to take Patty home. They'd met as students at the College of the Pacific in Stockton, California, but she'd grown up in the islands (she'd named their cat *Popoki*, Hawaiian for cat) and still had family on Maui.

So, with the promise of a $700 payday and a family reunion, Duane and Patty packed suitcases, took their two kids in hand, and left their tract home in Granada Hills to board a flight headed even farther west.

◆

A FEW DAYS BEFORE the Hula Bowl, Putnam received a transpacific phone call from Paul Schissler, the Pro Bowl's promoter. Schissler had been an LA sports figure for years, having owned and coached the Hollywood Bears, the team that signed Kenny Washington when the NFL still shunned black players. Before that, he'd coached four losing NFL seasons in the mid-1930s, including with the Chicago Cardinals. He'd run the Pro Bowl since its start after the 1950 season, and he was running it now, a voice from thousands of miles away with a recommendation for Putnam.

"You can take your time coming back," Schissler said.

Practice had begun for the Pro Bowl, and Schissler noted that Putnam wasn't there for it. The game was supposed to include the world's best sixty players, not its best fifty-nine. If Putnam was going to skip practice and assorted publicity, he could just enjoy that vacation in Maui. The word had come down from the commissioner, Bert Bell himself. Schissler was just making the phone call.

Putnam was furious. First, he wanted to talk to Bell directly, "To see what the score is." Other players had participated in both games, he said, including Otto Graham and Crazylegs Hirsch. "I'm the first one to be punished," he told a reporter. "Nothing happened to them." Then, he said he might ask the new players' association to weigh in, take some action against Pro Bowl officials. "I'm just a lineman," he said. "I don't make much money."

Putnam knew, though, that his complaints would take time to be heard and any actions by the players' association wouldn't get him back on the Pro Bowl roster, not for that game in January 1957. The Pro Bowl would need another offensive guard. So, even though he was steamed, while Putnam had Schissler on the phone he made a suggestion.

"John's right there in town," he said.

◆

WHEN BOB GAIN REMEMBERS playing in Pro Bowls, he recalls the strange looks he got from bellhops in the hotel lobby as he crossed the polished floors carrying so many boxes of Jezebel brassieres.

Gain, the Browns' defensive lineman who had also played for the University of Kentucky against my dad and Santa Clara, played in five Pro Bowls—all in Los Angeles. The city gave birth to the game, and Los Angeles would hold onto the Pro Bowl for decades. The idea had come from George Preston Marshall, Washington's owner, who had mentioned it to Schissler. Schissler, in turn, brought it to the Los Angeles Newspaper Publishers Association, who agreed that it was a good idea, one they would sponsor if proceeds went to charity.

So each year, coaches voted for the best players, and the commissioner's office tabulated the results. One team represented the Western Division; the other, the Eastern. Fans could tell them apart because the best of the West always wore blue helmets, and the best of the East wore red. A coach from each division was assigned to work with each team. The teams always stayed at either the Biltmore or the Ambassador, and each year they switched locales. For out-of-state players, especially those like Gain from Cleveland, the Pro Bowl was a vacation from grim winter weather.

"A buddy of mine said, 'If you get to the Pro Bowl, you'll love it,'" Gain recalled. "'There's no scrimmages, a little contact.' The Pro Bowls were light, too. If we did something, and the coach didn't like it, we'd tell them, 'Go to hell!' We didn't play for them!"

Gain invited his wife to come along, though she never did. Instead, she'd give him her measurements and send him to Los Angeles's garment factories to buy lingerie for her, wholesale. In particular, she wanted those Jezebel brassieres.

"If you bought them in downtown Cleveland, you'd pay six, seven, eight dollars for a bra," Gain said. Wholesale in LA, he'd pay a buck a piece. He could buy a dozen or more, easy. And he did.

"When I walked through the lobby with all those tied together," he said, "you could see the bellhops looking at me funny."

◆

DAD'S PRO BOWL? THERE'S not much to say about it. About the Pro Bowl, there rarely is. The West won, 19–10, behind four field goals kicked by Baltimore's Bert

Rechinchar. But, as Gain explained, the results of the Pro Bowl—the game itself—didn't matter so much. In most players lives', certainly in my dad's, what mattered about the Pro Bowl was, first, its prestige and, second, the payday: $700 for every player on the winning team; $500 each for the losers.

My parents took that seven hundred out shopping. They drove through Los Angeles from department store to furniture stores, from Sears to J. C. Penney, and in the end purchased their first bedroom set. The wood was stained a shade or two lighter than mahogany. Mom particularly liked that the headboard came with sliding doors. It cost them about $500 of that Pro Bowl money. Thereafter, they called it their "Pro Bowl Bedroom Set." They never got rid of it. One day, it would still be in use at my sister Anna's home.

◆

AT WHICH EVENT WOULD my dad find more to make him smile?

Shoulder-to-shoulder with celebrities at the Cocoanut Grove for a Rams banquet? Jerry Lewis on stage, all knees and elbows and grating voice? Marjorie Merriweather Durant offering cheek pecks for him and my mom?

Or would he find more charm through the doors of a junior high school, on the night of a mother-son banquet?

It was April 12, 1957, a Friday. my mom was pregnant with their second child—my sister Mary—and having trouble with bleeding, so doctors said she ought not to travel. My dad kissed her goodbye—kissed Jay, too— then drove east to Highland, which was something like a town, east of Los Angeles and north of Redlands, tucked tight against the mountains. The Parent-Teacher Association there had asked him to serve as the featured speaker for its banquet at which sons honored their mothers, what the *San Bernardino County Sun* said was "always the highlight of the school's program."

The event was scheduled to begin at 7:00 p.m., and those coming early to the school's quiet parking lot arrived with dusk, the dry desert air cool enough to make a man grateful for a jacket. Inside, the aromas of the evening's dinner—Swiss steak, not chicken—had begun to suffuse through the school hallways. Here there were boys wearing their best, shiniest shoes, and mothers with makeup just so.

Jerry Lewis or Jerry Cox? Jerry Cox was the eighth grader who stood bravely in the school's auditorium to give "a special invocation honoring the mothers." One hundred and thirty-six people attended, mothers coming as guests of their sons. Instead of the Harry James Orchestra, the assembled enjoyed the Eighth Grade Girls Ensemble and the Ninth Grade Girls Sextet, both "under the direction of Mrs. Kathryn Callahan."

Then came the time for my dad, introduced as a Pro Bowler since last January, now a Ram and once a Cardinal, who had served in the Army and was cocaptain of that Santa Clara team that upset Kentucky in the Orange Bowl. Ladies and gentlemen...

And the polite applause.

Dad would not have spoken long. Likely, he would have consulted a few notes, reminders of what to say, things he'd thought about on the drive from Los Angeles. It was a mother-son banquet, so likely he thought about my mom and Jay, the mother and son he knew best. And of his own his mother, Elizabeth, that stern Irish woman who in those first months after the move from Pittsburgh kept him dressed in knickers, as Pittsburgh boys dressed, even though the Los Angeles kids found knickers to be hilarious and a great reason to pound the snot out of him. He was nine years old, so he didn't have that much snot to get pounded, and his mother knew that. She knew no kid his age could do him lasting damage. She sent him out in his knickers and let him suffer the little-boy punches, and when he came home she cleaned him up, and sent him out again—still wearing knickers. *Mothers*, he could tell these Highland boys, *if they love you and understand the world the way an Irish woman understands the world, will let you get hurt, because they know pain has limits. They know you can take it.*

After his talk, the mothers and sons and their featured guest ate their Swiss steaks, and probably my dad signed some autographs, answered questions, and encouraged the boys who professed to play football, too. He raised his glass of iced tea or milk or Kool-Aid, whatever it was he drank that night, when John Kennedy, a ninth-grader, offered his toast to the mothers, and again when Mrs. Floyd Porter, immediate past president of the PTA, offered a toast to the sons.

Later, they all watched a film of highlights from the 1956 Rams season.

Had there been highlights? It's easy to imagine a Van Brocklin quip: "If our fifty-six highlight reel won an Oscar it would be in the category 'best sixteen-second film.'"

Then, it was time to say goodbye, and mothers and sons rose and moved toward the parking lot, lit that night by a moon nearly full. There, if the boy was a young gentleman, he opened the door for his mother, though she, of course, sat behind the wheel. Soon, they'd all be home, except for my dad, whose drive back to Los Angeles would last a couple of hours through that moon-bright night.

Thank you for coming, the mothers had said. Thank you, said the boys. Out here, he was a celebrity. He wasn't Hollywood, and he didn't need to be glib or fashionable or witty. He didn't need to have big plans or ideas that would change the world or Southern California's landscape—or that would even change football. For the boys of Highland and their mothers, he needed to be polite and to enjoy their company, and he needed to be a Ram. For them—and for him, too—that was enough.

◆

IN THE PHOTOGRAPHS TAKEN at the Rams offices on Beverly Boulevard, a young man shakes Sid Gillman's hand. Gillman is older, thicker, wearing a sport coat with a plaid shirt and no tie. Southern California formal, ca. 1957.

The young man, on the other hand, looks as if he just flew in from Madison Avenue in New York City: suit coat buttoned, white shirt pressed, the pocket handkerchief squared like it was folded with a ruler. The knot in his tie is so small it hides inside his collar. A tie tack finishes the look.

To their right is a large split-leaf philodendron, the only decor. The light from flash bulbs is harsh. It's a conventional grip-and-grin shot, a staple of unimaginative journalism. The men smile at each other. Gillman looks as if he's laughing at his own joke. The young man's smile is polite; it gives little away.

It's April 8, four days before my dad is to speak to the Highland Junior High mothers and sons. The Rams have just announced the hiring of a new top assistant for Dan Reeves, a position that in years to come will be called a general manager, and the team has invited the press for photographs and questions. If the reporters and photogs have any age on them, they know this young fellow. He's a Southern California native, born in South Gate a few miles south of Los Angeles. A few years back, right out of the University of San Francisco, he worked for the Rams as a publicity guy and later for their scouting operation. He left to become a partner at an up-and-coming West Coast public relations company, where he'd handled—among other clients— the 1956 Olympics in Australia. Now, at age thirty-one, he's back on Beverly Boulevard to take over the Rams day-to-day operations and to make personnel decisions.

His name is Pete Rozelle. One day he'll become the most influential figure in NFL history.

But for now, he's here because Bert Bell, the NFL commissioner, asked him. The Rams have been without an assistant to the president since Tex Schramm—weary of the owners' bickering and Reeves' drinking—quit the job in January to join the sports division of the CBS television network. Not surprisingly, Reeves and his co-owners couldn't decide on a replacement. Anyone Reeves supported, Edwin Pauley spurned. Anyone Pauley wanted, Reeves rejected. Bert Bell, like Schramm, tired of the gridlock. He intervened, suggesting young Rozelle, whom he remembered from his days with the Rams. A few nights later, Rozelle received a phone call from the NFL commissioner.

"We checked around," Bell told him, as Rozelle recalled in an interview conducted in 1991. "You are the first thing the Ram owners have agreed upon since Garfield was shot. So do you want to take the job?"

The Rams were coming off their worst season in Los Angeles. The quarterbacks were unhappy, and the season had ended with no definitive answer to the question of who would call plays each game. Average home attendance had dropped. Players had organized to demand more money and team-funded medical care. Owners feuded, and one drank too much. And LA's mayor had recently led a delegation to spring training in Vero Beach, Florida, to convince the Dodgers that Los Angeles was ready for major league baseball. Who could predict how the arrival of the Dodgers might affect the Rams' bottom line?

All those challenges awaited the man who would be assistant to the Rams' president and none would be easy to solve. But the money the Rams offered was twice the pay Rozelle was making at the public relations agency.

Do you want the job? Bell had asked. Rozelle's answer was yes.

So the Rams called a press conference, photographers took aim, and Rozelle shook Sid Gillman's hand.

CHAPTER 14

Not A Very Nice Thing To Do

"Victory is sweet. It is also bittersweet. The Los Angeles Rams learned this yesterday. Veteran linebacker Larry Morris broke his ankle in the first quarter of Friday's 45–14 conquest of the Washington Redskins and will probably be sidelined for the season... The Ram casualty list also included regular guard John Hock, victim of a ligament strain, which will probably inactivate him for a month..."
—Jack Geyer, *Los Angeles Times*, August 18, 1957

BEFORE, IT HAD BEEN a tendon in the knee. Now, a ligament. Had he heard a pop? Most people hear a pop when a knee ligament sprains, but it's hard to hear anything when you're wearing a helmet and seventy-five thousand fans are shouting and you're grunting and some guy with a burgundy-colored jersey is bringing a shoulder at full-speed. Had he heard a pop? Does it even matter? He *felt* the difference. A knife pain and the joint wobbly, then more stabbing every time he put weight on the leg. Even later, with the knee iced and braced, the whole leg felt so loose.

The way the doc explained it, the ligament stretched too far. Probably some fibers tore. Not a complete rupture. Hard to know, though. X-rays won't show that sort of thing. Exploratory surgery, though, would have allowed a peek inside the knee. Whatever the doctor did, whatever he learned, three or four weeks of rest and rehabilitation was the early and optimistic estimate for my dad's knee. That would take the team through its exhibition season. He'd be back in time for the games that mattered.

A small consolation. At twenty-nine years old, he knew he didn't have much football left in him. Every game felt like a gift, especially for a guy whose knees sometimes seemed made of driftwood, dry and brittle and hollow. He'd kept them working with surgery and liniment and stretching, with ice and massages and whirlpools, and it was a sort of miracle, really, that for two seasons he'd only had to cope with pain and stiffness.

This sprain was different. For the first time in two seasons, he couldn't just grit his teeth and drag the joint back into service. This would take time. Only a month, true, but football time runs faster than other sorts. Football time rushes by. It can't be stopped or even slowed. The gridiron isn't Disneyland, where a ticket-buyer might find a never-ending century of horse buggies and gas lamps. The gridiron isn't Hollywood, either, where actors and actresses use makeup and lighting and scalpels to stave off the future and stretch their youth. Football time is relentless and overwhelming and quick. Vicious and sudden as an arm bar tackle across the head.

Sit on the bench for even a month, and the game might damn well move on without you.

◆

AT AGE EIGHTY-TWO, A person like my mom has lived so much life that some bits can't be recalled. You might not remember, for example, which of your husband's knees was the one he hurt that season, or in which game (but probably it was the right knee, because that one was always the worst). You might not remember whether he needed crutches. Or how he managed to climb the stairs to your second-floor apartment. You remember a second surgery, maybe that was in 1957. The operation could have been exploratory. What you remember with certainty is that after a second surgery, doctors took you aside for a private talk, but you don't remember if that was in a hospital hallway or in an office, or when exactly. You don't remember which doctors they were, if they worked for the Rams or not. You remember that you were pregnant with your third child, because at that point the children were arriving once a year. You remember that those doctors—at the hospital or the office, who knows?—gave you an instruction about your husband, something other than to massage the knee or to give him these pills twice a day and these others every eight hours. You don't remember all the details—that was more than fifty years ago!—but you remember exactly what the doctors said you had to do.

You have to tell him, they said, *he shouldn't play football anymore, because if he does, he won't walk normally, ever again.*

You remember what you thought: that asking his wife, of all people, to give him that news—it wasn't a very nice thing to do.

◆

IN A HOLLYWOOD STUDIO remade to appear like the small bedroom of an LA apartment, the cameras stand in four or five places to capture the scene from various angles: close-up, distance, my dad in the bed, my mom at the doorway. The casting department advertised for a pretty young actress to play my mom's role, and the director wanted someone with Audrey Hepburn's spunk, only more maternal and more Irish. A Susan Hayward type, maybe, only younger, with Hayward's reddish hair and round cheeks and the small chin that made a heart of her face.

The director has already decided that this scene won't include any background music. It will be a scene of silences, of quiet. Dad believed in doing things quietly, never making a fuss. So there will be no fuss in this scene. Later, the sound editors will add the voices of toddler-infant play—Jay and Mary, distant and quiet, as if from another room, another life.

One camera watches Dad lie in bed with his right leg elevated on pillows and the knee wrapped with so much bandage over so much swelling it looks as if he's got a football swaddled there. It's good-sized, this Pro Bowl bed, with its headboard that has sliding doors. My dad's in a white T-shirt, which is tight and shows his Charles Atlas physique, and he's working a newspaper crossword puzzle. It's light duty, the puzzle, you can tell from his expression; it's nothing he's fretting about. Now and then he flips the pencil to erase, and he blows at the eraser shreds, then slaps the newspaper to get rid of the ones that stick. Another camera catches Mom arriving at the doorway. She's pregnant with my sister Sue but still several months from delivery. With both hands she holds a tray. On the tray is a plate with a sandwich and beside that a sweating bottle of beer. A small fan whirrs, sitting on a windowsill.

"How's anyone supposed to know Texas's third largest city unless you live in it?" he asks, and he chuckles. "Do you know Texas's third-largest city?"

"Aren't all Texas cities the largest?" She fixes the tray over his lap, making sure the fold-down legs are secure. He scooches back, setting aside the crossword puzzle at the same time, and she adjusts the pillow under his leg. After a thank-you, he tries a bite of the sandwich.

"I brought your pain pill, too," she says.

"I don't need that."

"But the doctor says."

So he reaches for a water glass from the side table and gulps down the pill. A moment later, he sips from the beer bottle.

"Anything else?" she asks, taking his hand. Here, a camera closes on her face, and it's clear that her expression doesn't match the tone of her voice. The voice is full of cheer, but the face is sober. Her eyes dart from his face to his knee, from knee to face.

"A slice of chocolate cake?" he asks, and she nods, then kisses his hand as if her kiss might break him into pieces.

At the doorway she turns back to face him. She folds her arms across her pregnant belly, wrapping herself tightly, as if for protection, as if holding herself together. Is this the time? If it is, she must be fierce and quiet as she tells him. Her husband is a fierce and quiet man, and it will be best if she is, too. The breath she takes in, then, is huge, as if breath is a prayer and gives strength.

This is the time. She speaks his name, and the camera catches him turning to her. He raises his eyebrows in question even as he swallows a mouthful of sandwich.

"The doctors asked me to tell you something," she says. "I don't know why they wouldn't tell you themselves. But they didn't. They asked me."

Then she tells him. Exactly what they said, and no more.

He's not grinning anymore, but the look that's taken hold of his face isn't awful, either. If this news gives him pain, his expression will hardly show it. His brow furrows a bit, his lips purse. For a moment, his jaw expands as if he's clenched his teeth, but just as quickly the muscle relaxes. He seems not to breathe. Then he does.

"Well," he says, "that's the way things go." Then he looks at her. "I'm sorry they asked you to do that. Thank you for telling me. It was important."

She nods. Then she turns to leave the room. "I'll bring you cake," she says.

◆

"I'M SURE EVERY YEAR John was ready to retire," said Duane Putnam, thinking about his old friend. He's certain, because every year he, too, thought about retirement.

Football wasn't so lucrative that a Putnam or my dad could sock away savings for those decades after they and football parted ways. When football ended, they would need another career. Every year in football meant another year away from building their resumés with the sorts of experiences men in their twenties could usually claim.

Also, the work of a football player wore a body down. Injuries played a part, but so did the day-to-day exertion. "It was always running," Putnam said. In preseason, in regular-season practices, in games, if you weren't repeating plays and working on timing, you were running. That's how coaches kept you in shape, and it didn't matter if you were a big guy or a little guy. "You always had to run," Putnam said. "After ten or eleven years, your legs get a little tired of that."

Then, if you are a John Hock or a Duane Putnam, you think about retiring. You hear from doctors that you might not walk normally again, and you have every good reason to retire on the spot.

Why, then, do you come back for more?

◆

FOR DECADES AFTER HIS football career ended, my dad kept a black and white photo of himself with four other Rams, taken one evening during training camp in Redlands. It's a joy-filled photo, snapped after a day of practices as the players entertained themselves on the quiet campus. The five men crowd together on a dormitory porch—probably Melrose Hall—and behind them a window is open to gather breezes. Each man wears slacks that are probably khaki-colored and T-shirts that look white, and on each T-shirt are iron-on letters across the chest that read "LA RAMS." All five appear to be backed up against a railing, in front of an audience, with Duane Putnam in the middle, the only one seated, his hair in a brush cut, and he holds a small acoustic guitar on his lap. Over his shoulder, a fellow blows harmonica. Putnam is laughing, and the three others, including my dad, seem to be desperately holding a note, strangling some off-key harmony while trying not to laugh. My dad's arm wraps around the back of the harmonica player, his hand rests on the fellow's shoulder. My dad's head tilts back; he is giving full and jolly voice to whatever he is singing badly.

Here's something to consider about that photo and perhaps why my dad held on to it for so long, kept it framed and so often in view. It isn't just a photograph of five men goofing around like boys. It isn't just five friends entertaining themselves and others. It's five men who live with an every-day intensity marked by sweat and pain, shared violence, and even this: earned moments of equally intense giddiness.

◆

HERE NEXT IS THE testament of John Houser, a robust man in his seventy-eighth year, broad-faced and tall and slightly stooped, thus giving the impression that he looms over you. A man with the stiff knees of an ex-NFL lineman, a preacher's passion, and a salesman's gift of gab, who joined the Rams as a rookie in 1957:

"I'm John W. Houser, Jr., and God Almighty for years, I was called Joe. If you were to go to my high school, which is a boys school out in Chino, you'll see they knew me as Joe. As a matter of fact, there's a citizenship award out there on a plaque…and it's got my name on it, Joe Houser, which didn't bother me much when I was seventeen going on eighteen. Then at the University of Redlands where I went to school, gee whiz, the coaches and everybody knew me as Joe. So when I finally joined the Los Angeles Rams, the nickname came along with me, but that's when I tried to reverse the process, because I signed a contract with *John*, and that's when I started realizing it wasn't going to get me too far, legally… It's a nickname that came about when I was a very young youngster—actually a baby.

"The Rams conducted their training camp, preseason training camp, at Redlands, and unbeknownst to me at the time, my coach just happened to say to the Rams, who were touching base with him, preparing for training camp, 'Would you be interested in one of our local boys trying out for the team?' The Rams said, 'Bring him on!' They're thinking this would be PR for them using the school, using the facilities. I was walking across the campus quad one day, Coach says, 'Hey Joe, I wanna talk to you.'

"'Yeah, Coach, what do you want?'

"'How would you like to have a try out with the Los Angeles Rams?'"

The big man with the boyish face, the Pride of Redlands, got his opportunity. He tried out at tight end, but the pro quarterbacks threw with such zip he couldn't catch the passes. So then the Rams tried him on the line, put him at guard. Lo and behold, he made the starting lineup.

Houser: "Mainly with the help of John Hock. He got his knee busted. And that's kind of a backdoor way of getting to be a starter."

◆

AT REDLANDS, A TINY college with not much of a football team, John Houser played tight end and running back and center and tackle. But he'd never played guard— and that's the position the Rams thought he'd fit. But he was all "fumble feet," he said, stumbling and stuttering around. On the practice field, Duane Putnam helped by showing him the footwork, explaining the timing. Then, at lunch, he'd sit with my dad, who would give him lessons of an hour or longer about the men Houser would face in the next exhibition game. My dad offered tips about the likes of Leo Nomellini of the 49ers (they called him "The Lion" because he roared when he played), Dick Modzelewski of the Giants (small at six feet tall, but solid as a concrete plug), and Art Donovan of the Colts. Donovan, my dad told him, would line up nearly six yards away from the line and let you rush him, then sidestep you like a matador. Offensive line judo. "You had to be under control," Houser said, "or you'd be brushed aside, and he'd make a fool out of you."

The scouting reports kept Houser on the field and mostly succeeding—but not always. Once that season, against San Francisco when Houser faced Leo "The Lion" Nomellini, Van Brocklin called for a long pass play. That meant Houser had to keep Nomellini occupied for five seconds, the time it would take Elroy Hirsch to run down the field. "You're supposed to pop him," Houser explained, "then, when he comes back, pop him again." Two pops equals about five seconds. But Nomellini feinted inside, and when Houser followed him Nomellini spun around pop-free and sacked Van Brocklin before Dutch could take five steps. "Look, rook!" Van Brocklin roared. "We're paying you ten thousand a year to keep that SOB off my back!"

That confused Houser, who as a rookie was actually making only $5,500. "Yeah, Dutch," he answered anyway, "but they're paying him twenty-five thousand to get you."

After those failures, Houser would find himself on the sidelines standing next to my dad, who would say in his calm, quiet un–Van Brocklin way, "Well, that didn't work."

◆

IN THAT SUMMER OF 1957, my dad came back after missing three games and began again the burdensome work of a shuttle guard, this time sharing the duties with John Houser. Dad stayed with the team even after Sid Gillman, midway through the season, named Houser as the starter at right guard because, as the newspapers reported, "John Hock has not recovered fully from an earlier injury."

He stayed through all that, and even stayed after my mom gave him the doctors' warning, a warning that placed him at the juncture of two equally difficult truths: his knees could cripple his career, and his career could cripple his legs.

That summer, he tilted toward the career.

It wasn't money that kept him on the field, because the pay was mediocre. It wasn't his meager celebrity, which only troubled his sense of self. It wasn't the thronging bellow of Rams fans on Sundays.

But my dad had seen his father lose his job at US Steel in Pittsburgh, and toil at a service station and for a soap company. He'd seen his wife grading students work. He himself had peeled potatoes in the military and sold rabbit skins door-to-door. He knew about work. He knew that football, like no other job available to him, demanded that he give himself—every iota of mind and soul and body—to his labor.

Perhaps that's why my dad found it difficult to give up the game—despite pain, despite the mediocre pay, despite the risk to a lifetime of walking. What other job could provide this every-day intensity? What other work could promise—as his hometown, as Los Angeles itself promised—that something spontaneous and thrilling would happen today, if only you stepped outside and gave yourself wholly to the great ongoing game?

Dad had signed a contract. That meant he could still play.

He would still play.

CHAPTER 15

LA Bums

NEARLY TWO HOURS BEHIND schedule the airplane at last appeared, a promise from the East, delayed but true. When people in this patient, eager crowd saw its flying lights flash out of the night sky they began to cheer. Then the Convair 440 Metropolitan touched down and taxied toward the celebrating crowd, its twin engines winding down and propellers slowing to a *thup-thup-thup*. It was October 23, 1957, so crisp an evening that Roz Wyman wore a long unbuttoned coat over her professional-style city councilwoman dress. And if moments ago she had felt the chill, now she likely felt only exhilaration, because the airplane turned, and on the fuselage, just behind a logo of a giant baseball, were painted the happy words, "Los Angeles Dodgers."

The future she'd dreamed for her city had just landed.

Two bands, including a bunch of fellows in top hats, played welcoming fanfares. A man lifted his son to his shoulders so the boy could see. A woman in glasses and a cardigan gawked as she petted a small dog she clutched to her chest. Nearby, a strange sight: In a wooden chair built several sizes too big, like a movie prop for the film *The Incredible Shrinking Man*, released earlier that year, a grown man sat, dwarfed. The fellow wielded a super-size bat twice his height, grinned, and waved a placard that read, "WELCOME O'MALLEY & LADS TO A BIG TOWN."

Wyman, just twenty-seven years old, and Kenneth Hahn, a county supervisor and political ally, stood ready as the plane parked, waiting for its door to open and its steps to lower. And when those steps came down, the two politicians, each wearing a baseball cap, climbed up to be the first to greet Walter O'Malley, their new neighbor.

There had been times Roz Wyman thought this would never happen. She'd been working to bring major league baseball to Los Angeles for most of four years, with special attention given the last three years to the Dodgers. Some nights she'd arrive home after a day of phone calls and letter writing and wrangling and her husband would ask, *What do you think? Will they come?* and a pit would grow in her stomach, and she'd have the sense, as she once said, "that after I beat my guts out" the Dodgers would decide not to come. Yes, O'Malley's unhappiness with Ebbets Field was legendary, and the failed efforts to find a new home in Brooklyn were well-publicized. But Brooklyn's famed "Bums" had been part of the borough since the nineteenth century. *How do you leave after all that time?* she wondered. How do you leave a place like Brooklyn? How do you leave New York?

Even in the wake of that skepticism and doubt, she gave the long hours. In small moments of apprehension, she might have believed the Dodgers would never leave Brooklyn, but she always believed Los Angeles needed major league baseball. So Wyman kept pushing and pushing, even up to the night of October 7, just three days after her twenty-seventh birthday, when all of her efforts almost fell apart.

That night, the city council was to vote on a binding deal negotiated with O'Malley's representatives and meant to bring the Dodgers west. The council needed ten votes from its fourteen members who were present, and Wyman wasn't at all sure that nine of her peers would vote with her. At City Hall, as the council debated, she paid careful attention to each member's concerns and worked to allay them. Moreover, she was four months pregnant, and she had already lost one pregnancy. "It was terrible," she recalled of the stress that day. "It was hard on me."

Then, the mayor, Norris Poulson, interrupted her work with an urgent message. He wanted her to come to his office but wouldn't say why. She ignored him, believing the situation with the council to be too tenuous. Poulson insisted, sending note after note and, eventually, a Los Angeles police officer. Finally, she slipped away to his office. He told her he wanted to telephone O'Malley.

Poulson was in a tizzy. To that point, the city's negotiators had only been talking with people who worked for O'Malley. Sure, they said he'd like the deal. But they weren't him. Poulson wanted to hear from O'Malley himself that he'd go for it. Politically, a lot was at risk. The deal—a huge land swap, deeding hundreds of acres of city property to the Dodgers—was likely to be controversial among Los Angeles voters. If the council approved the deal and O'Malley rejected it, wouldn't Poulson and the city council look like a bunch of provincial suckers?

But Poulson was too nervous to talk himself with O'Malley. So he handed Wyman the phone. She tried to hand it back. "Oh, no," he told her. "I don't want to talk at all."

Then a voice came on the line. Roz Wyman said hello. "Mrs. Wyman," said Walter O'Malley. For all Wyman's efforts, this was the first she'd ever actually talked to the Dodgers' president and primary owner.

"Mrs. Wyman," he said, "I want to thank you for all you've done. I know it's been difficult."

Not knowing what else to say, Wyman asked about the weather in New York.

She didn't want to ask about the deal, because, unlike Poulson, she didn't want to know what O'Malley thought. Ignorant of that knowledge, she could tell her peers on the council a simple, limited truth: His people say he'll like it. But if she asked and if O'Malley offered no assurance, what would she tell others on the council? She couldn't lie. She could only hope they wouldn't say, "Mrs. Wyman, does Mr. O'Malley agree to this deal?"

"Ask him! Ask him!" said the mayor.

And if some council member put her on the spot that way, and she said, "He offers no assurance," then the votes might go away and all her years of work could vanish the way blue sky disappears on a smoggy day, and Los Angeles would remain a city of the second rank.

"Ask him!" the mayor said.

Wyman breathed and steeled herself. She had to say something; there had to be a reason for the call. "Mr. O'Malley," she said, "I take it if we vote this deal through, you will come?"

He told her that he didn't know.

"I'm certainly giving it serious consideration," he said. "Do you have the votes?" She said she thought she had the votes.

He reminded her, then, that he was after all a New Yorker, and he professed to still believe that New York might be better for the Dodgers than Los Angeles. He told her that baseball had never proven to be a big success in California. He said, "I don't know if we will come."

"That's a pretty disappointing answer," she replied. "We've gone a long way to get here." Nevertheless, she told him, she would go back to the council chambers and "fight this thing through."

And then they said their polite goodbyes.

She took a few moments to gather herself, then returned to the debate, which lasted for a couple more hours. Remarkably, no one straight-out asked her if she knew what O'Malley thought of the deal. At last, exhausted and with some confidence, Wyman called for the vote.

It was 10–4. The council approved the contract with the Los Angeles Dodgers.

The next day, the Dodgers released a statement announcing that the team would move to Los Angeles for the 1958 season.

Wyman, giddy with the news, didn't know why O'Malley had refused to commit in the hours before the vote, but that didn't matter so much. What mattered was that the Dodgers had decided to come to Los Angeles. A New York institution would uproot itself and settle in the nation's opposite corner. The City of Angels was now major league.

Wyman, Mayor Poulson, County Supervisor Hahn, and half a dozen of Wyman's fellow yes-voting council members then held a ceremony to sign the contract with the Dodgers. One councilman brought a bat; Wyman and a few others wore baseball caps with wide pieces of tape affixed across the crown, and on the tape, in thick marker, they'd written, "LA BUMS".

The contract they signed called for Los Angeles to deed more than three hundred acres in Chavez Ravine to the Dodgers; in turn the Dodgers would give to the city an LA minor league ballpark they owned, which amounted to much less acreage. The Dodgers, with all that extra land, would then build a fifty-thousand-seat stadium, and they'd do it with no public funding except the swapped land. The team also agreed to pay about $300,000 a year in property taxes for the site. Other minor aspects of the deal included the Dodgers funding a youth recreation center.

About two weeks later, O'Malley stepped off the Corvair airplane with a baseball in each hand, and he tossed those into the crowd. Wyman shouted into a microphone, "Welcome to Los Angeles!" and Hahn presented O'Malley with a proclamation. Reporters from KTTV and KTLA recorded the speeches, and newspaper photographers snapped away, their flash bulb pops sparkling off the shiny brass of tubas and trombones.

And then another man hurried toward the plane and handed O'Malley an envelope before rushing away.

"What's this?" O'Malley asked Wyman.

She answered quietly. "You have just been served," she said. Then she added, "There may be a few lawsuits."

Out in the crowd, plenty of people waved signs saying, "Hello, Dodgers!" and the like. But there were a few, too, that weren't so cheerful. These signs were held by people who thought the giveaway of Chavez

Ravine was too great a price to bring the Dodgers to Los Angeles. The city had acquired the property through a complicated series of events involving eminent domain condemnation, federal money for public housing, and a backlash against such housing by people who believed it would lead to communism. Now land on which various governments had spent millions of dollars, taken from private owners and once intended for poor people specifically and the public good generally, was about to go to a privately owned baseball team. Not everyone liked that. Blared one protester's sign:

"IT'S NOT THE DODGERS WE OPPOSE! IT'S THE DEAL!"

◆

HAVING BEEN BEATEN IN order by San Francisco, Detroit, and Chicago, the Rams arrived home in Los Angeles by plane that same week as the Dodgers. But instead of bringing major league status, the Rams brought with them a record of 1–3. At the airport, no crowds cheered them, no bands played. Some of the players, at least, had wives and kids to greet them.

That Sunday following Dodgers Week was a beautiful afternoon for football. Smog had cleared, sun shone, and the day was warm, reaching to eighty-eight degrees. Norm Van Brocklin trotted onto the field for pregame introductions before the crowd of more than seventy-seven thousand—and boos welcomed him home.

One victory against three defeats? the boos seemed to say. Why are we buying tickets? Will this season be a repeat of last year? Good heavens, will it be worse?

So far, the 1957 season *was* worse, with old, tired tensions persisting: controversy over who would call plays, over which quarterback—Van Brocklin or Bill Wade—ought to get more field time. Add to that some troublesome injuries, such as to my dad and Ron Waller, the rookie all-star running back from the season before, and the Rams lacked a spark. Critics had even called the offense—and Van Brocklin—"unimaginative."

Unimaginative? Was there any worse insult in the movie capital of the world, the epicenter of Googie architecture, the home of Disneyland? And to make this accusation of the Rams—the team that had invented the wide receiver, put logos on helmets, had tried three "bull elephant" running backs at once? The team that had first dared to go west?

Unimaginative!

They got boos while every day the biggest headlines proclaimed the Dodgers. Billboards extolling the Dodgers read "Good luck, team!" Everywhere Walter O'Malley appeared people applauded. The Dodgers had yet to play a game in the city, and already Los Angeles swooned for them.

The Rams—and particularly Van Brocklin—felt frustrated, angry. And on this Sunday, the last in October, facing Detroit's Lions, they played that way.

They'd already lost to Detroit that season, 10–7, and John Houser, the rookie from Redlands, remembered it well. Veteran offensive linemen had taken him for dinner to a Detroit restaurant called the Brass Rail, and as they ate their steaks they heard a lot of carrying on coming from a private room, separated from the main dining area by accordion-folding walls. At last they asked their waiter who it was having all that fun, and the waiter told them it was players from the Detroit Lions. When the Lions exited, recognizing the Rams and saying, "We'll see you guys tomorrow," the last bunch of them were two guys carrying out a third who looked to be inebriated. *And who's that?* the Rams asked their waiter. "That's Hunchy Hoernschemeyer," the waiter said. The next day, when the Rams kicked off, Houser looked down field and saw a Lion leaning on the goal post, puking. The Rams kicker sent the ball into the air, and the sick guy staggered under it, then ran it back forty-six yards. "Hunchy Hoernschemeyer," said the public address announcer. Houser turned to one of the veterans. "We should see what kind of booze that guy was drinking," he said.

It had been that kind of season.

But now Detroit was on the Rams' turf, and Los Angeles unloaded its frustrations.

The first time their offense had the football, the Rams needed only nine plays to score a touchdown, finishing the drive when Tank Younger ran into the end zone from three yards out.

On their second drive, they again needed only nine plays—this time to cover fifty-one yards and score a touchdown. Van Brocklin, making the calls, mixed passes with runs, and handed off to different running backs. He ended the drive himself by pushing the ball in from the one-yard line. The score was 14–0.

Then, Rams linebacker Les Richter intercepted a Detroit pass on the Rams' side of the field. The offense again worked its way to Detroit's one-yard line, but on their fourth and final down, the Rams still hadn't scored. From the sidelines, Gillman and his coaches were waving and shouting for a field goal attempt. That was conventional wisdom, after all. If you've got a lead, build on it with the easy three points. Don't risk failing and losing momentum.

It was the boring call. The *unimaginative* call.

Van Brocklin ignored the coaches. He wanted another touchdown, and he wanted it for himself. He took the ball on the snap from the center, then leaned left. Or, as the *Los Angeles Times* put it, he "stuck his helmet in the seat of Guard Duane Putnam's football pants and charged across."

Not only was it a touchdown, it was a touchdown with style. Swashbuckling. And with the extra point kick, the Rams led 21–0. Now, as the offense trotted off the field, thousands of fans rose to their feet to give Dutch and company an ovation.

Dad watched most of the action from the sideline. He was unaccustomed to this role, backing up another guard. Throughout his career with the Rams, if he was healthy enough to suit up, he had started. Now it was a knockout gorgeous Sunday in Southern California, a Marilyn Monroe of days, and he wore shoulder pads and cleats and a knee brace. Healthy enough to suit up, every muscle, every nerve, every day he'd lived since he'd joined the Rams four years earlier told him he should be playing, but instead he watched. He knew Gillman would eventually call his name, that he'd play a few downs, spell young John Houser when the rookie got winded or had his skull rattled. Until then, he'd stalk the sidelines. Blame it on the knee, sure, yeah—and maybe he *had* come back too soon after the ligament strain. Maybe he *did* need more time to strengthen the joint. Whatever the reason, though, Gillman, by putting my dad on the bench, even if only for a little while, had sent a message that number sixty-three wasn't the player he'd been.

Enough of that. It wasn't the time to contemplate or muse about such things. He still had to pay careful attention, help the kid, Houser. He needed to know what was happening on the field in case the coaches sent him in. Still, this was such a different experience than playing. Then, his body, his head, his heart—every part of him—had been caught up in the game. Now there were moments his mind could dart away from the action—and maybe light upon a thought or two. Maybe it was in one of those moments that he began to understand the growing reality.

Given the knees, the coaches, and the doctors, a decision about retirement might be made for him if he didn't make it himself.

◆

CONSIDER, FOR A MOMENT, the numbers. Consider their context.

Los Angeles was ga-ga for the Dodgers, and the Rams had lost three of their first four games. Yet a crowd of 77,314 showed to watch the football game against Detroit.

The Rams won that day. For their next game—the Chicago Bears at home—80,456 people showed, including former President Harry S. Truman. Rams co-owner Edwin Pauley had served various roles with the Truman administration—among them special assistant to the secretary of state. He'd long been a friend and fundraiser for Truman, and he had invited the president. Truman, in a tie and overcoat, watched from a corner seat in the press box. He munched on a sandwich, and he kept the teams' rosters and a pair of binoculars handy, even as the Rams lost.

Next, San Francisco's 49ers came to town. Though the Rams' win–loss count stood at a lousy 2–4, the crowd size again grew for this in-state rivalry, this time setting an NFL record: 102,368, nearly a full house. Never before had so many people watched an NFL game live.

No other team in the league could boast such astronomic attendance. That the Rams could draw those numbers with a depressing, dismal record meant something more was happening.

What was happening was Pete Rozelle. The calm, quiet man with the Madison Avenue wardrobe had come into his new job in the midst of a player revolt coupled with owner acrimony and peevishness. One of his first accomplishments was to persuade the owners to pay each player fifty dollars per exhibition game and to raise their per diem from six dollars to nine. He even convinced Reeves and the rest to pay part of the players' health insurance premiums.

Then he smoothed relations between the owners. They still weren't talking—especially Reeves and Pauley—but they weren't so much working at cross purposes, either. That made the day-to-day operations more efficient. Rozelle believed patience to be one of his skills, and he figured that if he approached each situation patiently he could ease tensions and find solutions.

Acting on what he'd learned in public relations, he then brought a more professional look to the team, giving attention to small details company wide. For example, he hired a graphic artist to modernize the look of the game-day programs. He also worked to create a retail outlet for Rams merchandise—selling everything from T-shirts to bobblehead dolls of players.

If he couldn't change what happened on the field, the former public relations executive could at least sell Los Angeles something other than a losing team. For the cost of a ticket, Rozelle was selling excitement, thrills—a modern spectacle. Gladiators clashing with Lions and Bears.

And as the crowds grew he was also selling a sense of belonging. For the cost of a T-shirt a fan could join the tribe. For the cost of a ticket, any Los Angeleno could join the crowds, then bear witness on Monday morning, say "I was there."

It's possible that Rozelle and the Rams ownership felt some urgency. After all, the Dodgers brought a shiny new game to provide competition for the Los Angeles sports fan's dollar. It's possible much of Rozelle's efforts were meant to secure a fan base before the Dodgers threw out their first pitch. But Roz Wyman doesn't think so. Years later, she believes the Rams owners likely wanted the Dodgers, too. She knew Ed Pauley better than the others, and to the best of her recall she believes he thought the more sports the better.

"It's like a market in the mall," she explains. "If you have more than one market, it's good."

Los Angeles was prosperous after all; plenty of people carried full wallets. And to each sport there was a season, so it would be rare when baseball and football found themselves in direct competition. If people could become accustomed to two sports, if they came to love two sports, wouldn't they support two sports? Look at New York or Chicago or Pittsburgh or Detroit. Why not Los Angeles?

There could be two of Hollywood's Teams, right?

◆

THERE ARE PEOPLE WHO look forward, imagine how things might be, and act on their imaginings to transform a city, a town, or how things work. Walt Disney was a leader in that club, and Dan Reeves belonged, and so did Roz Wyman and Walter O'Malley and Pete Rozelle.

There are also people who wake every morning and go to work. Though they dream, their focus mostly stays with today. Without this last bunch, everything the visionaries imagine would fall apart. In Los Angeles, in the 1950s, they were carpenters and TV repairmen and maids and grocers and soda jerks. They took visitors' money at Disneyland and belted kids into rides. In Hollywood, they built sets and hauled lights. They drove streetcars until there were no more streetcars. They emptied trash cans at the beach. They cut meat. They picked oranges from trees. While standing at conveyor belts, they connected engine parts. They packed brassieres into boxes for shipping. They taught long division to schoolchildren. They tossed beer kegs into trucks. They bought tickets to football games and brought their children and fed them hot dogs with ketchup. They cut their own lawns, they cooked their own dinners, they enjoyed a cold beer. Innovations begin with the Walt Disneys and Dan Reeves of the world, but their ideas depend on these others who know when to flip a switch or how to lift a crate, and at their best do that job with efficiency and skill. Call them the offensive linemen of the world. Snap a chin strap or punch the clock, these are people who grind through the same work day after day after day until the days behind them rise in a towering uncountable stack.

Eventually, the body becomes weary.

It was mid-November, 1957. When those 102,368 people set an NFL record for attendance, they watched the Rams beat San Francisco, 37–24. It was the third straight game my dad had not started, though for this one Gillman brought back the shuttle-guard system, so my dad and Houser played about the same number of snaps.

It's likely Dad had been thinking more and more about retirement, about what might come next in his life. In football years, he was growing old. He'd turned twenty-nine in the spring, and if he played another season, he'd be thirty, a year older. That Houser kid would just be a year better. Quite likely, Dad would back him up all year. If the knees let him. There were so many kids like Houser now, and so few old-timers. Even Putnam was talking about retirement. So were Van Brocklin and Tank Younger, and Will Sherman, the defensive back and cocaptain. When my dad had come to the Rams he was blocking for guys like Skeet Quinlan and Woodley Lewis and Vitamin Smith. Even their names sounded old. They were all gone now, traded or retired. Last year, he'd blocked for Ron Waller, and now there was an even younger kid—Jon Arnett, a rookie from USC, chewing up the gridiron grass with his quick moves.

It wasn't pain from the knees that would have given him thoughts of retirement. Pain he could handle. Pain was irrelevant. But if the knees—one or both—didn't work, couldn't do what he needed them to do, pain or no pain, it was over.

He had always loved that Los Angeles seemed so new, so dynamic. He'd come home from Japan to a city where change was the constant. Young and unmarried, all possibility lay ahead of him, and his city and its football team seemed that way, too. But now the city and team had both become something else—and it was hard to put a finger on what was different. The city had aged, somehow, in just a few years. The Rams had, too. Just like my dad, now married and with a family, the Rams and Los Angeles had begun to settle down a bit, to grow closer to a definition of themselves. The Rams were an institution, a team that could lose but still draw larger and larger crowds, even as the coaches and front office took more and more control. In the city, plans for highways had led to highways themselves, the culture of cars established. Those highways led to bulldozed fields that were now neighborhoods where people lived, making decisions about life insurance and their kids' teachers, and worrying about the belt that squeaked each time the Chevy started.

Millions of people had moved here over the last twenty years, and now millions were getting on with their lives. The decade was nearing its close. Pretty soon it would be 1958. Soon, Los Angeles would have the Dodgers and the Rams and a new baseball stadium. It was, as the man's sign read, a grown-up town.

My dad was twenty-nine years old. He had a wife and three kids. Maybe it was time for him to find a different role in this new era, in this grown-up city.

Teaching history at a high school—that appealed to him. Spending days with young men and the long-gone centuries, then changing into a T-shirt and carrying a whistle through the afternoon, instructing many of those same young men at football practice. That life sounded good. It sounded so good there were times a return to the Rams seemed like the fall-back position, what he'd do if he couldn't find a teaching job.

And if that were the case, if the Rams were the fall-back position, then this probably would be his last swing through an NFL season. Having beaten San Francisco on that record-setting day, the Rams were about to embark on a three-game road trip. Then two more back home. Five games to go.

It looked to be the start of my dad's last weeks as a Ram.

CHAPTER 16

The Most Quiet Part

B Y ALMOST EVERY MEASURE, the last game of
1957 meant nothing to the Rams. The team
had played eleven games, and its record was
5–6. The Western Division title lay beyond
reach, no matter the result of this final game. Victory
or defeat, the season ended on December 15 when the
Rams played Johnny Unitas and Baltimore Colts. But
Pete Rozelle and the front office staff had learned that
even a losing team, marketed properly, could draw
record crowds. They just needed to give this last game
some meaning.

For their most recent contest, the eleventh of the
twelve-game season, the Rams had drawn nearly
seventy-one thousand people to the coliseum. And

that figure gave Rozelle and his staff an idea. Add all the attendance from exhibition games, away games, and home games, and the total attendance came to 998,546. With some quick research, Rozelle and company realized that with one game to go, the Rams could be the first football team ever—college or professional—to play before a million fans in a single season.

All they needed was 1,454 people to show for the finale against the Colts. That figure was guaranteed, but they could use that "million fans" goal to sell even more tickets. Pitch it as an historic moment for the NFL in particular, and football in general. No other team, not in New York, not in Chicago, could claim this accomplishment. Los Angeles would be the first. And wouldn't fans line up to have a chance at making history?

Bingo. Touchdown. Now the game had meaning.

◆

THE NIGHT OF THE Ye Olde Rams banquet, four days before the season's final kickoff, Sid Gillman added some meaning of his own.

Microphone in hand, he prowled the stage in front of all those celebrities, players, and fans, looking for offensive linemen to call out. He started by inviting Ken Panfil onto the stage. Panfil, six foot six and some 250 pounds hopped up on stage. He was big-chested with a sweet smile and a face that could have belonged to a movie star if he'd had a smaller nose. He regularly started at tackle on my dad's side of the line.

"Look, folks," said Gillman. "Doesn't he look big enough to stop Gino Marchetti? No one has done it this year, but Ken has been playing good ball for us, and I think he can do it. Don't you?"

Marchetti was widely acknowledged as one of, if not the best defensive tackle in football. When the Rams and Colts met later that week, Panfil would line up across from Gino. Given the Baltimore reporters in the room, odds were certain that Marchetti would hear about Gillman's boast.

Panfil stepped down, and maybe those eating their banquet chicken noticed a little less sweetness in his smile.

But Gillman wasn't done. Next he summoned Duane Putnam, who was going to face his old Rams teammate, Gene "Big Daddy" Lipscomb. As Putnam stood in the glare of the lights, Gillman started on him.

"Here's the top offensive guard in pro football," he said. "He has to spot around eighty pounds Sunday, but we know he can do it. Putnam's target is Big Daddy Lipscomb. Watch Put cut him down. It should be a real battle."

Later, reporters did indeed bring Gillman's boasts back to Marchetti and Lipscomb. Said the latter: "The best thing that happened to me was being traded to Baltimore. They aren't going to scare us, that's for sure." And Marchetti promised Panfil would have a most uncomfortable day. "He won't be picking cherries," he said.

The Colts needed no such chest thumping as Gillman provided. They had beaten the Rams two weeks earlier in Baltimore, 31–14. Given their 7–4 record, a victory at Los Angeles would put them in position to go to the NFL championship game. It was, as *The Baltimore Sun* reported, the most crucial game in the franchise's short history. And though six Colts suffered sore throats from breathing a week's worth of Los Angeles smog, on the day of the game the players were all in top playing shape. Even as the game began, the Colts principal owner, Carroll Rosenbloom, strolled through the press box and said, "Boy, if ever a team is ready, it is the Colts today."

◆

DAD'S CREDO: DO THINGS quietly.

Come Sunday, the morning of the last football game he'd ever play, who would have known it was the end but him? To make an announcement would add noise to the day, people shaking his hand, saying goodbye, making a fuss the way people did over Tank, who'd told the newspapers he was through. Whisper it to even a few, and word would spread.

Dad would have kept it quiet. He wouldn't have told a soul.

In Los Angeles, where spotlights heralded movies and department store openings and where cameramen gathered as a woman in a sparkling gown stepped from a limousine, my dad's reticence would have confused a lot of people. In a city where even the mobster Mickey Cohen had once taken a photographer from *Life* magazine on a tour of his home, such self-effacement as my dad's struck an incongruous note, contradicted Los Angeles's narrative about itself, was so unique it could have drawn attention—if it weren't that everyone's attention was drawn to the spotlights and glitter.

Because it was a Sunday morning, he and my mom would have gone to Mass at Church of the Transfiguration as they always did. They would have dressed in raincoats and likely carried an umbrella or two, because two storm systems had collided over Southern California and the rain fell heavy, more than three inches up in the San Fernando Valley. On the radio were reports of cars stalling in deep water on the valley's west side, and of houses flooding in the Glendale foothills. Telephone cables in west Los Angeles were under water, limiting communication. The coliseum field promised to be muddy and slippery. Maybe there wouldn't be eighty thousand fans, as some had predicted. Maybe a bunch of folks would stay home.

Dad would want Mass on this morning, because he would want everything to be the way it always was. He'd want Latin and the sign of the cross and hymns and the body and blood. At the stadium, he'd want the weight of shoulder pads, and to rub something into his knees, and for Dutch to say some smart-ass thing, just as he always did. On that road trip, Dad had regained the starting role, so on this day—as on so many before—he would run out onto the field for the Rams' first down, in the company of the Dutchman and Crazylegs and Tank, and he'd line up beside everyone else wearing blue and gold. He'd listen to Van Brocklin's cadence, and at the moment of the snap he'd jump from that three-point stance and smack into old Art Donovan or somebody. Everything just as it always had been.

As it always had been in Mass, too, and after he'd knelt and taken the wafer on his tongue, he'd lift himself and walk past the Christmas poinsettias to the pew where he'd pray. And, maybe, what came then was the only difference for him on this morning, this day.

Maybe then, with hands folded and eyes closed and an organist blowing a hymn through the pipes, somewhere in the quietest part of him, my dad in his prayer thanked God for the games, every blessed one of them.

CHAPTER 17

Next Time

Nathan: Is there any, uh, particular attraction
in California?

Nella: No, nothing special. Just like everybody else, I'm
looking for the end of the rainbow.
—from *The Tall Men*, Twentieth-Century Fox pictures,
premiered September 22, 1955, in Los Angeles; with Robert
Ryan as Nathan Stark and Jane Russell as Nella Turner

C LOUDS ROLLED AND CHURNED that Sunday
morning, and at last let a flash of sun fall
on Anaheim, just enough light to convince
Monte and Juanita Craig to brave the rain
and drive into Los Angeles for the Rams game.

They filled a thermos and bundled up, she in a long plaid overcoat buttoned to the neck, he in a jacket with a cowboy look to it, a material like lamb's wool lining the collar. In fact, with his lean face and pointed nose, Monte, a Texas native, could pass for an older Hank Williams—if Hank had worn eye glasses.

Juanita kept her curly, short hair tucked behind her ears. She and Monte had moved with their two children, Bobby and Charlotte, from the Lone Star State as part of the great Southern California migration in the years around World War II. He found work as a radio and TV repairman, and the family settled on the eastern edge of Greater Los Angeles. Now, Bobby and Charlotte were grown, Monte and Juanita were each forty-six, and they hadn't missed a Rams home game all year.

They arrived early to the ticket window and bought general admission seats, as they usually did, then headed for a gate into the stadium. The odd thing, though, was that all the gates were closed but one. So they joined that line, which moved pretty quickly. Not much of a wait at all. Maybe just enough time to remark on how the clouds had crowded out that earlier, brief sun. Now the skies looked ready to open up and soak everyone.

Just as the Craigs reached the front of the line and stepped through the turnstile, someone grabbed Monte by the arm.

"You!" that someone said. "You're the Rams' millionth fan!"

Next thing you know, Monte and Juanita were grinning and posing for pictures at the gate with Rams president Dan Reeves. Standing behind them, a uniformed ticket taker in a cap and tie raised a yard-long poster that read "Mr. MILLION." Reeves handed Juanita a football, which was autographed by players and marked to commemorate the occasion of the "1,000,000th FAN."

"This is the most thrilling thing that ever happened to us," Juanita said.

Reeves congratulated the couple and delivered the news that they'd won an all-expenses-paid trip for two to the NFL championship game. Then the Craigs were escorted to the press box where President Truman had sat a few weeks earlier, and to seats reserved for them. Person after person shook their hands. Reporters asked them questions. Just like that, they had become celebrities of a moment; just like that, they'd become part of the great Southern California story. As so many others had, they'd followed a rainbow west, and they'd caught a lucky break. It was a story repeated so often it had become myth—the proverbial waitress noticed by a studio exec. But sometimes it was real, say, a football player whose buddy has to drop out of the Pro Bowl and hands off his spot. Sometimes those lucky breaks led to big change. Sometimes the story didn't end so well. Sometimes nothing much changed, except that the busy world took a moment to notice, and a person could later say, as did Monte and Juanita Craig, that you'd been favored with a most thrilling thing.

By definition, the Craigs' moment wouldn't last, not in a city and a decade where change was the constant, where it was all so new. Wasn't there always a prettier actress, a rookie lineman with healthier knees, another movie premiere, a highway opening, a shopping mall ribbon-cutting, another ball team arrived from thousands of miles away? To live that great Los Angeles story—to catch the break and gain your moment—meant also to watch it end.

The Craigs were neither movie stars nor politicians. Sitting in a press box was for them a rare treat. One day next season, they'd probably go to a Rams game and cheer with thousands of others in general admission, as they so often had, and that would be fine, a pleasant afternoon. But for now, from the press box high above the coliseum, Monte and Juanita looked over the whole thing: the sky smudged gray and tucked in to each horizon, a string of Christmas lights affixed to the Olympic torch-holder at the stadium's east end, mountains to the north, and in the west, at field level, the tunnel from which the Rams, in blue and gold, and the Colts, in white trimmed with blue, poured onto the field. Taken together, it was a breathtaking sight.

Imagine how much more impressive the view if the stadium were filled! Today whole sections sat empty. The rain storms had, after all, kept many away. The fifty-three thousand people out there constituted the lowest turnout of the year.

But wasn't that good news for Mr. Million and Mrs. Million-and-One, who might have missed their moment if just one other person had braved the rain, and who now turned their attention to the field as the Rams lined up and kicked off to the waiting Colts.

◆

NOW COME THE END of things. So many that day, and no one knew them all.

Tank Younger had announced his retirement, so even he expected this to be his last game. It wouldn't happen, though, as he'd planned. In another few months, the Rams would trade his contract to Pittsburgh, and he would play his last NFL season for the Steelers.

Likewise, Norm Van Brocklin would soon be traded to the Eagles, putting an end to the Rams quarterback controversy and his play-calling spats with Sid Gillman. Elroy "Crazylegs" Hirsch, probably the most popular Ram in Los Angeles, had insisted he'd be back for another year, but he would retire, too. It was to be the last game for a host of other players, including Bob Boyd and Will Sherman. Come the next season, there'd be only one familiar face left from that Rams team which had won the NFL championship in 1951: Dick Daugherty, a defensive back. He'd stay just that next year, then retire, too.

And, of course, it would be my dad's last game.

One other finale? The end of football's sole reign at the coliseum. In April, the Dodgers would arrive for their opening day, and they would control the space for months. When next the Rams took the field, their chalk lines would cross dirt base paths. The gridiron, so emblematic of Los Angeles's own grid layout, that predictable and comforting structure that had given rise to such imagination and magic, would exist in the same plane as a cockeyed baseball diamond.

For now, though, the rematch with the Colts and their second-year phenom, quarterback Johnny Unitas. The Rams had nothing to play for but pride. The Colts knew another victory would give them a shot at the NFL championship game.

But this game was to be played in Los Angeles where Hollywood writes the stories. Given all that was ending for the Rams in this last game of the 1957 season, it was a climactic moment in team history. And if it were a movie, wouldn't the script call for the Rams to win?

◆

FOUR PLAYS AFTER THE kickoff. One minute, forty-one seconds. That's all Baltimore and Unitas needed to score their first touchdown. Things looked worse for the Rams soon after, when Big Daddy Lipscomb barreled past Duane Putnam and sacked Van Brocklin. Dutch came up limping with a crumpled toe or two.

It was an exquisitely awful start to a meaningless game played on a dreary day at the end of a mediocre season.

But it was only the beginning, because—for whatever reason—Crazylegs, a football ancient at age thirty-four, and Dutch, who was thirty-one and had probably just broken a toe or two, played as if it were 1951 again—when their younger selves scored almost at will and the Rams had last won the NFL championship.

This day, as on those days' years before, Van Brocklin zipped passes to the sidelines and downfield, and Hirsch, more often than not, was the one to drag them in. When that combination wasn't at work, the Dutchman floated a few to the rookie, Jon Arnett, or he handed off to Ron Waller or some other running back, who—rather than crash through that gargantuan Baltimore defensive line—sprinted to the edges and around.

The Rams kept on that way through the first half. Though Putnam struggled with Lipscomb, the other Rams linemen—Panfil, Bob Fry and the Hock-Houser combo—kept the massive Colts linemen corralled. Then, the rain did indeed fall as the skies had promised, and all through the coliseum umbrellas popped open— gold, blue, orange, and pink bursts, like fireworks in the gloom. Stadium lights burned, though it was still afternoon. On the field, players slipped and splashed, and those pretty white and gold and blue uniforms became a confusion of mud. Wet dirt smeared across jersey numbers, ground into the knees of the pants, and soaked into the seats. In such weather, coaches will tell you, hands get slick and wide receivers can't make sharp cuts in the muck. The best strategy becomes the running game. Give up on the pass. But that would have been like asking Hirsch and Van Brocklin to give up on their best selves. Dutch wasn't about to do that. Not even late in the second quarter, with ten yards to the end zone, when a pass play to Hirsch went awry. In the next huddle, Van Brocklin called the very same play, and this time the ball settled softly into Elroy's arms for a touchdown.

The Rams led, 20–7.

◆

WHEN THE TEAMS RETURNED for the second half, they found the field littered with confetti left behind by a high school band that had entertained the crowd. As a high point to the show, the students had released a flock of pigeons, and a few of those lingered, too, *flup-flup-flupping* across the field.

The Rams received the kickoff. A few plays in, they returned to the huddle, but as they circled to hear the next play, something fell into their midst. Or flew. Who knows whether the players were more startled than the pigeon that landed in a flock of sweaty, muddy men.

"I thought for a moment it was a new kind of secret weapon the boys from Baltimore were trying to spring on us," Dutch joked later.

Van Brocklin's hand darted. *Zzzt!*—and the pigeon was his. Sometimes it's that kind of day—passes on the mark, bird in the palm. Dutch cradled the pigeon—

holding it at arm's length—and walked it off the field, its white wings beating. A photographer met him partway and took custody of what the *Los Angeles Examiner* later called "a living forward pass."

◆

THE TEAMS EXCHANGED TOUCHDOWNS—FOR the Colts, a ninety-nine-yard drive that took most of the third quarter; for Los Angeles, another Van Brocklin-to-Crazylegs pass. Then the Rams added a field goal for a 30–14 lead with less than six minutes to play.

From that point, the Colts became desperate, maybe even a little goofy. A trick involving a backwards pass led to a ninety-nine-yard touchdown, but Gillman would later dismiss the play as better suited to a school playground than the gridiron, calling it "intramural."

The Colts then attempted an on-sides kick, perhaps the most desperate maneuver in football. If the high-risk play worked, the Colts would wrest the ball from the Rams and have another opportunity to score. Chances were the play would backfire, though, giving the Rams an easy shot at a field goal, perhaps even a touchdown.

Which is exactly what happened.

So here came Van Brocklin and the Rams. With only a few minutes to go, the polite and courteous thing would have been to run a few plays, let the minutes tick away, maybe kick a field goal. With the Rams defense stifling the Colts again and again, three more points would give Los Angeles an almost-insurmountable lead.

Van Brocklin wasn't interested in being courteous. It's easy to guess why after all the crap he'd heard over the last two seasons from fans, after the arguments with Gillman, and after he'd been made to share his job with Bill Wade. Maybe this was the end of all that, and he was going to take the ball and throw it down the metaphorical throat of everyone who rankled him these last two years—and if the Colts got in the way, well, boohoo for them.

Or maybe he knew that with one more touchdown, he'd break his own team record for touchdown passes in a season, set in 1953 (my dad's first year), when Van Brocklin had thrown nineteen.

Or maybe it was just Dutch being Dutch.

It could have been all those reasons.

What's verifiable is that with just a few minutes to go and a 30–21 lead, the Dutchman came out gunning for one last touchdown. First, he passed thirty-three yards to Bob Boyd. A pass to a fullback gained another fifteen, and now the Rams needed only eight yards for a fourth touchdown. This time, Van Brocklin lofted the ball to a rookie, Lamar Lundy, who stretched his arms and gave Dutch his fourth touchdown pass of the day, and his record-breaking twentieth of the season. An extra-point kick made the score 37–21, and that's where it would stay.

Soon after, the final gun sounded.

The game ended. The season was over. An era closed.

With mud gritty on their faces and wet in their shoes, with rain dripping from their helmets, Hollywood's team—the lot of them, unglamorous as could be—walked off the field.

◆

LET THE CAMERAS FIND my dad, one last time.

The scene starts in the locker room, after the Colts' game. A close-up to open. With both hands, my dad slaps his clean face, especially around that rock-outcropping of a jaw. The sound is so crisp you can almost smell the aftershave. Around him is the din of men joking, laughing. The scrape and hiss of a beer can as it's tugged open.

"This one's for Putter," someone says, offscreen. "You get your ass beat by Lipscomb like that, you need a beer." Dad turns from his locker, and those glaring fluorescent lights shine down on him. The camera sits a little low, just enough to remind the viewer of my dad's size. He's just about dressed, and costume has put him in slacks zipped and fastened but the belt not yet buckled, a long-sleeve dark-blue sport shirt—unbuttoned, and T-shirt bright white. A squat, balding guy walks past with a cooler, and my dad grabs a beer can of his own, pulls the tab. At the next locker over, Putnam finishes a long draw of his own suds, looks at my dad, and shakes his head.

"Next time," says my dad, lifting his can a smidgen, a quiet toast.

"Next time," says Putter, and clinks his can to my dad's. Then he rubs a big hand over his brush cut. "To heck with next time."

The camera pans the room. Gillman's still gabbing with one or two reporters, and Tank Younger's walking here and there, getting fellows to sign his game ball. There's a glimpse of Ron Waller grimacing as he tries to move a knee that is wrapped and iced, another of the big rookie John Houser, and guys congratulating Ken Panfil for getting the best of Gino Marchetti. Then there's Crazylegs in front of a mirror, putting something in his hair and working it with a comb. Finally, the camera settles on Van Brocklin, sweaty undershirt still clinging to him, still wearing his muddy pants. He's sitting at his locker, legs splayed, barefoot, and with a beer in hand. He's laughing already, like what he's about to say is the funniest thing he ever thought of. "Hey, Lantern Jaw!" he shouts. "Hooker! You keep playing like you did out there against Donovan, you might have a future."

Dad grins. "Is that a thank you, Dutch?"

"Naw," says Van Brocklin. He's grinning, too, showing those gaps in his teeth. "You don't thank a man who does the job he's supposed to."

Now, the director waves a hand, a signal, and my dad leans over to pick up his duffle bag—a prop the director wants to connect back to the opening scene, when the big man in the Army uniform arrived home on a bright January day almost five years before. My dad stuffs the bag with his equipment, his muddy shoes, a few bottles of red liquid magic for his knees. It's slow going. He hesitates now and then. In the background, Van Brocklin's voice barks, "I think Lipscomb broke my goddamn toes."

"I'm ordering the biggest steak Don Paul's place serves," my dad tells Putnam. "Have the kitchen cook it until the fat's crisp."

"Burn it," says Putter.

"Then I'm ordering another."

Next, my dad's making his way through the locker room, duffle bag over his shoulder, shaking hands. Everyone's shaking hands, everyone's saying goodbye.

Outside, in a mist lit by a few sconces along the stadium wall, he meets my mom, gives her a kiss. She's carrying an umbrella big enough for the two of them. Together, they stroll to the parking lot, but even at a stroll he falls behind a half step. "Are you sore?" she asks. "Do you want me to drive?" He answers by opening the driver's side door for her, then stepping around the back of the car.

Off they go, heading north on the freeway, then west, then north again, past palm trees shining with bulbs of Christmas green and red, past neon Santas and reindeer, the car's windshield wipers beating away the mist, drops on the passenger windows gathering and fragmenting the evening light. He leans back, shakes his shoulders into a more comfortable position, ignores the complaints from his knees, and welcomes the drive through this familiar and all-so-new city, on his way to a familiar and all-so-new life.

CHAPTER 18

Epilogue

NOT LONG AFTER HIS four-touchdown game against the Colts ended the 1957 season, **Norm Van Brocklin** was traded to Philadelphia where his new coach deferred to the Dutchman when it came time to choose plays. Van Brocklin in turn led the Eagles to the NFL championship in 1960, a year he was also voted the league's most valuable player. Dutch retired after that season and became a head coach for two teams: the Minnesota Vikings and the Atlanta Falcons. In both cases, he started with bad teams and built them into solid—though never championship—franchises. His coaching record was 66–100–7.

After the Falcons fired Van Brocklin in 1974, he divided his time between commenting on games for television broadcasts and raising pecans at his farm in Social Circle, Georgia. When a reporter asked Dutch's wife, Gloria, if he could be happy on a farm, so far away from the game that had been his life, she answered, "Let me put it this way: pecan trees don't drop touchdown passes."

In 1971, two decades after he won the NFL championship with the Rams, he was inducted into the Professional Football Hall of Fame. He died eight years later, at age fifty-seven.

◆

WITH VAN BROCKLIN TRADED to the Eagles, **Bill Wade** became the Rams' primary quarterback for the 1958–60 seasons, a stint that included his own Hollywood moment: a guest appearance on *The Donna Reed Show*. In that idealized world of after-school milk and cake, in an episode that opened with Donna wearing a seamstress's tape measure around her neck along with pearls, Wade and other Rams helped convince a neighbor boy's mother to let him play football. An actor portrayed a Rams publicity man named Bert Rose, and it's likely the show was a coup for the real Rams publicity man, whose name really was Bert Rose, and his boss, Pete Rozelle. The episode, called "All Mothers Worry," ended with **Jon Arnett, Les Richter, Don Burroughs** and Wade, all decked out in suits and ties, joining Donna and her family for dinner. Wade had the episode's last line, saying politely in his native Tennessee twang, "Mother always told me when you're asked for dinner, be helpful!"

Wade joined the Chicago Bears for the 1960 season, and in 1963 he and the Bears won the NFL championship. He retired in 1966.

◆

JOHN W. HOUSER, JR., who as a rookie was my dad's fellow shuttle guard, played two more years with the Rams before he was acquired by the Dallas Cowboys for their inaugural season. He ended his playing career as a St. Louis Cardinal, leaving the game when he noticed his speed diminishing. "I got into the league as a big guy who was quick," he recalled in a conversation during the summer of 2013, "and I could get in the way or get out of the way as I pleased. Now, I couldn't get out of the way anymore. I could see myself playing one or two more seasons." He shrugged. "Just had a feeling that this was a time to get out."

He joined the Owens Corning corporation in sales and marketing, learned about fiberglass insulation and commercial roofing, and worked for that company in their Los Angeles and Denver offices. After he retired, he became active in the struggles of NFL old-timers to win compensation from the league and its players' union for lingering brain damage brought on by concussions. With a color-coded map of his brain in hand, Houser can point to the color that shows his trouble spots and quote the doctor who told him he had a better-than-average shot at dementia.

"The owners are waiting for us to die," he said in 2013. "Plain and simple."

◆

IN A 1958 RAMS game day program, a page of photographs shows Rams "on the lighter side," and includes one of **Ron Waller** inspecting a new bowling alley he and a business partner owned. Worried that football would do him some crippling injury, his wife's grandmother, the Post cereal heiress, wanted him to move into business, and the family backed him. The 1958 season, in fact, would be his last as a Ram.

In the spring after the Rams beat the Colts in front of their millionth fan, a misdemeanor drunk-driving charge against Waller's wife, **Marjorie Durant,** led to banner headlines in Los Angeles, especially after she accused the officers who stopped her of making "improper advances." A jury acquitted her of the charges.

Waller, meanwhile, was looking to buy an NFL franchise and bring it to Miami. But the Wallers separated in 1960, thus ending his opportunity to become an NFL owner. That same year, he joined a new team in a new league formed to challenge the NFL. Waller, the first player signed by the American Football League's Los Angeles Chargers, played for them one season. He and Marjorie divorced in 1961.

A decade later, Waller had become an assistant coach with the Chargers, and then, after his boss was fired, he coached the Chargers for the last six games of the 1973 season, going 1–5. He coached one more team in another upstart league that folded quickly. Eventually, he moved back to his native Delaware, settling about seven miles north of his hometown. He passed away in 2018.

◆

WALLER'S COACH IN THAT inaugural Chargers season was **Sid Gillman**. His tenure with the Rams ended after 1959's 2–10 debacle. But less than a month after Pete Rozelle fired him, Gillman had been named head coach of the Los Angeles Chargers in the new AFL.

In that league, Gillman made a great reputation as a football innovator and became, as his biographer Josh Katzowitz calls him, the "father of the passing game." With the San Diego Chargers until 1969, Gillman applied mathematics and precise timing to the design of passing plays, and thereby revolutionized football.

He also never stopped wearing his bow tie.

After his last head coaching job ended in 1974, Gillman still worked occasionally as a special assistant coach, including for the Chicago Bears and Philadelphia Eagles. He was inducted into the Professional Football Hall of Fame in 1983.

◆

PETE ROZELLE FIRED GILLMAN, but the Rams' 2–10 misery in 1959 may well have started with Rozelle himself, and a trade he announced via telegram to the NFL league office on February 28, 1959. The wire revealed that the Rams were trading nine players to the Chicago Cardinals—and getting one in return.

The trade was dramatic, but for the Rams it had a precedent. In 1952, they had traded eleven players for Les Richter, a linebacker from UCLA. But Richter then was at the start of a Hall of Fame career. Rozelle's nine-man trade brought the Rams a twenty-nine-year-old running back.

That running back, Ollie Matson, had been a star for the University of San Francisco when Rozelle was a student there. He'd won bronze and silver medals in track at the 1952 Olympic Games, and, for the Cardinals, he'd had a 924-yard-rushing season in 1956.

Maybe a great running back is worth nine players, but the Rams' fortunes suggest otherwise. Matson didn't disappoint, gaining 863-yards rushing and another 130-yards receiving in his first Rams season, but the team had been decimated. They'd lost valuable linemen, including Ken Panfil, Glenn Holtzman, Frank Fuller, and Art Hauser. The ensuing 2–10 record made a strong case that the Rams had lost more than they'd gained.

A month after Rozelle fired Gillman, he himself left the Rams—elected by the league's owners as a surprising compromise choice to succeed Bert Bell as the new commissioner.

Rozelle remained in the commissioner's chair until his retirement in 1989, becoming perhaps the most successful league commissioner in any sport ever. During his tenure he negotiated the NFL's first nationwide television contract, increased its number of franchises, merged the league with the AFL, and oversaw the birth and growth of the Super Bowl.

He, too, was inducted into the Pro Football Hall of Fame, in 1985.

It would require nearly a decade after Rozelle left the Rams for his old team to again become a playoff contender.

◆

THE OWNERS' SQUABBLES INTENSIFIED after Rozelle left. In 1963, **Daniel Reeves** finally bought out Edwin Pauley and others whose contributions had allowed the Rams to survive their earliest days in Los Angeles.

Reeves continued to work his way through coaches, though, giving the team to Bob Waterfield for two seasons, then to former Rams linebacker Harland Svare for three seasons. Not until George Allen coached the team from 1966–70 did the Rams begin to win again. But Reeves and Allen meshed like gin and milk, two beverages emblematic of their personalities. Reeves fired Allen in 1968, only to rehire him after players rebelled. Two years later, he fired Allen a second time. It was the last time Reeves would ever fire a coach. Reeves died from throat cancer in the spring of 1971 at age fifty-eight, which resulted in the sale and transfer of the Rams to Baltimore Colts owner Carrol Rosenbloom (husband of Georgia Frontiere).

He had been inducted into the Pro Football Hall of Fame three years earlier.

◆

OTHER RAMS FROM THE 1950s enshrined in the Hall of Fame are **Tom Fears** (1970), **Elroy "Crazylegs" Hirsch** (1968), **Dick "Night Train" Lane** (1974), **Les Richter** (2011), **Andy Robustelli** (1971), and **Bob Waterfield** (1965). **Tex Schramm**, the general manager for most of those years, was welcomed into the hall in 1991.

◆

FOR THEIR FIRST GAME at the coliseum, the **Los Angeles Dodgers**, in uniform, rode in a motorcade of open convertibles along their new city's Broadway from downtown to the parking lots of Memorial Coliseum, past thousands of cheering fans. Nearly eighty thousand people filled the stadium to watch the Dodgers beat the San Francisco Giants, 6–5.

From the start, the Dodgers excited Hollywood's imagination. Celebrities on hand for opening day included Zsa Zsa Gábor, Jimmy Stewart, Danny Kaye, Edward G. Robinson, Dinah Shore, Groucho Marx, Gene Autry, and a dozen or so others.

That opening day party was tempered somewhat by a looming election. Enough opponents had signed petitions to put the Chavez Ravine deal to a public referendum. Supporters of the land-swap organized a five-hour "Dodgerthon" on KTTV, and, again, Hollywood turned out. Some who appeared on the team's behalf included Jerry Lewis, George Burns, Dean Martin, Jack Benny, Debbie Reynolds, and Ronald Reagan. Clearly, much of Hollywood wanted a major league team.

The vote, held that June, favored the Dodgers by a few percentage points, but didn't end the controversy, especially after some people—mostly Hispanic— refused to leave their homes in the Chavez Ravine. In front of newspaper photographers, law enforcement officers carried a woman out by her arms and legs. Various books, films, and people still refer to the taking of the area from its mostly Hispanic residents as "The Battle of Chavez Ravine." Dodgers Stadium opened on April 10, 1962.

The Los Angeles Dodgers have since given four World Series championships to their adopted city.

◆

THIRTEEN DAYS BEFORE THE Dodgers were to play their first game in Los Angeles, **Roz Wyman** gave birth to her first child. Groggy just after, she reportedly asked three questions. The first was about her husband; the second, whether the child was a boy or girl (it was a girl); and the third: can I go to opening day?

Who would have told her no? So it was that she and her husband, Gene, sat next to Walter O'Malley and his wife on chairs brought down to the field's level.

Her strong stand fighting for the Dodgers and the landswap had cost her much political goodwill across the city. She had received death threats and notes full of vitriol, often focusing on her being Jewish or a woman—or both. Some Democrats said they'd never vote for her again. Allies within the party fell away. But she never stopped believing that helping to bring the Dodgers to Los Angeles was the best thing she'd ever done as a councilwoman. In 1958 the *Los Angeles Times* named her the city's woman of the year.

Later, she played a smaller role in bringing the National Basketball Association's Minneapolis Lakers to Los Angeles in 1960.

When Wyman ran for a fourth term on the council in 1965, she lost, but she and her husband remained powerful forces in state Democratic politics.

And if the Dodgers played at home yesterday, odds are good she was at the game using her season tickets.

◆

DUANE PUTNAM REMAINED A Ram until the new team in Dallas, the Cowboys, acquired him for their inaugural season in 1960. The next season he joined the Cleveland Browns, but the season after that he returned to wear Los Angeles's blue and gold, before retiring. Subsequently, he served as an assistant coach for several teams. He and his wife Patty finally settled in a suburb about halfway between Los Angeles and Redlands. In the same way Putter once regularly attended Mass with my dad, though he wasn't Roman Catholic, after he retired he would also go with buddies to Christian Reformed church services, though he wasn't Christian Reformed, either.

He and my dad remained good friends until my dad died in 2000. An amazing guy, the three time all-Pro Putnam died in March of 2016.

◆

MONTE AND JUANITA CRAIGS memories of a Rams game on a rainy day passed through the generations of their family, so that even decades after they had died, their grown-up granddaughter, Carri, could, at mention of the Rams, exclaim, without prompting, that her grandfather "was Mr. Million."

The game that is part of the Craig's family lore is not much more than a footnote in NFL history, but it had been for Monte and Juanita one of the most exciting days of their lives. Watching from the press box, they kept dry, even as all those colorful umbrellas bloomed beneath their view like flowers popping. Pigeons flew at halftime, and there were hot dogs to eat, and coffee to drink from a thermos, and that autographed football to bring home. On the field, so far below that the players looked like little plastic toys, the Rams' defense proved able to stifle Johnny Unitas when it needed to. The Craigs watched that, and they watched the Rams' offensive line, entangled with those behemoths for the Colts. And Jon Arnett, nicknamed the "Jaguar," zigging and zagging, and Crazylegs dancing along the sidelines, and the Dutchman—he of the stubby fingers and sharp tongue—*zinging* pass after pass exactly where it needed to be. By watching, by witnessing, the Craigs and every other fan in this stadium had given Los Angeles another reason to brag: the first city with a team to reach a million fans. Fifty-three thousand in the stadium that day, and maybe most weren't movie or television stars or politicians, but they were Angelenos, and they'd done their part to make something happen for their city. By buying a ticket and braving the rain, they—the crowd, the audience—had created this great scene: the concrete stadium with its white lights, the Southern California sky so strangely gray, my dad blocking to give Van Brocklin time, young Lamar Lundy reaching high to snag the Dutchman's final touchdown spiral, and all the players who endured weather and pain to make this sloppy, messy thing of beauty.

It was Los Angeles Rams football. It must have seemed as though it would last forever.

◆

"HE MISSED IT," MY mom says, quietly. "I'm sure he missed it. He didn't complain, though. But you knew he missed it. How could you not?"

Perhaps to take the sting out leaving the game he loved, Dad, **John Hock**, spent the spring of 1958 with seven other Rams, including Putnam and Ron Waller, barnstorming as a basketball team. Lamar Lundy, who at six foot seven had once been named the Purdue University basketball team's most valuable player, anchored the Rams at center. My dad and Les Richter, the linebacker, started at guard. "We don't know how good the boys are," said a Rams spokesman, "but it's a cinch they could be rough." The group played charity games, including one in Redlands to benefit high school student scholarships. They played and lost another, 59–46, to a similarly constituted group of San Francisco 49ers.

Dad would teach for a year or so, turn down a few NFL assistant coaching offers, including one from Sid Gillman of the LA Chargers. He would then take a job as a sales rep with Western Car Loading, a company that moved freight from coast to coast. Our family continued to grow with four girls and three boys, and my parents bought a house in Anaheim, about five minutes from Disneyland. On Sunday nights, if the kids were well-behaved, they'd allow them to stand on the family station wagon and watch the Enchanted Kingdom's fireworks explode in the distance. Their seventh and final child Jim was born in 1969.

Dad had worked his way up in the company, which transferred him to New York, residing in a little town called Mahwah ("the meeting place") in northern New Jersey. On the East Coast, he reunited with Andy Robustelli, now an executive with the Giants, who gave him an in to purchase season tickets with the team. Mom missed California, but Dad loved the trees of the east coast. To keep Mom happy, my dad would drive the family back and forth numerous times to Los Angeles, with a wooden box on top of their station wagon specially built to give each of the seven kids the exact same amount of room for their things. Dad loved being behind the wheel, enjoying country music on the radio and the greasy food served along America's highways and interstates. "My father would always say the best food is truck stop food," recalled my sister Anna. Simple and solid as always, just the way he liked it.

In January 2000, the Rams played in their first Super Bowl. They weren't Los Angeles's team anymore—having abandoned Southern California for St. Louis, their last game as the LA Rams falling on Christmas Eve day, 1994—but they still wore blue and gold, still displayed the Rams horns on their helmets. They may have represented a city with which he had no connection, but with those famous horns they remained his one and only team to the very loyal John Hock. So at age seventy-two, with my mom, myself, and family around him, he sat in the Georgia Dome in Atlanta to watch his team beat the Tennessee Titans, 23–16. It was an incredible memory, especially with my mom handing out my dad's playing cards to anyone we met.

The following September, Dad contracted an aggressive form of lung cancer. He had thought the cough was annoying, but nothing more than a nuisance cold. The doctor said he must have had some nearly superhuman pain threshold not to notice the melon-size tumor in his lung. For roughly three months after the initial diagnosis, my dad fought for life, expiring on December 9, 2000. Draining gallons of fluid from his lungs the days before his death, my mom knew that my dad did not want to go. The day before he died, he said to my mom, over and over, "too short...too short." But it was now his time. Cancer had won.

Fast forward to August 2016. The Rams are back in Los Angeles for their first preseason game after twenty-two years away. Nearly ninety thousand fans are in attendance for a welcome home celebration. The same tunnel eight, once the wives entrance that my mom used time and again to enter the Coliseum would now see her grandkids pass through it sixty years later. My wife, Kellie, and me, and our boys, William and John—named after his grandfather—used that same historic tunnel to say hello to the Coliseum for the first time. To watch the Rams return to their longtime home. Between the chills and the tears, the young boys feel their grandfather's powerful presence in the place he loved so much.

Dad is smiling. Smiling down from above watching Hollywood's team take the field once again.

CPSIA information can be obtained
at www.ICGtesting.com
Printed in the USA
LVHW100558271121
704595LV00001B/1